Thinking Skills
Managing and Preventing
Personal Problems

Thinking Skills
Managing and Preventing Personal Problems

Richard Nelson-Jones

Royal Melbourne Institute of Technology

Brooks/Cole Publishing Company
Pacific Grove, California

Brooks/Cole Publishing Company
A Division of Wadsworth, Inc.

Printed in the United States of America
10   9   8   7   6   5   4   3   2   1

Library of Congress Cataloging-in-Publication Data

Nelson-Jones, Richard.
    Thinking skills : managing and preventing personal problems /
Richard Nelson-Jones.
        p.   cm.
    Includes bibliographical references.
    ISBN 0-534-11796-1
    1. Conduct of life.   2. Reasoning.   3. Decision-making (Ethics)
I. Title.
BJ1581.2.N445   1989
153.4'2—dc20   89-36205
                                                            CIP

Sponsoring Editor: *Claire Verduin*
Editorial Assistant: *Gay C. Bond*
Production Editor: *Penelope Sky*
Manuscript Editor: *Pamela Evans*
Permissions Editor: *Carline Haga*
Interior and Cover Design: *Sharon L. Kinghan*
Interior Illustration: *Sue C. Howard*
Typesetting: *Metro Typography and Design*
Printing and Binding: *Malloy Lithographing, Inc.*

Preface

This book is for people who wish to think more effectively about their personal problems and decisions. My philosophical position is that of pragmatic existentialism: you are personally responsible for *making* your own happiness and fulfillment according to the quality of your choices, even in adverse circumstances. Thinking skills involve a series of choices that may be well or poorly made. To think effectively, you require a repertoire of thinking skills to apply to your problems and decisions. I describe those skills and encourage you to use them.

This is definitely a how-to book. No one else can do your thinking for you. There are 55 "thinksheets" to help you learn by doing. Use these thinksheets flexibly; for example, stay with them only as long as they work for you and, if necessary, modify them to suit your needs. I have included numerous real-life case examples; they cover a wide range of problems experienced by people who were sabotaging their happiness and fulfillment by making self-oppressing, instead of self-supporting, thinking choices.

A number of themes surface repeatedly. First, you can support or oppress yourself by how you think. I agree with Abraham Lincoln that "most folks are about as happy as they make up their minds to be." Second, you should use thinking skills for preventing as well as managing problems. Why land yourself in trouble unnecessarily? Third, using effective thinking skills requires courage and commitment. You affirm and define your existence by rising above your own fallibility and others'.

The book draws heavily on the insights of recent cognitive therapies. In the first two chapters I examine what thinking is and discuss how we acquire and sustain poor thinking skills. The following chapters are on specific thinking skills: owning responsibility for your choices; using self-talk; formulating realistic personal rules; perceiving yourself and others accurately; realistically attributing cause for what happens in your life; predicting and creating your future; and using visual thinking. If your skills in these areas are deficient you are likely to deal ineffectively with your problems. Two putting-it-together chapters then demonstrate how you can apply your thinking skills to making decisions, and to preventing and managing specific problems. The emphasis in the final chapter is on how to maintain the courage to keep thinking for yourself.

Appreciation is due to the following people: Claire Verduin, Gay Bond, Sharon Kinghan, Pamela Evans, Penelope Sky, and the other members of the editorial production team at Brooks/Cole Publishing Company; Dawn Butcher of the Royal Melbourne Institute of Technology word processing unit, for her help and courtesy in typing the manuscript; and, last but not least, all the cognitive theorists, researchers, and therapists on whose work this book is grounded.

I hope you enjoy using the book, and that it helps you to think more effectively when you are facing problems and decisions in your life.

Richard Nelson-Jones

Contents

Thinksheets

Thinking Skills
Managing and Preventing
Personal Problems

CHAPTER 1

Choosing How You Think

Most folks are about as happy as they make up their minds to be.

Abraham Lincoln

Choices, choices, choices. Whenever you think, you make choices. Humans are unique in their capacity for thinking and choosing; other animals operate on the basis of instincts. Humans have a capacity for self-awareness and for thinking themselves into and out of difficulties. This book is about learning to become better able to control your thinking. It aims to help you make thinking choices that support rather than oppress you, and, when appropriate, to help others do the same. It seeks to develop your skills of "straight" as contrasted with "crooked" thinking about your personal problems. Ultimately, it is a book about having the courage to think for yourself.

Here are some examples of people whose thinking choices adversely affect their happiness and level of performance.

Pam is a high school student who is shy. She worries constantly about what others think of her and whether they will reject her.

Roger and Joyce have a distressed marriage. Roger tends to attribute many of Joyce's actions to malevolent motives. He routinely fails to check out the accuracy of his perceptions.

Sue and Paul have been going steady for a year. Recently, they have not been getting on so well. Sue thinks, "If Paul loves me, he should know instinctively how to make me happy. I should not have to tell him." This attitude prevents Sue from telling Paul what she wants.

Dennis works in a clothing store. He is about to get a new boss, which he regards as a threat. He tells himself, "I'm damned well not going to let him get the better of me." He has yet to meet his new boss.

Betty is a college student approaching her final exams. She thinks she must get outstanding grades, or both she and her parents will think she is a failure. This belief, which ties her worth as a person to her academic achievement, contributes to severe exam anxiety.

In these and numerous other ways, people sabotage their own happiness and fulfillment through ineffective thinking. As the saying goes, they are their own worst enemies. Unfortunately, ineffective thinking often has negative consequences for others, too.

Writers throughout the centuries have attested to the importance of clear thinking. In the first century A.D., Epictetus claimed, "Men are disturbed not by things, but by the views which they take of them." Shakespeare concurred when he had Hamlet say, "There is nothing either good or bad, but thinking makes it so." Shortly afterward, the French philosopher Descartes declared, "I think, therefore I am (*Cogito, ergo sum*)," thereby establishing thinking as the central definition of human existence. The fact that humans have the potential to think does not necessarily mean that the potential gets fully used, of course. As Jonathan Swift, the author of *Gulliver's Travels*, observed, "An old saying and a true, 'much drinking, little thinking.'" We humans don't need drink to befuddle our thinking. We easily succeed without such excuses!

Perhaps I can use humor to further illustrate the point that our thinking can adversely influence how we feel and act. In this limerick, the student not only causes but sustains her problem through ineffective thinking.

> *There was a young student from Maine*
> *Whose thinking caused her much pain.*
> *With every transgression*
> *She swelled with aggression,*
> *And brooded again and again.*

In short, our negative feelings are generated less by events than by the ways we think about events. As the limerick points out, anger and self-pity are the outcomes of faulty thinking. Focusing on your thinking choices gives you a "handle" with which to combat a range of unwanted feelings—including persistent anger, depression, and excessive anxiety. Furthermore, if you *think* more effectively and *feel* better, you are more likely to act in self-enhancing rather than self-defeating ways.

WHAT ARE PERSONAL PROBLEMS?

One way to view personal problems is to consider them difficulties that challenge you to find solutions. Personal problems like excessive anger, relationship conflicts, shyness, loneliness, lack of concentration, test anxiety, boredom, unemployment, indecision, and working with difficult colleagues challenge you to find solutions. However, another way to view personal problems is as situations to be avoided or prevented. The problem then becomes how to avoid the problem. This second approach perceives personal problems as more often covert than overt. The challenge is to avoid making the thinking choices that set you up for unnecessary and more overt problems.

Preventing as Well as Managing Problems

We are all likely to have thinking difficulties that contribute to our personal problems. Some would deny it; others would readily admit that it is a daily struggle to discipline their thinking to avoid harming themselves and others. But thinking difficulties do beset us all.

Effective thinking skills can help you avoid problems as well as to deal with them more effectively when they occur. These skills can be compared to the skills of top golfers. Their aim is to go around the course with a minimal number of strokes. They use their skills in a "preventing problems" way to stay on the fairway and out of the rough. However, even the best of golfers end up in the rough. Then they use their skills in a "managing problems" way to get out.

Assuming you are rational, like a top golfer you want to go through life with a minimal number of avoidable problems. Effective thinking skills can increase your chances of staying on the fairway. For instance, if you are skilled at perceiving yourself and others accurately, you may prevent avoidable conflicts. However, inevitably you will find yourself in some conflicts. Then you must use your thinking skills to manage those problems in the most constructive way.

By the end of this book you should have a greater awareness of the thinking difficulties that humans impose upon themselves. You should also have gained some useful self-help skills for preventing and managing your problems and making decisions of living. Let's try to stay out of the rough and to stop being our own worst enemies.

WHAT IS THINKING?

A variety of mental processes are subsumed under the word *thinking*. The following list shows over thirty mental processes that could be considered thinking. The list is far from exhaustive. Furthermore, it is possible to think about the process of thinking! Indeed, if you are to control your thinking, you must become aware of, and able to influence, your thinking about how you think.

Some Processes of Thinking

Anticipating	Creating	Judging
Attributing	Deciding	Knowing
Being aware	Distorting	Memorizing
Being curious	Dreaming	Perceiving
Believing	Evaluating	Problem solving
Choosing	Fantasizing	Reasoning
Concentrating	Forgetting	Reflecting
Conceptualizing	Imaging	Remembering
Concluding	Introspecting	Understanding
Considering	Intuiting	Visualizing

Thinking and Choosing

Thinking in this book is viewed from an existential perspective. That is, thinking is an integral part of human existence: humans are condemned to be thinkers and choosers. We actively create our lives through our choices; indeed, our lives may be viewed as the sum of the consequences of our choices. Humans cannot *not* think. Choosing from among various options is the central feature of the processes of thinking. Just as we cannot not think, we cannot not choose. As noted Viennese psychiatrist Viktor Frankl (1969) observed, "During no moment of his life does man escape the mandate to choose among possibilities" [p.85]. Our mental processes involve making thinking choices at various levels of self-awareness and self-control. For instance, people can choose to observe much of their mental functioning and, if they find it is not working for them, choose to alter it. I do not mean to imply that this is invariably easy, but it is usually possible.

Some people's thinking processes are more effective than others'. The late Abraham Maslow used to say that mental patients were not sick, but rather "cognitively wrong." He meant that their mental processes entailed poor thinking choices, resulting in behavior that got labeled as mental illness. "Neurosis, psychosis, stunting of growth—all are, from this point of view, cognitive diseases as well, contaminating perception, learning, remembering, attending and thinking" (Maslow, 1962, p. 189).

American psychiatrist William Glasser (1984), the originator of reality therapy, also emphasizes the role of choosing in our lives. He views people as control systems that are in a continual process of making choices in their attempts to control their lives. For example, people choose the misery they feel; however, better choices are available if they learn how to make them. Glasser does not explicitly mention thinking skills, but he clearly implies that by using better thinking skills humans can avoid much of their distress.

Albert Ellis (1962, 1980), the originator of rational-emotive therapy, is perhaps the most prominent psychologist in recent years to focus on the way people choose to think themselves into negative emotions such as anger, anxiety, and depression. Ellis is concerned to help his clients toward freedom of choice based on rational thinking. Rationality means thinking in ways that contribute to the chosen goals of survival and happiness. Irrationality means thinking in ways that block or interfere with the attainment of those goals. In particular, Ellis focuses on the way people choose irrational belief systems, with which they then persistently reindoctrinate themselves. Like a broken record, they stay stuck in the same groove.

Perhaps enough has been said by way of introduction to show that people thinking themselves into personal problems is a very common notion in contemporary psychology. In imitation of Ellis's "rational humorous" songs, and with apologies to Rodgers and Hammerstein, let me illustrate this point by parodying the lyrics of one of the latter's most famous songs. My intention is not to belittle the misery felt by depressed and suicidal people, but rather to show how their thinking may contribute to it.

Climb ev'ry mountain,
Count ev'ry blow,
Savor ev'ry put-down,
Till your mood feels low.

Climb ev'ry mountain,
Heighten ev'ry fear,
Wallow in self-pity,
Till suicide feels near.

Comedy and tragedy are not far apart in the context of inadequate thinking choices. Many jokes focus on other people's thinking deficiencies: for instance, British jokes about the Irish, U.S. jokes about Poles, New Zealand jokes about Australians. For example, a New Zealand prime minister once observed, about the emigration of New Zealanders to Australia, that it raised the intelligence level of both populations! It is easy to poke fun at the notion of others dim-wittedly creating their own problems. However, people in psychological pain are more to be sympathized with than laughed at. They require help to enable them to make more effective thinking choices.

Other Dimensions of Thinking

Besides choosing, a number of dimensions of thinking may be inferred from the list on page 3. They include the following.

Pictures and words   Thinking involves visual images and fantasies as well as thoughts expressed in words. Think of someone you love. Does your mind conjure up an image of the person, words, or a mixture of both?

Accurate and inaccurate perceptions   Perceiving means apprehending through both the mind and the senses. Most of your perceptions of yourself, others, and the environment may be accurate. However, other perceptions may be either distorted or denied altogether.

Levels of awareness   Thinking processes operate at different levels of awareness. Though humans are capable of accurate perception and reasoning, frequently they fail to use that capability fully. Defensive thinking implies that individuals are unaware not only of the outcomes of their defensive thought processes but also of the processes themselves. Further examples of unconscious thinking processes include dreaming and the wellsprings of creativity. Maslow (1962) distinguishes between primary and second-ary process cognition, or thinking. He makes a plea for acknowledging constructive as well as destructive unconscious primary thinking processes.

Some thinking processes occur on a level of awareness that is neither conscious nor unconscious. Psychiatrist Aaron Beck (1976) has proposed the notion of "automatic" thoughts that are influential in contributing to negative phenomena such as anxiety, phobias, and depression. Such thoughts pass almost unnoticed unless people are instructed to focus on them.

Rational and irrational thinking   Thinking choices can lead to conclusions that are realistically and accurately drawn from verifiable premises. However, often human thinking is not based on logical reasoning. Consequently, to varying degrees it becomes irrational and self-defeating.

Personal experiencing and valuing   Thinking for yourself implies that each of you has a unique capacity both for experiencing innner and outer events and for placing a value on that experiencing. But certain thinking choices are not based on your own personal experiencing and valuing. For example, you may treat other people's beliefs and values as if they were your own. The poet W. H. Auden wrote, of the effects of the totalitarian state, "And terror like a frost shall halt the flood of thinking." His words are also pertinent to the way in which you fear of others or of yourself may distance you from acknowledging, let alone stating, what you truly think.

Thinking, Feeling, and Action

The relation of thinking, feeling, and action may be considered in many different ways. Here are three interrelated viewpoints, two of which are depicted in the figure on page 7. All three help to highlight different aspects of the relation of thinking, feeling, and action.

Thinking, feeling, and action interact with each other.   Thinking often accompanies or results from feelings at varying levels of awareness. Conversely, you may choose to regulate your feelings by altering the way in which you think about yourself, others, and the environment. The connection between thinking and action is also two-way: thinking influences action, and action influences thinking. Likewise, feelings and actions influence each other.

Thinking, feeling, and action are integrated with each other.   This viewpoint is holistic; that is, there is no mind/body split, no dichotomy between human thinking and animality. Writers such as Carl Rogers and Abraham Maslow view high-level human functioning as integrated. Rogers (1961) observed that as humans become more able to perceive their significant biological experiencing, they act more rationally and less defensively. In most animals, instinct provides the link between feeling and action. Humans are different in two significant ways. First, their instinct is relatively weak; second, their capacity for thinking and self-awareness can override what instinct they have. Thus, in varying degrees humans may cease to think, feel, and act in an integrated way.

INTERACTION

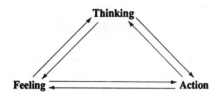

INTEGRATION

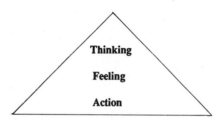

Two viewpoints on the relation among thinking, feeling, and action

Feeling and action are results of thinking.   This is the position advanced by writers like Ellis, Beck, and the so-called cognitive behaviorists. It is based on a simple ABC framework.

A. The activating event
B. Your thoughts
C. Your feelings and actions

What you feel and do (C) can be either helpful or harmful. This is due not so much to what happened (A), as to how you think (B) about what happened (A). In short, feelings and actions are heavily influenced by how you think about events. An extension of this model is that the consequences of action and feeling (C) provide feedback, enabling you to alter your thinking (B).

There is no simple answer to questions concerning the relation of thinking, feeling, and action. Neither can we say whether changed actions follow from changed thoughts or the reverse. In reality, cognitive and cognitive-behavioral therapists sometimes intervene to change clients' behavior before trying to change their thinking. Beck, who works with depressed patients, often starts by encouraging them to engage in some basic activities. He hopes thereby to alter their thinking about their capacity to influence their environments (Beck, Rush, Shaw, & Emery, 1979). Sometimes a good way to alter your thinking is to change your behavior in real-life situations that have caused you difficulty in the past. Later in this book you will be introduced to experiments in which you change your behavior to test the accuracy of your thinking and then, if necessary, alter that thinking.

WHAT ARE THINKING SKILLS?

As the preceding section has shown, the verb *thinking* subsumes numerous mental processes. However, in this book the focus is on thinking skills that help you manage your problems and decisions of living better. Consequently, though intellectual skills overlap the thinking skills useful for daily living, the former are not emphasized. Nevertheless, this is very much a book about using your brain!

What Are Skills?

The word *skill* implies proficiency in some activity. It also implies the ability to conceive of and implement an effective sequence of choices, so as to achieve a desired objective. For instance, to be a good decision maker you have to conceive of and implement the choices needed to make good decisions. The fact that we view thinking as a skill does not mean that applying that skill need be mechanistic or boring. Effective thinking skills may free you to be more spontaneous as well as help you to regulate unwanted feelings.

It is unhelpful to think of yourself as either having or not having a certain skill. Rather, think of yourself as having skills strengths and weaknesses, or a mixture of the two. If you make good choices in a skills area—for instance, making decisions—you have a skills strength. If you make poor choices, you have a skills weakness. In all thinking skills areas, you are likely to have both strengths and weaknesses in varying degrees. For example, in the skills area of making decisions, you may be good at identifying and collecting relevant information, but poor at evaluating the consequences of each alternative. The object of counseling, training, and self-help in thinking skills is to augment your strength and lessen your weakness in one or more skills areas. Put another way, it is to help you think about your thinking so that you become a better chooser.

Defining Thinking Skills

To gain maximum happiness and fulfillment, you require a repertoire of thinking skills. Your repertoire is the stock of skills that you are able to use when necessary. Here is a definition of thinking skills for the purposes of this book.

Thinking skills are sequences of choices, made via various mental processes. Your repertoire of thinking skills comprises your strengths and weaknesses in each skills area.

But it is insufficient just to know what a thinking skill is. You have to use it when required. Effectively using your thinking skills helps you to both prevent avoidable problems and manage unavoidable problems constructively.

Reservations About a Thinking Skills Approach

Some of you may have reservations about an approach that encourages you to discipline your thinking skills. Your objections may include the following.

- *It's too intellectual.* Focusing on how you think may take you too far into your head rather than help you get in touch with your feelings and take appropriate actions. Many very clever people behave foolishly in their personal relations.
- *It's too mechanistic.* A thinking skills approach allows insufficient scope for individual differences, free will, intuition, and creativity. Instead, people are reduced to being mechanical thinking boxes, somewhat like computers.
- *It's too superficial.* People's problems are often the result of emotional deprivations in their upbringing. As such, they may require long-term counseling: focusing on tightening up their thinking is insufficient. Furthermore, most people's behavior is influenced by numerous genetic and contextual factors. These factors include sex, age, intelligence, biochemistry, health, socioeconomic status, culture, chance, other people's behavior, and so on. To say that people can be much more in control of their lives if they think more effectively fails to take into account the importance of those other factors.
- *It's too hard.* What most people want is an easy life within the confines of a conventional world view. Few people have either the desire or the capacity for genuine independent thought. It is asking too much to expect the average person to discipline his or her thinking.

Each of the above reservations is a partial rather than a whole truth. Focusing on thinking skills can be a counterproductive intellectual exercise. However, working on how you think can liberate you to experience your feelings more fully and to behave more effectively. Because something can be done the wrong way does not mean you cannot be successful doing it a different way. The same holds true for the objection that a focus on thinking skills is too mechanistic. Improved thinking skills can release rather than restrict your capacity for creativity and independent thought.

The charge of superficiality, too, is a partial rather than a whole truth. Some people may indeed require nurturing emotional relationships to lower their anxiety level to the point at which they can usefully work on their thinking. And though genetic and environmental factors do place limits on your control over your life, you still have numerous opportunities to choose how you exist. Endeavoring to replace "stinkin' thinkin'" with effective thinking can help, even though sometimes you may have to make the most of poor conditions. And it's true: thinking for yourself *is* hard. But because it may be too hard for many does not mean that it will be too hard for you. There is a difference between hard and impossible.

BEING PERSONALLY RESPONSIBLE FOR YOUR THINKING

When you are being personally responsible you are in the process of making the choices that maximize your happiness and fulfillment (Nelson-Jones, 1984, 1988). Personal responsibility is a positive concept: you are responsible *for* your well-being and making your own choices. Compare this to the common meaning of responsibility; responsibility *to* others, including living up to their standards. Though taking personal responsibility is difficult, it is also liberating. It frees you to concentrate on how you can be most effective. It entails neither focusing on other people's faults nor feeling that you need say "my fault" all the time.

This book aims to help you adopt and implement a fundamental attitude of personal responsibility for how you think about your personal problems. Viewing thinking skills as sequences of choices allows you to do this. The focus is on your present and future behavior. Your past thinking choices merit attention only to the extent that you can learn from them.

Assuming personal responsibility for your thinking does not mean only thinking about yourself. Humans are social animals, and as such, interdependent. The borderline between meeting the needs of self and others wavers. Nevertheless, the degree to which you think effectively about your personal problems determines the possibility of synergy rather than conflict in establishing that borderline. Humans have the capacity to transcend narrow self-interest, both in their loving relationships and by taking a wider interest in the welfare of their species. Ineffective thinking not only releases humans' negative potential; it also restrains their positive potential. Conversely, effective thinking blocks the bad and encourages the good.

In his influential book *The Courage to Be*, theologian Paul Tillich (1952) wrote, "The courage to be is the ethical act in which man affirms his own being in spite of those elements of his existence which conflict with his essential self-affirmation" [p. 3]. Tillich viewed the world through a religious framework. Nevertheless, his words are congruent with the message of this book. To rephrase Tillich, the courage to be entails assuming personal responsibility for affirming your being through the adequacy of your thinking choices. You do this despite conditions in yourself and in your circumstances that block your self-affirmation. It is within your power to improve how you think about your problems. The choices are yours!

CHAPTER HIGHLIGHTS

How you think influences how you feel and act, and vice versa.
Thinking involves many different processes and is visual as well as verbal.
Choosing is the central feature of the processes of thinking.
To gain maximum happiness and fulfillment, you require a repertoire of thinking skills.
You are personally responsible for your thinking choices and for developing and using appropriate thinking skills when faced with personal problems.
Effective and independent thinking can require courage.

CHAPTER 2

Learning How Not to Think

Yet each man kills the thing he loves,
By each let this be heard,
Some do it with a bitter look,
Some with a flattering word.

Oscar Wilde

Parenthood: A relationship that allows an older generation to pass on its anxieties and distortions of reality to a younger generation.
Childhood: An eighteen-year custodial sentence in which children acquire the vices of their elders under the guise of learning their virtues.

The purpose of this chapter is to help you understand how you learned to make your present thinking choices when faced with personal problems. You will review how you attained your present level of thinking skills and, in subsequent chapters, look at ways of improving specific skills. This chapter's discussion is divided into two parts: acquiring deficient thinking skills and sustaining them. As you read, you may come to see that although others may have shaped your past thinking choices, you are now responsible for them in the present and future.

ACQUIRING DEFICIENT THINKING SKILLS

How did you learn to make poor thinking choices? How can you learn to make good ones? If you are to think effectively about your problems, ideally you require a sense of security as well as good thinking skills. Here's a simple equation:

EFFECTIVE THINKING = SECURITY + SKILLS

By security I mean a sense of self-worth, which tends to lessen anxieties that interfere with your thinking. Let's review how you learned your thinking skills and then discuss some ways in which you may have acquired a degree of debilitating anxiety.

Stages in the Development of Thinking

The branch of psychology that focuses on thinking is called cognitive psychology. To date, cognitive psychologists have focused on the development of intellectual and moral thinking rather than on the development of thinking about personal problems, though the latter may involve moral issues. Much of their work has examined the development of children's thinking; for example, Piaget's (1970) developmental stages of logical thinking. However, attention has also been focused on the development of thinking in adolescents—for example, Kohlberg's stages of moral thinking (Kohlberg & Gilligan, 1971)—and in young adults—for example, Perry's (1970) stages of intellectual and ethical thinking.

The work of Piaget helps us particularly to understand how—because their capacity for independent critical thinking takes many years to develop—children are at great risk of acquiring faulty thinking habits from adults. Piaget stated that the developmental stages of thinking are sequential: they appear in a fixed order, each one necessary to the formation of the following. Piaget stressed that these stages are not simply congruent with biological maturation; they also reflect children's experiencing of their physical and social environments.

Briefly, Piaget's three stages in the development of children's logical thinking are as follows.

1. *A sensorimotor period (to 18 months old):* Babies develop from creatures of automatic reflexes to beings having a primitive form of representative imagery for problem solving.
2. *A period of representative intelligence leading to concrete operations:* This has two subperiods.
   a. *Preoperational subperiod (18 months to 7 years old):* This begins with the formation of processes such as language and mental imagery.
   b. *Concrete operations subperiod (7 to 12 years old):* Children have developed some basic logical rules. However, their thinking is still firmly based on concrete reality.
3. *Period of formal operations (12 years and older):* Children can transcend concrete reality and think about what might be. They can act on propositions that are about other propositions, not just about concrete reality.

Although Piaget's work on the development of logical thinking is still being refined by research, it explains in part why you may engage in faulty thinking when faced with personal problems. For instance, much of your significant learning about personal problem solving was absorbed from your parents and others before you fully acquired the capacity for logical thinking. This may have predisposed your reactions to problems in later life to be more automatic than rational. Many people—possibly 40 to 50 percent—may never attain the stage of formal operations. Furthermore, even those who have developed the capacity for logical thinking may fail to use it when experiencing the anxiety generated by certain problems.

Learning from Observation

The term *social learning* implies learning that takes place within a social context. Learning from observation is one of the main methods of social learning: psychologists use the term *modeling* to describe such learning. You learn from listening to and watching people like your parents who demonstrate behavior, including their thinking skills. Modeling requires both an observer and a model. It is more likely to be effective if the observer (1) attends well, (2) retains the material efficiently, and (3) witnesses outcomes he or she personally values.

The effects of modeling are less direct when thinking rather than action skills are observed. With action skills, the old saying "Monkey see, monkey do" is more likely to apply. Not only are thinking skills not visual in the sense that action skills are, they are seldom clearly verbalized. People seldom talk aloud about their thinking processes when faced with personal problems. More often they talk and behave in ways that covertly convey their thinking skills strengths and weaknesses. For example, parents frequently think in overgeneralized terms, with great emphasis on how they and others "should," "ought to," or "must" be. To the extent that this reflects rigid and punitive standards, they model a style of thinking that contributes to their children acquiring skills weaknesses.

Having no models who think effectively about their personal problems robs children of a valuable source of learning. Even worse, children may acquire deficient thinking skills from poor models. Eric Berne (1972), the originator of transactional analysis, pointed out the ways in which different parents think and react when something goes wrong in their families. In some families, parents may react by searching for rational solutions to problems. In other families, parents may get angry, feel hurt, or become depressed. The latter fail to model thinking skills for coping adequately with personal difficulties.

Many kinds of people may have acted—for good or ill—as models for your thinking choices:

- *Parents*, including stepparents and surrogate parents
- *Brothers and sisters*, especially if they are older
- *Teachers*, whether known in class or through extracurricular activities
- *Peer groups*, or people of roughly your own age
- *Famous people*, such as well-known sports figures, entertainment personalities, and historical or religious leaders
- *Fictional people*, in books, on TV, and in movies
- *Advertising characters*, thinking and behaving in ways that influence your purchasing decisions

Usually your parents are the most important early influences on your thinking. Most of you carry your parents around in your heads long after leaving home. Think of the ways in which your parents, or substitute parents, handled personal problems, whether their own, with you, or with other family members. To what extent do you consider the thinking skills strengths and weaknesses with which you now handle personal problems to have been influenced by their examples?

Learning from Consequences

As children act on their environments, those environments respond with consequences. When a child behaves well according to parental standards, parents are likely to say "good boy" or "good girl." By doing so, the parents send a message not only about a specific behavior, but about how the child should view that behavior in the future. Furthermore, depending on how the message is sent, it may also communicate either affirming or "put-down" implications about the child's worth.

Many parental messages help children to develop adequate thinking skills for coping with future personal problems. Earlier I mentioned Berne's observation that, in some families, parents search for rational solutions when things go wrong. Children of such families are likely to learn not only from modeling but also from being encouraged to think rationally about their own problems. Another positive example would be that of a child, teased and bullied in primary school, whose parents offer emotional support by sensitively eliciting the child's thoughts and feelings. These parents might also help their child and reward him or her for developing realistic thinking skills that cope with the problem of being teased.

Psychologist Claude Steiner (1974) writes, "When problem solving is discouraged by parents, children develop a reaction of mindlessness, stupidity, passivity, and incapacity to think in the face of difficult situations" [p. 151]. Such training in mindlessness may even include providing negative consequences for the child's use of skills involving awareness, intuition, or rationality. Unfortunately, as the following limerick illustrates, some parents' own insecurities and thinking difficulties get in the way of their capacity to help their children think effectively.

> *There are parents, regardless of season,*
> *Who won't let their kids use their reason.*
> *They rule them with fear,*
> *No objections can bear,*
> *For to think for yourself is high treason.*

It is not only parents who provide positive and negative consequences that develop or retard their children's acquisition of effective thinking skills. Teachers, friends, relatives, and many others do so, too. Young people's peer groups exert particularly strong pressure to gain approval by thinking in conformist rather than autonomous ways.

The kinds of thinking skills you are encouraged to acquire may differ depending on whether you are a girl or a boy. Skills requiring intuition and sensitivity to the needs to others may be more encouraged in girls. Skills requiring analysis, independence, and willingness to take a stand or to take risks may be more encouraged in boys. Traditionally, the role of the woman was that of the social harmonizer in the home. Women also tend to disclose more and to form closer friendships than men. Consequently, males may receive more negative feedback when trying to develop the thinking skills required for close personal and family relationships, while women may manifest more thinking skills weaknesses in environments requiring assertion, such as in business. However, the thinking that sustains traditional gender roles has recently been strongly challenged (though not universally). Also, in many countries, the proportion of women both in the work force and in higher education has increased markedly. In sum, the consequences for the development of thinking skills are now less related to gender than they have been in the past.

Acquiring Inadequate Concepts and Information

It is a great help, in thinking about personal problems, to have a realistic conceptual framework within which to understand them. For instance, the late George Kelly, a noted personality theorist, is reputed to have said that asking a psychologist to describe a problem without the concept of anxiety was like asking a jockey to win a race without a horse! If you do not understand anxiety, you are disadvantaged in understanding yourself and others. Each major counseling and personality theory thus offers a language and set of concepts for comprehending human behavior. Clients and people in general also require realistic conceptual frameworks to guide their thinking, feeling, and action choices.

In all probability most of you grew up with conceptual frameworks that both helped and hindered you in effectively thinking about your problems. In general there is little systematic training, at home or in school, in how to think through personal problems. Most people are left to pick it up as best they can.

Children often grow up with considerable gaps in their information about essential aspects of life. However, if you are to think realistically about personal problems, you require as much relevant information as is necessary to make good choices. Sometimes with the best and sometimes with the worst of intentions, adults subject children to lies, half-truths, and omissions of truth. All of these blunt their awareness of life. For instance, parents may be dishonest some if not much of the time. They may engage in impression management, concealing information that contradicts how they want their children to see them. Also, they may be too embarrassed to talk about how children are conceived and born, their own sexuality, or their financial position. Their own anxieties about subjects like death may cause them to use euphemisms with their children rather than gently yet honestly confront them with reality. Government, education, and the media may also present—or fail to present—information in ways that restrict people's awareness of reality.

Acquiring High Anxiety

The Roman poet Horace wrote, "At the rider's back sits dark Anxiety." The same topic is approached in a humorous way by comedian Mel Brooks, when he jokes that he suffers from high anxiety. Anxiety is a part of our animal nature. Just as you cannot avoid choosing and thinking, you cannot escape your potential for anxiety. Ultimately the fear of death, nonbeing, or destruction is the underlying fear from which all other anxieties stem. I prefer to use the term *survival anxiety*, because anxiety has a survival value in that it alerts you to realistic dangers to your existence. Unfortunately, all people suffer in varying degrees from what I term *high anxiety.* I mean that it is higher than that required to cope efficiently with life's challenges, either general or specific. Thus it is disproportionate and debilitating rather than facilitating.

There is a two-way relationship between high anxiety and thinking skills. People who are highly anxious may block their awareness of the information they require to think effectively. For instance, they may have tunnel vision, which allows them to rigidly focus on only a few aspects of a complex situation. They may also block their awareness of their own thoughts and feelings. Or they may lack an adequate sense of themselves against which to evaluate inner and outer information. However, poor thinking skills not only result from high anxiety: they may also contribute to it. Poor thinking skills for personal problems can result in negative outcomes, which in turn may engender lack of confidence and anxiety.

There is also a close connection between a high sense of security and low anxiety, as I mentioned earlier. Here are some behaviors that parents can use to help their children feel secure and worthwhile. The opposite of each behavior may create insecurity and high anxiety.

- *Showing commitment:* Children need to feel they can depend on their parents' commitment to them. They require a secure base from which to explore and learn.
- *Expressing affection:* Children need to feel that their parents love and cherish them. Both verbal and tactile assurances are important.
- *Understanding thoughts and feelings:* Children need to feel that their parents are emotionally accessible and that they understand their feelings and thoughts.
- *Acknowledging separateness and difference:* Parents need to be sufficiently secure to respect their children as separate and different from themselves.
- *Practicing direct communication:* Messages need to be sent as clearly as possible, without "hidden agendas," "power plays," or "put-downs."
- *Being open:* Parents should reveal themselves as three-dimensional human beings and admit their fallibility. They should avoid impression management, lies, omissions of truth, and half-truths, and acknowledge reality rather than denying or distorting it.
- *Working through problems:* Parents need to be prepared to work through family problems as they arise, on a basis of mutual respect.
- *Providing suitable learning opportunities:* Helping children feel and become more competent by providing them with learning opportunities geared to their stage of development is essential. This includes the provision of relevant information.
- *Offering encouragement:* Encouraging children rather than discouraging them as they learn skills and competencies, including thinking skills, is of the greatest importance.
- *Modeling personal responsibility:* Ideally, parents help children learn from their example that ultimately each person is responsible for making the choices that lead to his or her unique happiness and fulfillment.

Some people's feelings of insecurity and of high anxiety are very pronounced. They may require a long-term counseling relationship. At first the emphasis may be on providing a corrective emotional experience, one of nurturing and healing, before teaching them how to think through their problems. In practice, the division between nurturing and teaching is seldom clear-cut.

SUSTAINING DEFICIENT THINKING SKILLS

Nearly 300 years ago the British philosopher John Pomfret wrote, "We live and learn, but not the wiser grow." It is useful to distinguish between acquiring deficient thinking skills and sustaining them. The past cannot be relived. If you are to overcome your thinking skills weaknesses, your focus must be on how you are sustaining them now. Often they are well-developed habits acquired many years before and sustained ever since. When Eric Berne (1972) developed the notion of scripts, he postulated that people's lives are preordained from their early years by a script that they follow faithfully. I view the concept of a life script in terms of how you sustain poor or good thinking skills. Poor thinking skills constrict choice, thus giving people's lives the appearance of being directed by a script.

The main distinction between acquiring and sustaining deficient thinking skills is that in acquiring them, the empahsis is on what others did to you. In sustaining them, the emphasis is on what you do to yourself. Though environmental factors play a part in your choices, you have by now internalized your weaknesses and risk perpetuating them through further poor choices.

What You Do to Yourself

How do you sustain your thinking skills weaknesses? Here are some factors contributing to the process.

Inadequate conceptual framework   Because thinking effectively about personal problems is rarely taught systematically, there may be gaps in your conceptual framework. You may have no concept of thinking as comprising a set of skills. Or you may have gaps in your knowledge of specific skills.

Faulty self-perceptions   You may view yourself as a consistently rational human being. Such a view may block you from acknowledging incoming information that contradicts it. Your perceptions of yourself are what you regard as "I" or "me." Your self-picture reflects your sense of security and of your competence to cope with life. The more insecure you are, the more likely you are to have rigid self-perceptions that are not amenable to change through feedback. Instead of having what Rogers (1961) terms "openness" to your experiencing—both inner and outer—you deny and distort information that contradicts your view of yourself. Such conflicting information may cause insecure people to feel highly anxious. To retain your self-perceptions and sense of security, you may engage in defensive "security" operations. One result of those operations is the retention of deficient thinking skills, since they remain unexamined. Another result is that you remain insecure.

Self-reindoctrination   Much of your thinking takes place in the form of "self-talk." The self-talk of many people faced with personal problems is highly repetitive. Their thinking resembles a record player stuck in the same groove. Ellis (1962) points out that people retain their emotional disturbance through illogical self-verbalizations. Repetitively self-verbalizing your illogical beliefs both represents and sustains deficient thinking. Counterproductive self-reindoctrination is more likely if your self-perceptions allow little room for the adequacy of your thinking to be challenged.

High anxiety   High anxiety may block your awareness of both your thoughts and feelings. Also, it erodes your sense of self so that you lack a sound inner basis on which to evaluate inner and outer information. High anxiety can cause you to feel unnecessarily threatened by feedback that contradicts your self-perceptions. These feelings in turn may trigger off security operations whereby you "operate" on the feedback to reduce its threat. These security operations take place beneath your conscious awareness. Thus you sustain the illusion of security at the price of relinquishing some of your hold on reality. I have rewritten the lyrics of the first verse of Cole Porter's song *High Society* to illustrate this point.

> *Just dig our problems mounting high,*
> *They're now approaching beyond the sky.*
> *We've been for years fleeing reality—*
> *My goodness gracious, now we are going to be*
> *In high, high, high anx-ie, high anxiety.*

High anxiety also makes you fearful of change. Maslow's (1962) distinction between safety and growth choices is relevant to this point. You may prefer the safety of your existing thinking skills, however deficient, to the growth entailed in changing the way you think and, in turn, act.

Secondary gains and payoffs   In this context secondary gains and payoffs are the inner rewards you get for hanging on to your deficient thinking skills. For instance, angry Annie blames everybody but herself for her misfortunes. If she is going to attain the real gain of accurately attributing responsibility for her misfortunes, she will have to relinquish the secondary gain of being able to blame others all the time. She sustains an easy and convenient habit that enables her to avoid having to change her own thinking and behavior. Ellis acknowledges that sometimes people's resistance to change may stem from pleasurable payoffs. However, he adds that their resistances very frequently ". . . stem from low frustration tolerance: their stubborn refusal to go through immediate pain to get future gain. Their main payoff is instant comfort, which undramatically and insidiously prevents them from working at therapy and surrendering their disturbances" (Ellis, 1980, p. 11). Ellis's observation is relevant for people outside as well as inside of therapy.

Insufficient awareness of personal responsibility   Many people are insufficiently aware that it is their personal responsibilty to make the most of their lives. Sustaining poor thinking skills is largely a matter of what you do to yourself rather than what others have done in the past or what your environment has done to you. This means that improving your thinking skills is closely linked to the degree to which you assume personal responsibility for making it happen. In general, however, becoming personally responsible is much easier said than done.

What Your Environment Does to You

The earlier section on acquiring deficient thinking skills focused on external influences. Many of those external influences may persist, thus helping you sustain deficient thinking skills. Here are some negative environmental influences that may prevent you from changing.

Deficient modeling   People who have modeled poor thinking skills for you in the past may continue to do so. For instance, a parent who demands a perfectionist's standard of achievement will continue to do so. Many men may continue to be afraid to show feelings of vulnerability and caring. Many women may continue to think or behave passively. The media continue their relentless pressure on both genders to think like good consumers and to value youth, success, and sex disproportionately.

Inappropriate consequences   Thinking skills weaknesses may persist because they have provided positive results. For instance, you may have been able to manipulate people into believing they are persecuting an innocent victim (such as yourself) when the reverse may be the case. Anger and the thinking that accompanies it may have gotten you what you wanted. However, your gains may have been at the expense of mutual respect in your relationships and of learning to develop the thinking skills to manage your anger better. And just as using poor thinking skills may have positive consequences, using good thinking skills may have negative consequences. For instance, however well you present your ideas, thinking for yourself may threaten others. Their negative responses may make it harder for you to think independently.

Lack of information and opportunity   You may continue to lack the opportunity to acquire a realistic conceptual framework within which to think about your problems. Significant people in your environment may continue to brush you off with impression management, lies, omissions of truth, and half-truths. Once you have acquired deficient thinking skills, you may not have access to those people, such as skilled counselors, who can help you overcome them. What some people require is a relationship in which the counselor offers not only support and understanding, but also confrontation and education. Frequently such relationships are not readily available.

CONCLUDING COMMENT

In this chapter I have stressed that the way in which you think mainly reflects your learning history. But although your good and poor thinking choices have been learned, you continue to sustain them, for good or ill. Because they are mainly sustained by inner processes, you need to take control of your thinking. Undoubtedly, you already do this to some extent. I'll next turn to some specific skills for improving your thinking when faced with personal problems.

CHAPTER HIGHLIGHTS

Your thinking skills strengths and weaknesses have been learned.

Both maturational and social learning factors influenced the development of your thinking.

You learned your thinking skills strengths and weaknesses from (1) observing others, (2) the consequences your actions provided, (3) the concepts and information you received, and (4) how secure you were helped to feel.

Once learned, many of your thinking skills strengths and weaknesses have been sustained by you.

You sustain your deficient thinking skills through (1) an inadequate conceptual framework, (2) faulty self-perceptions, (3) self-reindoctrination, (4) high anxiety, (5) giving way to secondary gains and payoffs, and (6) being insufficiently aware of your personal responsibility for the authorship of your life.

You are helped by others and by your environment to sustain deficient thinking skills through (1) deficient modeling, (2) experiencing inappropriate consequences, and (3) a persisting lack of information and opportunity.

You can learn to take more control of your thinking.

CHAPTER 3

Owning
Responsibility for Choosing

I choose, therefore I am.

Adaptation from Descartes

To make the growth choice instead of the fear choice a dozen times a day is to move a dozen times a day towards self-actualization.

Abraham Maslow

People who effectively cope with their problems and decisions of living possess a skill: the skill of owning their responsibility for choosing within the constraints of reality. Those who cope ineffectively add their denials and distortions to existing real-life constraints. The poet T. S. Eliot once wrote, "Human kind cannot bear very much reality." Frequently, humans choose to follow what I facetiously call the Nelson-Jones Reality Principle: "If you cannot accept reality, create it!" However, the price of creating your own reality can be high. It sows the seeds of alienation from yourself, others, and the environment.

In this chapter I focus on four interrelated skills needed to own responsibility for choosing to create your life within the constraints of reality. They are choice awareness, responsibility awareness, existential awareness, and feelings awareness.

CHOICE AWARENESS

Here is a vignette of a woman who has just come in for counseling.

> Katie is in her early forties, the mother of four children from 4 to 16 years of age. Six months ago her husband, Peter, left her to live with his secretary, Penny. Katie is furious with him for "abandoning" her and the children. Additionally, Katie is now having a difficult time with her eldest daughter, Sandra, who at 16 has decided to live with her father for the time being. Katie used to have a good relationship with Sandra but is now very angry with her and says that she has become "selfish" and "hard." Her relation-

ship with her other children is deteriorating too, not least because they see her pushing and shoving Peter when, unannounced, he comes around to visit them. Katie has a huge chip on her shoulder and feels herself to be very much the victim of others' bad behavior. She feels angry, anxious, depressed, confused, and powerless.

Katie is similar to many people of both genders who come in for counseling. They feel that their lives are beyond their control. They have relinquished, at least temporarily, their capacity to make effective choices within the constraints of reality. Even if her husband has behaved very badly, in the final analysis Katie is *choosing* to allow her emotions to be controlled by his behavior rather than *choosing* to work to free herself from his negative influence. Furthermore, she has probably *chosen* to allow her relationship with Sandra to deteriorate. An important part of counseling people like Katie is to help them become more aware that (1) they are always choosers, (2) their choices always have costs and consequences, and (3) within the constraints of reality, they can learn to increase the odds that their choices will have good rather than bad results.

Three Areas of Choosing

There are three main areas in which humans can be choosers: in relation to themselves, to others, and to the environment. But these areas overlap. In each, people as choosers are confronted with existential conflicts between their needs and the givens of their existences. Central to all choosing is this conflict between freedom and responsibility. Sartre (1956) has described humans as being "condemned" to freedom. Choices are difficult to make. However, the price and challenge of this freedom is the responsibility for making your life.

Choosing in relation to yourself   When you choose in this area, you are choosing how you feel, think, and act. Though physical reactions may be involuntary and beyond your control, psychological reactions are potentially within your control. Much of this book is devoted to helping you understand that how you choose to feel is related to how you choose to think and act. I hope to help you explore your inner world, seeing not only the surface choices but also the underlying or *underchoices* that you make. These underchoices frequently block your ability to truly own your life and fulfill your potential.

Choosing in relation to others   In any two-party relationship, there are really at least four relationships: each party's relationship to self as well as to another. Furthermore, since people exist in social networks of family, friends, community leaders, and others, there may be numerous contextual relations within which any two-party relationship exists.

Choosing in relation to others confronts you with some of your limits as a chooser. First, you are confronted with your ultimate isolation even when you are with others: for instance, no one can die your death for you. A second and related fact is that there are absolute boundaries between "me" and "you." To a large extent you can control how you choose in relation to yourself. But with others, the most you can hope for is to influence how they choose to think, feel, and act in relation to themselves and to you. This limitation can be hard for many to accept.

Choosing in relation to the environment   Your relationship to the environment is in part a relationship with the natural order, which can appear to be cruel and meaningless. The paradox of life is that, because of the natural order, we are dying as we live. Of course, though death is biologically inescapable, many erect psychological defenses against the awareness of their own mortality. The natural order can also be capricious; life can involve inescapable suffering. Additionally, the natural order does not provide much of a meaning structure beyond the survival instinct. Maslow (1970) has observed that humans have "weak, subtle and tender instinctoid needs" that are at risk of being "overwhelmed by the tougher, more powerful culture, rather than the other way about" [p. 82]. Thus if humans are not actually condemned to a search for meaning in the face of an indifferent universe, they often may feel close to this state.

Consciousness Raising to Facilitate Choosing

Throughout the remainder of this book you are provided with thinksheets designed to develop your thinking skills by giving you the opportunity to practice them. The first of these focuses on body language, but its underlying purpose is to raise your consciousness about how you may be failing to fully exercise your capacity to choose. The first thinksheet is in two parts.

─────────────── **THINKSHEET 1** ───────────────

Choosing Your Body Language

1. *Describing, being aware, choosing*
    a. Either on your own or with a partner, spend a minute or two *describing* what body language means to you. Your partner should remain silent when you do this.
    b. Spend a minute or two doing a Gestalt-type awareness exercise in which you say, either to yourself or to a partner, "Now I am *aware . . .*" before mentioning each aspect of your body language that you are aware of. For example, "Now I am aware that my arms are folded."
    c. Spend a minute or two saying "I *choose* to . . ." about each aspect of body language that you choose to display. For instance, if your arms are folded, say "I choose to fold my arms," or, if you change your seating position, say "I choose to . . ." and then add how you have chosen to move your body.
    d. How did you experience this describing, being aware, choosing sequence? If you have a partner, tell him or her.
    e. Reverse roles, so that the partner who listened can experience the exercise.
2. *Yes/no: Confronting your conditioning:*   People in Western cultures have been

(continued)

THINKSHEET 1 (continued)

taught to move their heads up and down when they say "yes" and side to side when they say "no." Hold a conversation with yourself or—preferably—with a partner, in which each time you say "yes" you shake your head from side to side and each time you say "no" you nod your head up and down. How do you experience doing this and what does it tell you about how you have learned to make choices?

I frequently start my workshops with the exercises of Thinksheet 1. In this sequence most people, when they get to choosing, choose to move their bodies to positions that are more comfortable for them. They feel empowered and freer to make, albeit in a simple way, choices that work for them. The exercise succeeds even in New York French restaurants! I demonstrated it in one to Sheenah, a former student, who is now a highly successful Park Avenue psychotherapist. She was aware that her arms were tight and there was tension in the back of her legs. When she moved on to choosing, she leaned back, opened her posture and uncrossed her arms. In other words, she had an "aha" experience. The yes/no exercise helps people realize that many of the constrictions on their choices are learned habits, of which they are unaware until they are confronted with them. This is true of many of the thinking skills weaknesses that interfere with choosing.

Thinksheet 2 will help you become aware that you can choose how you think about and respond to others. The idea is to get you thinking and responding in a new way, opposite to your initial inclinations.

THINKSHEET 2

Choosing the Opposite Response

1. Think of someone who makes you feel angry. Now imagine yourself going out of your way to do something to make that person happy. How might he or she react?
2. Think of someone who makes you feel inhibited. Now imagine yourself talking and relating to that person in a relaxed and outgoing way. How might he or she react?
3. Think of someone you want to avoid. Now imagine going up to that person and initiating a conversation in a friendly way. How might he or she react?
4. Think of someone with whom you have had an argument. Now imagine going up to that person and acknowledging that you were wrong. How might he or she react?
5. Think of someone from whom you take more than you give. Now imagine giving that person something really pleasing. How might he or she react?

Thinksheet 2 was designed to raise your consciousness of yourself as a chooser. However, it is also relevant to handling personal problems. Often you can gain insight into a problem by viewing it in a way diametrically opposed to your normal point of view. Did this happen for you in any of the exercises in Thinksheet 2?

RESPONSIBILITY AWARENESS

In recent years much attention has been given to the concept of causal attribution in the field of psychology. The term refers to the ways in which people attribute causes and meanings to their own behavior, to others' behavior, and to environmental events. The aspect of causal attribution focused on here is how people can choose to assume rather than avoid responsibility for their lives. This choice falls into two overlapping areas: acknowledging responsibility for the authorship of your life, and acknowledging responsibility for your everyday problems and decisions.

Responsibility for the Authorship of Your Life

Psychoanalysis, behaviorism, and humanism are all prominent schools of thought in contemporary psychology. However, in each one, a major assumption supplies a "cop-out" that enables you to avoid personal responsibility for the authorship of your life. Psychoanalysis allows you to attribute your difficulties to unconscious and instinctual determinants of behavior. In traditional behaviorism, the cop-out is provided by the concept of environmental determinism: you are merely a product of your environment. The humanistic position, represented by person-centered therapy, maintains the cop-out that parental and cultural influences have been stronger than your own self-actualizing tendencies. Fortunately, counselors and psychotherapists from these theoretical branches tend not to practice what they preach very strictly. Instead, they also share the existential view that people are responsible for *making* their lives through their choices.

To the extent that you have been "condemned" to freedom, you have also been condemned to the responsibility to fashion your life out of that freedom. Are you always responsible for your choices? The answer is "yes," but with qualifications. In the previous chapter, you saw how your learning may have interfered with your capacity to be an effective chooser. You also learned of the maturational lag: that your capacity for reasoning developed later than your need to make choices that would help you live most effectively. However, a distinction was made between what others did to you to help you acquire your deficient thinking skills and what you do to yourself that helps sustain them. Thus the burden of responsibility is passed back to you.

Many social factors may work against people's assuming personal responsibility. Adverse conditions such as poor housing, unemployment, poverty, racial discrimination, and lack of educational opportunity make it difficult first to learn to make and then to keep making the choices that are most advantageous. However, remove those adverse social conditions, and problems of personal responsibility are still likely to be rife, if less oppressive. Also, even in the most appalling conditions, people still make choices that control the quality of their inner and outer lives. In his inspiring book *Man's Search for Meaning*, Viktor Frankl (1959) relates how, in Nazi concentration camps, some individuals chose to score personal victories by turning their tragedies into triumphs of the human spirit.

Earlier in this chapter a distinction was made among choosing in relation to yourself, others, and the environment. All three strands are drawn together in the following personal responsibility credo.

Personal Responsibility Credo

I am personally responsible for my choices regarding how I think, feel, and act in relation to myself, others, and the environment.

Within the realistic limitations of my existence I, make my life through my choices.

I am always a chooser.

My choices always have consequences, for good or ill.

My choices always have costs.

The sum of my life is the sum of the consequences of my choices.

Responsibility for Your Everyday Problems and Decisions

It is one thing to accept your overall responsibility for making your life, but another to apply this goal successfully to your daily problems and decisions. In attempting to do so, it is important that you attribute responsibility and cause accurately. Two of the main faulty choices you can make are to attribute too much or too little responsibility to yourself.

Attributing too much responsibility to yourself   Some people choose to attribute too much responsibility to themselves, which can contribute to sustaining depression. Beck and his colleagues have observed that this is a common pattern among depressed patients (Beck, Rush, Shaw, & Emery, 1979). To counteract this tendency, he advocates a "reattribution" technique. Together with his patients he reviews the relevant evidence to make appropriate attributions of responsibility.

Unemployment is a typical situation in which maladaptive internal attributions of responsibility may contribute to low self-esteem and depression. Here it is useful to distinguish between responsibility for the cause of the problem and responsibility for its solution. Some unemployed persons may feel like failures because they wrongly attribute being unemployed to personal inadequacy rather than to structural or technological changes beyond their control. Those feelings of failure may be prolonged if they also attribute difficulty in getting rehired to personal inadequacy rather than to the realities of the job market. (Of course, I do not mean to imply that there are no instances in which internal attributions for becoming and staying unemployed are appropriate.)

Attributing too little responsibility to yourself   There is a widespread tendency among humans not to notice their own contribution to their distress, and to attribute responsibility elsewhere. There is an old joke about a psychological researcher who had trained a frog to jump when he said "jump." One day he decided to extend his research by cutting off one of the frog's rear legs and then saying "jump." The frog jumped sideways. Then he cut off the second rear leg and said "jump." The frog did not move. The psychologist conveniently concluded that the frog had suddenly gone deaf! He was not the sort of person to accept his own responsibililty for what he had done.

Scholarly findings support the validity of the point of that joke. For example, when Johanna Watson (1986) reviewed the attributions of 70 sets of parents referred for psychiatric assistance, she found their attributions about the causes of their children's emotional disturbances to be highly defensive. Parents commonly viewed the child's behavior as caused by something within the child, such as the child's "nature" or "just the way he or she was born." Fully 89 percent of the fathers and 76 percent of the mothers saw themselves as being of neither primary nor secondary importance in their child's level of adjustment. Of fathers who attributed their child's disturbed behavior to the family, 65 percent said their wives were the major contributors, usually charging them with being too "soft" on the child. Of mothers who attributed the disturbed behavior to the family, 39 percent accused their husbands, usually citing their lack of time for or disinterest in the child.

As this research suggests, a common pattern in relationship conflicts is that either or both partners make a convenient leap of logic, blaming the other rather than looking at their own behavior. Psychiatrist Thomas Szasz (1973) has written, "In the animal kingdom, the rule is eat or be eaten; in the human kingdom, define or be defined" [p. 20]. Unfortunately, this kind of defensive thinking is all too common in marital and family conflicts. Hence, the high psychological casualty rate among both adults and children. However, the carnage does not stop there: children frequently replicate for their own children the thinking, feeling, and action skills weaknesses of their parents.

―――――――――――― **THINKSHEET 3** ――――――――――――

Exploring How Accurately Others Own Responsibility for Their Lives

For each of the following examples, write down the following:

1. whether these persons are choosing to attribute too much or too little responsibility to themselves, and why you choose to think this
2. how they might change their thinking to behave more effectively in the future
Examples
   a. Brett is a 17-year-old who is shy with girls. He never makes the first move; instead he expects a girl to demonstrate clearly her interest in him before he considers asking her out.

(continued)

THINKSHEET 3 (continued)

b. Tony is the father of two daughters, ages 15 and 13. Recently he struck Joy, his 15-year-old, because "she made me so mad."

c. Sally is a 50-year-old spinster who until recently was secretary to a charitable organization. A month ago she resigned after an argument at a board meeting. She went out of her way to tell her friends that "I had no choice but to resign."

d. Tina is furious with her 16-year-old daughter, Tanya, for going to her boyfriend Keith's house one lunch hour when no one else was there. Tina is afraid of Tanya having an unwanted pregnancy. The two are currently not on speaking terms.

e. Arthur is a lazy teacher who is quick to notice when other teachers are being lazy. He thinks, "Why should I bother when others are getting away with it?"

THINKSHEET 4

Exploring How Accurately You Own Responsibility for Your Life

Do the following exercises in written form:

1. Explain the extent to which you think you accurately own responsibility for your thoughts, feelings, and behavior when faced with personal problems and decisions.

2. Describe a specific, recent situation in which you feel you succeeded in accurately owning responsibility when faced with a personal problem or decision.

3. Describe a specific, recent situation in which you feel you failed in accurately owning responsibility when faced with a personal problem or decision.

4. Explain whether your tendency is to attribute too much responsibility to yourself, too little, or a mixture.

EXISTENTIAL AWARENESS

Either he's dead or my watch has stopped.

Groucho Marx (feeling a patient's pulse)

The reports of my death are greatly exaggerated.

Mark Twain

An awareness of your mortality is the aspect of existential awareness on which I focus here. You are responsible for your choices within your life span. Though the exact length of your life is uncertain, your awareness that it is finite underscores your responsibility for its quality.

Many Western cultures have problems with the notions of aging and death. Youth and sexual attractiveness often appear to be valued more than wisdom and maturity. Death is muffled by euphemisms like "passing away" and "going to one's maker" rather than openly acknowledged as an integral part of life. Death threatens many people who are anxious about nonbeing.

Diminished Existential Awareness

In a number of ways, people exhibit an insufficient existential awareness of their mortality. Here are some personal beliefs that help them to do so.

Death can be postponed.   Some people lead their lives as though they had unlimited time. Kassorla (1984) calls them people with 500-year plans. The first hundred years is for doing things for their parents, the second for their neighbors, the third for their children and families, the fourth for some other pressure group that they value; by the fifth they might get around to doing something for themselves. Since they feel no urgency, many opportunities for choosing to live more fully are squandered. Such people are asleep to the existential reality that they have only one life, which is taking place *now*, is limited, and is "ticking away" all the time. They have not grasped the existential truth that to live is to die, and that they had better make the most of their lives.

Death cannot happen to me.   The illusion of immortality may be more common among younger than older people, though not always. Certainly, many young men in the past have gone off to wars buoyed up by images of glory and patriotism, unprepared for death and suffering. Also, many young people take unnecessary chances with their lives on the road. The behavior of some persons at risk for AIDS provides another example of a lack of existential awareness. Though many individuals engage in "safer" sex, still others allow themselves to be carried away sexually and fail to take precautions.

Death is transient.   Some people fail to realize the permanence of death. They engage in "magical thinking" to deny its power. Here is an example.

> At 17, Jack felt his whole life proved he was a failure. His alcoholic father had left home when Jack was 10. He had frequent fights with his mother, left school at 16, and started drinking heavily. He agreed to seek counseling after a suicide attempt in which, in a drunken rage, he had slashed his wrists with a knife. In counseling he mentioned that, prior to his suicide attempt, he had wondered what being dead was like and thought that it might be an interesting experience. After this experience he thought he could return to life.

My reward is in heaven.   One of the main functions of most religions is to help people handle their anxieties about death and dying. Sometimes people's motivation to improve their present lives on earth is weakened by the prospect of compensatory benefits in their future lives. This point was made by Karl Marx when he commented that "Religion . . . is the opiate of the masses." The prospect of rewards in heaven has been held out to soldiers in "holy wars" throughout the centuries, most recently by leaders such as the Ayatollah Khomeini.

Advantages of Existential Awareness

That an awareness of death can heighten one's awareness of life is illustrated in Yalom's (1980) case study of Eva. Eva was a 45-year-old, deeply depressed patient with advanced ovarian cancer. Her father had died many years earlier of a lingering cancer, of which no one had dared to tell him. In contrast, as a result of therapy, Eva confronted her physician and demanded all the available information about her cancer. Furthermore, acting on the premise that existence cannot be postponed, she led as full a life as possible, including taking a much-desired trip to Africa.

Yalom observed that many patients with cancer report that they live more fully in the present, no longer postponing life until sometime in the future. Furthermore, many become more able to count their blessings. Thus, awareness of death can not only heighten people's need to make the most of their lives, but can also help them experience more deeply many of the gifts of life they had previously taken for granted.

Viktor Frankl, the founder of logotherapy, also emphasizes the importance of acknowledging our "responsibleness" for choices within life's finiteness. He writes that the categorical imperative of logotherapy is this: "So live as if you were living already for the second time and as if you had acted the first time as wrongly as you are about to act now!" (Frankl, 1959, p. 173). He observed that in Nazi concentration camps some people behaved like swine and others like saints. All had both behaviors latent within them; which one became actualized depended less on the conditions than on their personal decisions.

Existential awareness involves not only an awareness of nonbeing, but also an awareness of being. You can be physically alive but psychologically deadened. Rather than making direct contact with yourself, others, and the environment in the present, you may be dwelling on the past or fearful about the future. The degree to which you can make effective thinking choices is a major determinant of your ability to exist fully in the present.

Consciousness-Raising Concerning Death, Dying, and Finiteness

In many ways, helping service professionals try to raise people's consciousness concerning death, dying, and finiteness. Their techniques include the following.

Imagining your death   You are encouraged to imagine the process of dying and your death. You may also be encouraged to explore the impact your death might have on others. This kind of imaginal exercise forms part of the training for AIDS counselors in San Francisco's Shanti ("inner peace") Project.

Reminiscing about contacts with death and dying   People can be encouraged to share their feelings about their contacts with dying people. They should be helped to link these memories with their thoughts and feelings about their own deaths.

Making contact with dying people   Arrangements may be made for people to interact with the dying. Three possibilities are (1) visiting a hospice, (2) observing meetings of a group of terminally ill patients, and (3) introducing people with terminal illnesses into everyday groups.

Thinksheet 5 is designed to raise your awareness of your finiteness, the passage of time, and your responsibility for being an effective chooser for the remainder of your life.

THINKSHEET 5

Confronting Your Finiteness

1. *Your past: Milestones*   Draw a line down the center of one or more pages. Go down each page, drawing a horizontal line to alternate edges for every five years of your life to date. The first line, to the left, represents 0 to 5 years; the second line, to the right, represents 6 to 10 years; and so on. Above each of these lines, write down what you consider to have been personal milestones that caused you to become the sort of person that you are today.
2. *Your present: Physical signs of aging*
    a. Make a list of any physical signs of aging that you presently recognize in yourself; for instance, graying hair, extra weight, increasingly poor vision, or wrinkles.
    b. What is your attitude toward these signs of your mortality?
3. *Your future: How much time do you have?*
    a. To what age do you expect to live? Give reasons for your prediction.
    b. Get a pocket calculator and work out:
    • how many hours there are in a year
    • how many minutes there are in a year
    • how many days you expect to live
    • how many hours you expect to live
    • how many minutes you expect to live
    c. What are your thoughts and feelings now that you have confronted yourself more precisely with the time you may have left on this earth?

FEELINGS AWARENESS

Much of this book emphasizes that you can influence how you feel through how you choose to think and act. Another skill is that of learning to acknowledge and be aware of your feelings. Central to your ability to think effectively is your ability to become aware of and own your significant feelings. This does not mean that you are encouraged always to express them. Rather, feelings tend to be the "parents" of choices. You can decide whether to develop them, to regulate them, or to treat them as unimportant.

Two aspects of feelings awareness are dealt with here: listening to your body and listening to your inner valuing process. Both require that you become aware of your bodily sensations, though the first aspect might be viewed as more physical and the second more psychological. However, to oppose them as a simple mind/body split would be misleading.

Listening to Your Body

Listening to your body is a logical skill to address after discussing existential aware-ness. The latter topic confronted you with one aspect of the natural order: the inescapability of death. The former confronts you with another fact of the natural order: that you are a human animal. Many people who think ineffectively are also out of touch with significant physical sensations: for instance, their need for relaxation and their sexuality. On the other hand, people who live effectively are frequently healthy animals. They may have been initially endowed with good health, but in addition their animality has not been seriously affected by psychological difficulties. Maslow (1970), reporting the findings of his study of self-actualizing people, observed that they tended to be good animals who ate and slept well and enjoyed uninhibited sex lives.

If you are truly to own your responsibility for choosing, you have to be aware not only of your physical death but also of your physical life. You are centered in your body, and your physical capacities comprise many of the significant limitations of your existence. Thinksheet 6 cannot convey the full extent of the importance of your animality, but it may help sensitize you to the fact that responsible choosers acknowl-edge that they are grounded in a physical, not just a psychological, existence.

THINKSHEET 6

Listening to Your Body

This thinksheet is best done on your own prior to discussing it with anyone else.

1. Sit in a quiet place with your eyes closed, and for the next 3 to 5 minutes focus on the sensations of breathing.
2. Sit in a quiet place, close your eyes for about 5 minutes, and try to tune into your bodily sensations. Focus on what your body is feeling rather than on what you are thinking. In other words, focus on physical sensations.
3. Sitting in a quiet place with your eyes closed, focus on the physical sensations in the following parts of your body for about a minute each.
   a. your head
   b. your arms
   c. your torso
   d. your legs
4. List the ways in which your physical sensations—for instance, fatigue—may influ-ence how you think. Be as specific as possible.

Listening to Your Inner Valuing Process

Carl Rogers viewed virtually all people as being, to a greater or lesser degree, out of touch with their inner valuing process. Since this valuing process represents people's essence or core, being distanced from it makes it difficult for them to make choices that reflect what they truly feel rather than what they have been taught they should feel. The main thrust of Rogers's person-centered therapy was to reunite clients with those parts of their inner valuing process from which they were alienated. Rogers's view of that process was not just reactive, however: it was also active. It took into account people's "actualizing tendency" to maintain and enhance themselves, which he considered to be the central human motivating drive (Rogers, 1980).

When your own responsibility for your choosing, your wants and wishes should ideally be representative of you as a unique individual rather than "borrowed" to please others, such as your parents or partner. At times you may be fully aware that you are making choices to please others rather than yourself. This may be entirely rational; you know what you want for yourself, but decide to take others' wishes into consideration. Or it may indicate a lack of self-assertion; you know what you want but are too afraid to go for it. On other occasions, your position may be less clear. For instance, you may either have difficulty discovering what you truly want, or you may think you know, but continue to experience a nagging feeling of discomfort. Also, some people are so out of touch with their valuing process that they deny many of their feelings altogether.

Assuming responsibility for your choosing requires that you be emotionally responsive both to yourself and to others. Frequently your wants and wishes emerge as feelings fragment that you may glimpse if you are attentive, rather than as full-blown emotions. You need to develop the skill of inner listening and of sorting out the wheat from the chaff among your feelings. Many of the thinking skills discussed in this book can be used to remove blocks to the acknowledgment of your true feelings. Some of you may choose to seek professional counseling, for either "remedial" or "growth" purposes, or for a mixture of the two. For instance, you may come to acknowledge that you are unaware of your feelings and sense little identity of your own. Alternatively, you may consider yourself reasonably emotionally responsive, but want to become even more so.

Thinksheet 7 is designed to help you become more aware of the importance of listening to your feelings and intuition when faced with problems and decisions of living. It focuses specifically on gaining access to your feelings. However, in real life, your actions may be based on a considered judgment that simply takes your feelings into account. Learning to be emotionally responsive can be a long and arduous process. For some of you, Thinksheet 7 may raise more issues than it answers.

THINKSHEET 7

Listening to Your Feelings

This thinksheet is best done on your own prior to discussing your experiences with anyone else.

1. *Your past: Learning emotional responsiveness*
   a. Take a piece of paper and draw a line down the center. At the top of the left-hand column write HARMFUL MESSAGES and at the top of the right-hand column

(continued)

THINKSHEET 7 (continued)

write HELPFUL MESSAGES. In each column list messages you received while growing up that harmed or helped you in becoming aware of your feelings, intuition, and wants and wishes. These messages may have been received from observing others or from the consequences of your behavior.

  b. How aware do you think you are now of your feelings, intuition, and wants and wishes? Give reasons for your answer. In what ways, if any, do you wish to change? Write down your answers.

2. *The present: Focusing on your feelings*
  a. Choose a problem or decision that has been bothering you recently.
  b. Both physically—in terms of absence of distractions—and psychologically clear a space in which you can focus on how you are feeling about that problem or decision.
  c. Spend from 5 to 10 minutes of quiet time with your eyes shut, just experiencing what you feel in relation to the problem or decision. Do not try to analyze or think your way through the problem. Instead, just experience the flow of your feelings.
  d. At the end of your quiet time, assess whether you think and feel any differently about the issue than you did at first.

CONCLUDING COMMENT

Owning responsibility for your choosing is a complex task requiring much awareness, skills development, and practice. There is still much truth for both sexes in the following quotation from *Julius Caesar:*

> *Men at some time are masters of their fates:*
> *The fault, dear Brutus, is not in our stars,*
> *But in ourselves, that we are underlings.*

CHAPTER HIGHLIGHTS

You make choices in relation to three main areas: yourself, others, and the environment.
Many people are insufficiently aware of themselves as choosers.
You are responsible for the authorship of your life.
You are responsible for your choices in everyday problems and decisions and for attributing responsibility accurately rather than attributing too much or too little responsibility to yourself.
You may be insufficiently aware of your existential finiteness.
Developing a realistic awareness of death can heighten your quality of living.
You are a human animal and as such need to acknowledge and understand your physical sensations and limitations.
You need to be sensitively attuned to your inner valuing process and not distort or deny any significant feelings.

CHAPTER 4

Using Self-Talk

*People who talk to themselves are not crazy. It is what they choose to keep
telling themselves that determines sanity or insanity.*

The ways in which you choose to talk to yourself can significantly influence how you
feel and act. Negative self-talk can significantly affect your confidence and
competence.

> Sally, a single woman in her early thirties, is a salesperson for a kitchen manufacturer.
> At the start of her second session of counseling she relates how anxious she is about
> having received an invitation to a formal party this Saturday. She describes her fears in
> the following words, relating them to her experiences at sales seminars. "I think that
> this is my main problem at the moment because it has always been a big problem. Every
> seminar I go to I always think on the coffee breaks I'm going to have nobody to talk to
> and I can't mingle . . . and that's my biggest problem—mingling . . . and I always think
> no one likes me so nobody wants to talk to me."

Though Sally was emotionally deprived while growing up, her current negative self-talk
about nobody liking her or wanting to talk to her sustains her problem of meeting
suitable men. A feelings consequence of Sally's self-talk is high anxiety in social
situations. A behavioral consequence is that in company she oscillates between inhibition and loudness.

People talk to themselves even when they remain silent. This is illustrated by the
joke about the psychoanalyst who had a client who remained silent for three sessions. At
the end of each he charged the client $100. Halfway through the fourth session, the
client requested permission to ask a question and said, "Do you by any chance need a
partner?" In other words, his self-talk went like this: "This analyst has a good racket
going. Let's see if I can get in on it, too!"

WHAT IS SELF-TALK?
Defining Self-Talk

Self-talk is the verbal aspect of thinking. It goes by numerous other names, including the following:

- Self-dialogue
- Inner monologue
- Inner dialogue
- Inner speech
- Self-verbalization

Basically, it is what you say to yourself during your waking hours. Though images or pictures may accompany self-talk, they are not self-talk. Sometimes you are aware that you talk to yourself when confronted with a problem or decision of living. On other occasions, you may be either less aware or unaware of what you say to yourself. You can become more aware of your "hidden" sentences if you go into counseling, join a thinking skills training group, or work through a book such as this.

What Is the Self?

Your self is what you call "I" or "me." It is the center of your personal universe. Your self has three major components.

1. *Your Natural Self:* Each person has a fundamental inner nature, or inner core of genetic aptitudes, drives, instincts, instinct remnants, and human potentialities. This is your animal nature. Some of your animal nature is shared by the entire human species; for instance, your need for food, shelter, physical safety, belonging, and love. But some of your animal nature is unique to you: your individual aptitudes, inner valuing process, and drive to realize yourself. This inner nature or inner core of your personhood I call your Natural Self.

2. *Your Learned Self:* This self is the product of your social learning history. It reflects the ways you have been taught to view yourself and your skills strengths and weaknesses. In Chapter 2 I reviewed some of the ways you acquired your thinking skills. In an ideal world, your Learned Self would be in accord with your Natural Self. It would give you the skills to fulfill your nature within the constraints of reality. However, in the real world, most of you have learned ways of thinking about yourself that block the attainment of your human potential. Your Learned Self can do you good or ill; it usually does both.

3. *Your Choosing Self:* Whereas your Natural Self represents your genetic endowments and your Learned Self reflects your past learning history, your Choosing Self represents your capacity to *make* your life through your choices in the present and future. Thus you not only have a self but are also continuously creating your self. A great advantage of having a Choosing Self is that it enables you to discard the habits of

thinking and self-talk of your Learned Self that block fulfillment of the inner core of your Natural Self. Another advantage is that you can choose aspects of your Natural Self that you wish to develop. This may be particularly important for the development of social interest and a concern for others that goes beyond immediate self-interest.

Self-Support or Self-Oppression

You can use self-talk either for self-support, self-affirmation, and realizing your human potential or for self-oppression and blocking your growth as a person. In everyday language, you can choose to be either "your own best friend" or "your own worst enemy."

Within each of you, in varying degrees, there is conflict between the self-talk that affirms your Natural Self and the self-talk of parts of your Learned Self. The latter may use self-talk against you in ways that lead to negative emotions and to self-defeating actions. If your Natural Self wins the conflict or makes progress in it, you are likely to lead a freer, happier, more spontaneous, and more fulfilled life. The costs for those who are losing the struggle can be high: increased strife, alienation, and escape into alcohol, drugs, promiscuous sex, violence, and even suicide. Less dramatic costs are evident in the many people leading lives of quiet despair.

Choice Points

All the thinking skills presented in this book involve self-talk. My aim is to help you become more aware of how you currently use self-talk for good or ill, and to show you where the choice points are for altering your self-talk in your own best interests. In Chapter 1 I mentioned the simple ABC framework used by writers like Ellis (1980) and Beck (Beck & Greenberg, 1974) to show that feeling and action are influenced by how you think. Here is that framework again:

A. The activating event
B. Your thoughts
C. Your feelings and actions

At B you have a choice about what you choose to say to yourself or think. By learning the appropriate use of self-talk, you can learn how best to think about your thinking. By making the right thinking choices at critical choice points, you can assume more control over how you feel and act. Focusing on your self-talk helps you work from inside to outside. When you alter your inner environment of thinking choices you lay the groundwork for dealing effectively with your outer environment of people and external events. In this chapter, much of the emphasis is on coping self-talk. However, all the other thinking skills, in their different ways, also use self-talk and help you to cope better with your problems and decisions of living.

USING "I" SELF-TALK

Thomas Gordon (1970), the author of *Parent Effectiveness Training*, suggests that children are much more likely to listen to parental requests if they are sent as "I" messages that own thoughts and feelings ("I'm feeling tired. Please play elsewhere"). "You" messages ("You are a naughty child") put children on the defensive. The notion of "I" messages or self-talk can usefully be applied to your inner self-talk as well as to your outer talk. By "I" self-talk I mean using words and phrases starting with the personal pronoun "I," in ways that help you to assume rather than to avoid personal responsibility for your thinking choices. Here are some ways in which "I" self-talk may help you to support rather than oppress your self.

• *Avoid putting yourself down with "you" self-talk.* Just as "you" messages ("*You* dummy. Can't *you* do anything right?") can put others down, in self-talk they can put you down. For instance, when Fran, who is taking a 3-hour essay examination, notices that she has started to answer one of the questions incorrectly, she is at a thinking choice point. On the one hand, she could use "you" self-talk: "You idiot. Why did you make such a stupid mistake? You have really screwed it up." On the other hand, she could use "I" self-talk: "I've made a mistake. What can I do to put it right in the time available?" The latter self-talk is more likely to help her than the former.

• *Use verbs that acknowledge your responsibility as a chooser.* It is possible for you subtly to box yourself in with certain verbs, thereby relinquishing your freedom to choose. For instance, your self-talk may include verbs like "can't," "must," "ought," "should," and "have got to" that imply less choice than you may actually have. Alternative verbs that acknowledge you have a choice include "won't," "want to," "prefer to," and "choose to."

• *Own your feelings, thoughts, and actions.* In your self-talk, just as in your conversation, you may make statements starting with words like "you," "people," "we," and "it," that camouflage your acknowledgment of your feelings, thoughts, and actions.

The following examples illustrate contrasting modes of self-talk.

Owning a feeling: You find one of your colleagues to be difficult.

Non-"I" self-talk: "He is a horror."

   "I" self-talk: "I feel hurt by his criticism."

Owning a thought: You have doubts about the effectiveness of a political leader.

Non-"I" self-talk: "Nobody seems to think she is doing a good job."

   "I" self-talk: "I do not think she is doing a good job for the following reasons . . ."

Owning an action: You have left yourself very little time in which to complete an assignment.

Non-"I" self-talk: "It always happens that I'm pushed to meet deadlines."

   "I" self-talk: "I've made a mistake in not leaving myself enough time to do the
            job properly."

You may have observed a trend in the above examples. All the non-"I" self-talk statements locate the source of your feelings, thoughts, and actions outside of yourself. All the "I" self-talk statements locate control of your feelings, thoughts, and actions in you. In each instance there is a choice point at which you decide how you talk to yourself.

• *Avoid unnecessarily rigid self-perceptions.* Your self-picture is a unique collection of many different self-perceptions, through which you describe and define yourself. Those self-perceptions cover your body, sexuality, style of relating, feelings and emotions, tastes and preferences, academic prowess and achievement, work and leisure abilities and interests, and philosophy and values. Some self-perceptions—for instance, "I have blue eyes"—are tied to your genetic endowment and are uncontrollable. Other self-perceptions are a matter of choice. For instance, people who say "I am a poor letter writer" or "I am an indifferent cook" may be making accurate statements about how they now perceive themselves but inaccurate inferences about how they will be in the future, since they may choose to change. The pitfall here is describing aspects of yourself as if they were unalterable when they are not.

THINKSHEET 8

Using "I" Self-Talk

Write out your answers to the following questions.

1. What does self-talk mean to you? What does using "I" self-talk mean?
2. To what extent do you think you oppress or restrict yourself by failing to use "I" self-talk in the following ways? When possible, illustrate your answers with specific examples.
   a. putting yourself down with "you" self-talk
   b. using verbs that acknowledge no choice
   c. not being open about your feelings, thoughts, and actions
   d. having rigid self-perceptions
3. If necessary, set yourself specific and realistic goals for improving your use of "I" self-talk. What might they be?

COPING SELF-TALK

Coping self-talk has been used successfully for a range of problems and with many different groups. The problems have included managing stress, anger, test anxiety, shyness, impulsiveness, and pain. The groups of people trained in coping self-talk have included nurses, teachers, police officers, probation officers, and athletes.

Top athletes face considerable stress when they compete. Below are examples of possible negative and coping self-talk, provided by Dr. Peter Fricker (1987), a psychologist at the Australian Institute of Sport, for a swimmer who is standing on the starting block at a major international competition.

NEGATIVE SELF-TALK

If I don't win this, there goes endorsement; there goes family pride, national limelight; I won't get a telegram from the Prime Minister.

COPING SELF-TALK

I know how to swim and to swim fast because I've been doing it twice a day for the past 10 years. All I have to do is to get in there. Okay, my technique means I've got to concentrate on getting my right arm in the water at that angle and a nice movement in the water under my body. That's all I've got to think about. If I just get in and do that as well as I can and as fast as I can, I'll be right. That's the process of swimming [p. 1].

Put simply, the negative self-talk focused on the possible *outcome* of the race, while the coping self-talk focused on the *process* of swimming fast. The goal for negative self-talk was glory. The goal for coping self-talk was "doing as well as I can."

What Is Coping?

The term *coping* in relation to a personal problem means to grapple successfully with it. Coping involves thinking, feeling, and action. To cope effectively you need to be able to draw on your repertoire of thinking skills, including coping self-talk, to manage the stress or problem at hand. Your use of thinking skills has two main objectives: reducing the feelings of distress associated with the problem and taking appropriate action to change the situation. Thus coping self-talk is of two major types: *calming* self-talk and *coaching* self-talk. The former helps you calm your anxieties, while the latter keeps you focused on the task at hand. Staying focused on the task, rather than engaging in self-talk irrelevant to it, also contributes to calming your anxieties.

Coping self-talk is about *coping*, or doing as well as you can, rather than about *mastery*, or being perfect and having no anxiety. Coping is therefore a much more realistic goal than mastery. Altering your goal from mastery to coping is likely to increase your self-support and to decrease your self-oppression. You now have an attainable standard toward which to strive. This can increase what Stanford University psychologist Albert Bandura (1977) calls your self-efficacy, your conviction that you can successfully execute the behavior required to produce a given outcome.

The notion of coping is also relevant to learning and implementing thinking skills. Mastery self-talk about the learning process would demand that you make steady progress on schedule. There would be no room for or tolerance of setbacks and failure. Coping self-talk about learning assumes that difficulties and mistakes are an inevitable part of the process. You cope with them as best you can, and you learn from your mistakes. With coping self-talk you are more likely to persist, since you tell yourself that mistakes are learning experiences rather than failures. Furthermore, once you have learned the thinking skills and are implementing them in your daily life, coping self-talk is an important way in which you can encourage yourself to keep using them.

Awareness, Choice, and Action

It is now time to see how you can apply coping self-talk to your problems. I will present this technique in three stages: awareness, choice, and action. Awareness means becoming more aware of your current use of self-talk and knowing when it is more harmful than helpful. Choice means identifying your thinking choice points for self-talk and also how to talk to yourself. Action means building up your coping self-talk skills to help you influence your feelings as well as act more effectively when faced with actual problems.

Awareness of Your Self-Talk

Becoming Aware of Self-Talk

The Canadian psychologist Donald Meichenbaum (1977, 1983, 1985, 1986; Meichenbaum & Deffenbacher, 1988) has perhaps been the most prominent advocate of using people's self-talk to help them better cope with their problems. It is unlikely that you consciously tell yourself various negative things when confronted with problems. Rather, making unhelpful self-statements may have become an ingrained style of thinking, similar to how you think automatically when you drive a car.

Before we look at specific ways in which you may use negative self-talk, work with Thinksheet 9. It is designed to increase your awareness of your self-talk when faced with stressful situations and problems. Right now, just concentrate on recognizing that you actually use self-talk, rather than trying to decide whether it is negative or coping.

──────────── **THINKSHEET 9** ────────────

Becoming Aware of Using Self-Talk

1. *Self-talk about a past situation:* Think of a specific situation in your recent past that you experienced as anxiety evoking and stressful. Close your eyes and visualize the scene. Just replay the events in slow motion and try to relive your thoughts and feelings. What thoughts did you have, or, put another way, what were you telling yourself in the situation? When you open your eyes, write down as much of your self-talk as you can remember.
2. *Self-talk about a future situation:* Think of a specific situation approaching in the near future that you expect to be anxiety evoking and stressful. Close your eyes and picture the scene. Visualize, in slow motion, what you anticipate happening and try to imagine your thoughts and feelings about it. What thoughts were you having, or,

(continued)

put another way, what were you telling yourself about the situation? When you open your eyes, write down as much of your self-talk as you can remember.

A number of methods can help you to stimulate both your recall and your anticipation of your self-talk. Thinksheet 9 uses visualization, or what Meichenbaum (1985) terms imagery-based recall. Other methods include keeping a self-monitoring diary and conducting experiments in which you intentionally place yourself in difficult situations in order to collect self-talk data.

Perceiving the Value of Coping Self-Talk

As with any other thinking skill, you are more likely to use coping self-talk if you perceive its value in overcoming a problem than if you do not. You need to see both that your thinking influences how you feel and act and that your lack of coping self-talk has contributed to the persistence of a particular problem.

Using coping self-talk on a problem does not preclude using other thinking skills as well. For instance, shy people may also need to alter self-oppressing personal rules that demand that they be accepted by everyone. Additionally, such people may need to acquire better skills for acting on the environment; for instance, improving their conversational skills, voice quality, and amount of eye contact. In sum, you are more likely to see coping self-talk as valuable if you regard it as a necessary part of, rather than the whole of, your approach to a problem.

Characteristics of Negative Self-Talk

The two main characteristics of negative self-talk are that it is neither calming nor coaching. Though these characteristics overlap, we'll examine them one at a time. Various skills weaknesses actually contribute to raising rather than lowering your anxiety. Negative self-talk behavior that contributes to rather than calms emotional distress includes the following.

- *Emphasizing mastery rather than coping:* When you set your standards unrealistically high, you automatically lower your expectation that you can be successful.

    Roger is a good student, except when it comes to exams. Then he tells himself, "If I don't get straight A's, I have as good as failed."

- *Catastrophizing:* You can easily convince yourself that if you do not get what you want, it is a catastrophe.

    Mary Beth is returning to the work force after raising a family. Before her first job interview she thinks, "If I don't get this job it will prove that I am unemployable, and that will be a catastrophe."

- *Adversely reacting to your physical symptoms:* You can convert your feelings of anxiety into panic attacks by what you tell yourself about your physical symptoms of anxiety. Even without achieving full-blown panic attacks, many people heighten their anxiety and apprehension by adversely reacting to bodily sensations such as tension, nausea, breathlessness, palpitations, choking, hot-and-cold flushes, and sweating.

> Bob, a bedding salesman, is afraid of public speaking. His sales director has asked him to give a presentation to a group of buyers from a large bedding chain store. When the time comes Bob thinks, "I can feel the tension in the pit of my stomach and my throat feels dry. This obviously means that I am going to have difficulty managing. At worst, things may get out of control and I will blank out totally."

- *Being overly self-conscious about what others think:* You can freeze up with anxiety by talking to yourself as though you are the center of other people's universes.

> The dress Eartha wanted to wear to a party did not come back from the cleaners on time. Consequently, she wore another dress that was not quite as nice and thought, "People can see that I'm not looking my best. If I just had that other dress on, I could relax and enjoy myself."

- *Putting yourself down:* You may talk to yourself in language you "wouldn't even use to a dog."

> Julio is learning a new game of cards. He gets increasingly angry that he is not catching on as quickly as the others. He tells himself, "You fool. You oughtn't to be so stupid. Why do you always have to mess things up?"

- *Focusing on setbacks and not owning successes:* You can harm yourself as much by what you do not tell yourself as by what you do.

> Maria and Marge have been good friends for some years. Recently Maria has felt that Marge has been taking less interest in her and that their friendship is threatened. Both women have experienced tension in their relationship. Maria tells herself about all the problems, but neglects to tell herself that they still have good times together, such as last Saturday, when they played tennis and swam.

The second main characteristic of negative self-talk is that it does not help you coach yourself. Three of the ways in which you can undermine effective self-coaching are as follows.

- *Not setting yourself clear goals:* Because you have not clarified in your own mind what you want to achieve, you are unable to describe the steps necessary to achieve it.
- *Not breaking down tasks:* You may have set yourself clear goals but failed to break the task down into incremental, smaller steps more easily achieved. Consequently, you experience difficulty in talking yourself through the specific steps necessary to achieve the subgoals and, hence, the overall goal.
- *Not concentrating on the task at hand:* As in the earlier example of the competitive swimmer, success is more likely to come if your self-talk focuses on the process at hand now rather than on a future, possibly unrealistic, goal such as glory.

────────────── **THINKSHEET 10** ──────────────

Exploring Your Negative Self-Talk

1. With regard to *either* your overall style of self-talk when faced with personal problems *or* a specific situation in the recent past that was anxiety evoking and stressful, identify your use of any of the following kinds of negative rather than coping self-talk.
   a. Negative behavior increasing emotional distress:
      - emphasizing mastery rather than coping
      - catastrophizing
      - adversely reacting to your physical symptoms
      - being overly self-conscious about what others think
      - putting yourself down
      - focusing on setbacks and not owning successes
   b. Negative behavior decreasing self-coaching effectiveness:
      - not setting yourself clear goals
      - not breaking down tasks
      - not concentrating on the task at hand
2. Summarize what you perceive to be your current style of self-talk when faced with personal problems.

──

Thinking Choices and Coping Self-Talk

Coping Self-talk Cues

A number of cues or triggers tell you when it may be appropriate to use coping self-talk. They coincide with your choice points. Coping self-talk is best engaged in before, during, and after anxiety-evoking situations. Consequently, one obvious cue to use coping self-talk is when you have a difficult situation coming up. Another cue is when you become aware that you are using any of the kinds of negative self-talk just described. When you experience persistent negative feelings and engage in self-defeating actions, you should consider it a signal. Coping self-talk need not be restricted to anxiety-evoking situations, however; remember that it also has a coaching function, which is applicable to many situations.

Calming Self-Talk

When you use coping self-talk you tend to intersperse calming with coaching self-talk. Following are examples of each type and then examples in which they are combined. Calming self-talk implies both the presence of supportive and the absence of negative self-talk. Negative self-talk that is likely to contribute to emotional distress has already been reviewed. Now the emphasis is on the do's rather than the don'ts of self-talk. Here are two important kinds of calming self-talk.

- *Telling yourself to stay calm:* Sample self-statements include "Keep calm," "Slow down," "Relax," and "Just take it easy." Additionally, you can instruct yourself to "Take a deep breath" or "Breathe slowly and regularly."
- *Telling yourself you can cope:* Sample self-statements include "I can handle this situation," "My anxiety is a signal for me to use my coping skills," and "All I have to do is to cope." If you have coped with a situation better than usual, acknowledge it: "I used my coping skills and they worked."

Coaching Self-Talk

Coaching self-talk is no substitute for the action skills that enable you actually to accomplish a task. However, it can help you cope with anxiety-evoking and stressful problems in the following ways.

- *Clarifying your goals:* Be specific. For instance, if you have purchased a faulty record, your goal might prompt this coaching: "On Tuesday afternoon I will return the record to the store and request that it be replaced."
- *Breaking down tasks:* You need to think through a step-by-step approach to achieving your goal, including how you might handle setbacks. Once your plan is clear, you need to be able to coach yourself through the steps of implementing it.
- *Concentrating on the task at hand:* While keeping your goal in mind, focus on talking yourself through each process of the steps involved in attaining it. You are like those pilots who talk themselves through difficult landings. Concentrate on the task at hand and discipline yourself not to think extraneous thoughts.

Examples of Coping Self-Talk

Coping self-talk may be used before, during, and after anxiety-evoking and stressful situations. Often, calming and coaching self-instructions are combined; for instance, "Calm down. Just take one step at a time." You need to think through the self-instructions that work for you. Here are examples of possible before, during, and after self-talk for coping with shyness, anger, test anxiety, and a job interview.

- *Coping with shyness in a stressful social situation*

BEFORE

"Now calm down. Think of some things I can talk about."
"I can cope with this situation if I take it easy."

DURING

"Relax. Everybody is not looking at me."
"My anxiety is manageable. I know I can cope."

AFTER

"Well done. I managed to control my negative thoughts."
"I'm pleased that I'm making progress in handling social situations."

- *Coping with anger in a potentially provocative situation*

  ### BEFORE

  "Remember, stick to the issues and avoid put-downs."
  "I can cope with this encounter if I don't let my pride get in the way."

  ### DURING

  "My anger is a signal telling me to remain task oriented."
  "Calm down. I can feel in control as long as I keep my cool."

  ### AFTER

  "Though we didn't resolve anything, at least I handled myself well."
  "I'm learning to cope better without getting aggressive."

- *Coping with test anxiety*

  ### BEFORE

  "I don't have to be perfect. All I have to do is the best I can."
  "What are the specific skills I need to take this test effectively?"

  ### DURING

  "Now calm down, relax, and take some slow, deep breaths."
  "Read the test instructions carefully and plan the time accordingly."

  ### AFTER

  "I survived. I didn't feel so bad after all."
  "When I control my self-talk, I can control my fear."

- *Coping with a job interview*

  ### BEFORE

  "Let's think through how I can best present my case."
  "Relax. Even if I don't get the job, it's not the end of the world."

  ### DURING

  "Speak firmly and calmly and answer the questions asked."
  "It's okay to be anxious. I know I can manage these feelings."

  ### AFTER

  "I did it. I managed to contain my negative thoughts and got the job."
  "Even though I didn't get the job, I did well to be selected for the interview, and I'm doing better each time I use my coping self-talk."

Thinksheets 11 and 12 are designed to build your skills in formulating coping self-talk and in using it when you are faced with personal problems.

THINKSHEET 11

Formulating Your Coping Self-Talk

Write out your answers to the following questions.

1. What is the difference between calming self-talk and coaching self-talk?
2. Give two specific examples of each of the following:
   a. Calming self-talk
   b. Coaching self-talk
   c. Coping self-talk that combines calming and coaching self-instructions
3. Referring to the previous pages, provide one additonal self-instruction for before, during, and after each stressful situation.

THINKSHEET 12

Applying Coping Self-Talk to a Personal Problem

Write out your responses to the following questions and tasks.

1. Identify a personal problem of your own in which coping self-talk might be appropriate.
2. Set clear goals for what you want to achieve.
3. Take three index cards for before, during, and after self-talk. One side of each card is for negative self-talk, the other for coping self-talk. At the top of one side of your before card write NEGATIVE SELF-TALK BEFORE and at the top of the other side write COPING SELF-TALK BEFORE. Label your during and after cards the same way.
4. On each of your before, during, and after cards, write at least two negative self-talk instructions and two coping self-talk instructions that apply to your problem. Read your coping self-talk instructions at least twice daily for a week.
5. What do you think might be the emotional and behavioral consequences of using your coping self-talk instructions, in contrast to your negative self-talk instructions, for managing your problem?
6. What other skills might you require to manage your problem most effectively?

Coping Self-Talk and Action

So far I have attempted to increase your awareness and to clarify some of your thinking choices when using coping self-talk. Now I'll discuss building a bridge between knowing what to do and actually doing it.

Taking a Gradual Approach to Learning

One way of learning and consolidating your coping self-talk skills is to go from the simple to the more difficult. You can gradually learn to use coping self-talk either within a problem area or across problem areas: for example, start by using coping self-talk for a less anxiety-evoking job interview before using it for a more anxiety-evoking test-taking situation. The principle of graduated learning and practice is the same for both attempts. You build up your confidence and skills by practicing and succeeding at less anxiety-evoking challenges before moving on to more difficult ones. One way of distinguishing more from less difficult tasks is to rate each on a difficulty scale of 1 to 10. You can then order the tasks in a hierarchy.

Rehearsal

If you can, rehearse coping self-talk as you role-play situations with other people. However, many of you are likely to be working on your own. If that's the case, using coping self-talk during visualized rehearsal can be an effective method of learning. For instance, Vince, a shy teenager, can imagine himself before, during, and after anxiety-evoking social situations. As he visualizes progressively more difficult scenes, he employs coping self-talk. Before moving on, Vince replays each scene until he is convinced that his coping self-talk has helped him manage his anxiety and stay focused on the task. He also develops coping self-talk for handling setbacks: for instance, "I am still learning, and I'm not going to succeed all the time."

Practice

Although you use self-talk all the time, you may need to practice faithfully to replace your oppressing self-talk with supporting self-talk. In Thinksheet 12 you identified a specific problem in your life for which coping self-talk might help. If you think it was too difficult a problem to start with, identify another one for Thinksheet 13 that would give you a reasonable chance to succeed in using coping self-talk to alter your behavior. Be open to modifying your coping self-talk if you are uncomfortable with it and it does not work for you. Again, genuine learning rarely occurs without setbacks and difficulties. Use coping self-talk to encourage yourself in handling them, as well as to acknowledge your successes, thus motivating you to persist.

———— Thinksheet 13 ————

Translating Coping Self-Talk into Action

1. Rank two situations in the same problem area, one more anxiety evoking and one less so, for which coping self-talk might be appropriate.
2. Formulate two before, during, and after coping self-instructions for each of your two situations.
3. Rehearse, using your coping self-instructions, as you visualize each situation. Begin with the less threatening one. Replay the scenes as often as necessary. Do not move on to the second situation until you are sure you have managed your anxiety and remained focused on the task of the first situation.
4. Try using this same coping self-talk as you deal with these two situations in real life.

Modify your self-talk, if necessary. Reward yourself with praise when you improve at controlling your anxiety and remaining focused on the task.

CONCLUDING COMMENT

Since you use self-talk all the time, it is important that you start increasing your coping self-talk and decreasing your negative self-talk *now*. Remember, it is not the fact that you talk to yourself but what you choose to keep saying to yourself that makes you crazy!

CHAPTER HIGHLIGHTS

Self-talk is the verbal aspect of thinking.

Your self has three major components: your Natural Self, your Learned Self, and your Choosing Self.

You can choose to use self-talk to either support or oppress yourself.

'I" self-talk is generally preferable to "you" self-talk.

Coping self-talk is of two major types: calming self-talk and coaching self-talk.

Calming self-talk helps you manage the emotional distress associated with anxiety-evoking and stressful situations.

Coaching self-talk helps you instruct yourself through the different steps involved in the successful execution of a task.

Negative self-talk means thinking in ways that contribute to self-defeating emotions and actions.

You need to become aware of how you currently use negative self-talk.

You can choose to replace your negative self-talk with coping self-talk.

You may also need to use additonal thinking and action skills when faced with personal problems.

When learning to use coping self-talk for your problems, take a gradual approach, rehearse and practice.

Start using more coping self-talk *now*.

CHAPTER 5

Choosing Your Personal Rules

The Golden Rule is that there are no golden rules.
George Bernard Shaw

Human beings govern themselves with rules. In this chapter my main focus will be on your inner rules. Wessler and Hankin-Wessler (1986) call these rules by which people live "Personal Rules of Living." I modify their term slightly to call them personal rules *for* living or, more briefly, personal rules. These are your principles or guides for your own conduct, the conduct of others, and for the environment.

Your internal directives are manifestations of your personal rules. They are the internal orders or commands that you give yourself, which frequently place pressure on and inhibit you. I will discuss these directives in the second part of this chapter.

Personal rules and their accompanying self-talk can be used for self-oppression or for self-support. The poet W. H. Auden once wrote "Weep for the lives your wishes never led." Sometimes you may allow your Natural Self to be inhibited by restrictive rules from your Learned Self. Your personal rules underlie how you approach specific problems. In the previous chapter, examples of coping self-talk were provided for managing shyness, anger, test anxiety, and a job interview. However, along with the negative emotions and actions implied in each of these situations were some underlying self-oppressing personal rules. For example, the shy person says "I *must* be liked by everyone"; the person prone to anger feels "Others *must* treat me the way I want"; the one experiencing test anxiety claims "I *must* achieve at a high level"; and the job interviewee insists "I *must* get the job." The reasons that personal rules like these are self-oppressing rather than self-supporting will be discussed later.

The issue of personal rules goes beyond its relevance to specific problems; it is relevant to a problem shared by all people: the conflict between individuals' past traditions and their present need to assert and define themselves as unique individuals. The past may have benign or harmful influences, but its ghosts are ever pervasive. The learning handed down by your parents and others is not to be rejected entirely. Instead, let your Choosing Self review parental and traditional rules and then own, live up to, discard, or reformulate them.

Personal rules are central to your ability to define and assert yourself in the present. Your personal rules can help or hinder you in resisting pressures to conform against your interests, whether that pressure is from friends, family, or a wider society. Coming to terms with personal rules can be an area of particular importance to members of socially stigmatized minority groups. For instance, some homosexuals may have to confront their own lack of acceptance of their sexual orientation. Also, they may have to change rules (concerning their need for universal acceptance, for example), that encourage their further putting themselves down if they are rejected by others.

Personal rules are also of fundamental importance to ethical and social living, since they moderate the potential conflict between self-interest and social interest. In this sense, personal rules are a new way of talking about conscience. Conscience may seem an old-fashioned term in this age, when the pursuit of hedonism, be it short-term or longer-term, is so highly valued. Conscience is not a concept that features prominently in contemporary applied psychology. However, I regard developing your conscience to be a vital part of developing your full humanity. Working with your personal rules, then, does not simply mean working through harmful internal voices from your past; it also means developing your human potential for social living.

WHAT ARE PERSONAL RULES?

Your personal rules are the dos and don'ts by which you lead your life. Each of you has an inner rule book that guides your living. You may be aware of some of your rules, but there are others of which you are unaware. Some of the latter may be fairly easy to bring to the surface; however, others may be more threatening and anxiety evoking. Consequently, you may have more difficulty acknowledging them.

Most people in Western cultures live under what might be termed an illusion of autonomy, meaning that they see their behavior as predominantly the result of their own free choice. Frequently, this is a truly illusory view: many humans are controlled by others' rules, which they follow *as if* they were rules of their own choosing. British psychiatrist R. D. Laing (1969) uses a metaphor of people going through life as if hypnotized: not only do they follow instructions, but they are unaware that they have been given any instructions.

Personal rules represent a form of self-talk, much of which goes on below conscious awareness. They are the filters, structures, or templates that result in some of the underchoices influencing your feelings, thoughts, and actions. For instance, Wayne, a college student, has this underlying personal rule: "I must always receive approval." Consequently, when he meets Ann, a warm and attractive fellow student, and considers asking her out for a date, he perceives her as a potential threat and tells himself that he cannot handle the chance of being rejected. Throughout, Wayne remains unaware of his personal rule demanding approval.

Another function of personal rules is to provide standards for judging your own and others' behavior. If your rules are self-supporting, they can motivate you and help you attain realistic goals. If your rules are self-oppressing, they leave you open to a triple dose of self-oppression. For instance, Steve sets himself an unrealistically high goal of winning a difficult tennis tournament. The first dose of self-oppression is administered when he doesn't win. The second dose is given because he has become anxious and depressed over not winning. The third dose is given because he now starts devaluing not only his tennis-playing ability but himself as a person—both because he has not won and because he is getting anxious and depressed about it.

COMBATING YOUR SELF-OPPRESSING PERSONAL RULES

I use the term *combating* deliberately, because self-oppressing personal rules tend to be deeply ingrained habits of relating to yourself, others, and the world. You usually have to fight hard, both to lessen their influence and to avoid losing the gains you have made. There is no true "cure" for self-oppressing rules: overcoming them is a constant struggle. Albert Ellis suggests that practically all humans have a strong biological predisposition to think irrationally and thus to disturb and go on disturbing themselves. Because of this, even those persons helped by the most efficient forms of psychotherapy find it virtually impossible to achieve and maintain good mental health. Ellis (1987) regards most of his clients as ". . . natural resisters who find it exceptionally easy to block themselves from changing and find it unusually hard to resist their resistances" [pp. 370–371].

Combating self-oppressing personal rules takes place in three stages: awareness, choice, and action. First, you increase your awareness both of their existence and of your specific harmful rules. Second, you learn to dispute your thinking and to reformulate self-oppressing rules as self-supporting ones. Third, you work hard at integrating changed rules with changed actions.

Increasing Your Awareness of Self-Oppressing Personal Rules

Inappropriate Feelings and Actions As Signals

How do you know if you have self-oppressing personal rules? They can be hard to see: some are so much a part of you that you are unaware of their existence. As when puffs of smoke at the Vatican announce election of a Pope, you have to understand the signals.

Persistent inappropriate feelings are one signal alerting you to a self-oppressing personal rule. The dividing line between appropriate and inappropriate feelings, of course, is not always clear. Life can be difficult, so appropriate feelings cannot simply be equated with "positive" feelings like happiness, joy, and pride. Some "negative" feelings like sadness, grief, fear, and anger can be entirely appropriate to the contexts in which they occur. You have to ask yourself questions like these: "Is this feeling appropriate for the situation?" "Is feeling this way helping or harming me?" "Am I taking responsibility for my feelings, or allowing them to be determined by others' behavior?"

Inappropriate feelings and actions are interrelated. If you feel excessively angry, you may act violently and worsen rather than improve your position. Again, appropriate questions are "Are my actions helping or harming me?" "Am I taking responsibility for my actions, or allowing them to be determined by others' behavior?"

If you are uncomfortable with the way you feel or act, your self-talk can take the form of "I feel this way because..." or "I act in this way because..." These self-statements can initiate your search to become aware of the relevant personal rule or rules contributing to your distress. I do not suggest that on every occasion you backtrack from inappropriate feelings and actions to look for self-oppressing personal rules. Life is too short. But it is a useful self-help skill when you are experiencing persistent and/or major distress.

Mustabatory and Absolutistic Rules

Masturbation is probably the most common form of human sexual activity, and I do not wish to give it a bad name. Nevertheless, Albert Ellis (1980) has coined the term *mustabation* to refer to rigid personal rules characterized by "musts," "oughts," and "shoulds." He has identified three major clusters of irrational beliefs or personal rules that create inappropriate feeling and action consequences.

1. I *must* do well and win approval for all my performances... (p. 5).
2. Others *must* treat me considerately and kindly... (p. 6).
3. Conditions under which I live *must* be arranged so that I get practically everything I want comfortably, quickly, and easily... (p. 7).

Some of the main characteristics of self-oppressing personal rules are as follows.

* *Demandingness:* You think of your wants and wishes as demands rather than as preferences.
* *Perfectionism:* You put pressure on yourself and others to be perfect. Nobody's perfect.
* *Overgeneralization:* You make rules for *all* situations rather than allowing flexibility for specific situations.
* *Self-rating:* You rate yourself on your total worth as a person rather than on how functional your specific characteristics are for achieving your goals.
* *Catastrophizing:* You think that it is or will be absolutely awful if you, others, or the environment are not as they should be.
* *Having a low tolerance of frustration:* You tell yourself that you cannot stand the anxiety or discomfort arising from imperfections in yourself, others, or the environment.

Ellis has further grouped the disturbances caused by the absolute demands people make on themselves, others, and the environment into two major categories: ego disturbance and discomfort disturbance (Dryden & Ellis, 1986). Ego disturbance refers to disturbances created by self-oppression; discomfort disturbance implies the emotional discomforts, such as anxiety, that people feel when their demands are not met. He advocates self-acceptance and a high tolerance of frustration as fundamental to rational living.

Below are some examples of self-oppressing personal rules set within the ABC framework. A is the event, B the personal rule, and C the consequences.

Leona is a prominent scientist.

A. I gave an uncharacteristically poor public speaking presentation.
B. I must perform perfectly well at public speaking at all times.
C. I feel inadequate and anxious because I have given a poor talk. I try to make out to others that my presentation was not too bad.

Tricia is in her mid-thirties.

A. A man I accepted a date with raped me.
B. There must have been a perfectly correct way for me to behave that would have prevented the rape.
C. I blame myself and feel anxious, depressed, and guilty. I have stopped going out with men.

Chuck, a talented musician, is enrolled as a business major.

A. I failed my first year in business.
B. I must always please my parents.
C. I feel alienated and depressed. I will repeat the year in business to see if I can do better.

Cindy is the mother of a teenage daughter.

A. My daughter and I have constant fights.
B. I must control what my daughter does.
C. I feel a failure as a mother and am consequently depressed and anxious. My daughter is increasingly rude to me.

Another clue to the presence of self-oppressing personal rules is the recurrence of certain central themes. Ellis has suggested on different occasions ten, eleven, or twelve central irrational beliefs that fit into the three major clusters listed previously.

Thinksheet 14 has been designed to help make you more aware that you have self-oppressing personal rules, and of what they are for one or more problem areas of your life. It is based on a worksheet developed by British psychologist Windy Dryden (Dryden and Ellis, 1986).

———————————— **THINKSHEET 14** ————————————

Becoming Aware of Your Self-Oppressing Personal Rules

1. Select a problematic situation from the past to work on. Use the ABC framework.
   A (*the event*): Describe the situation that contributed to your personal upset.
   B (*your personal rules*): Looking for "musts," "oughts," and "shoulds," list any
      demands you made of the following:
      • yourself
      • others
      • the situation
   C (*the consequences*): Describe how you felt and acted. Do you consider any of
      your feelings and actions to have been inappropriate?
2. Repeat this ABC exercise for a problematic situation in your present life.

Choosing to Dispute and
Reformulate Your Self-Oppressing Personal Rules

In the previous section you may have become aware that your underlying self-talk
conveys some self-oppressing personal rules. Also, you may have made some progress
in identifying them. Disputing and reformulating those personal rules are two skills that
can help you move toward self-supporting rules.

Disputing

Ellis (1980) considers the technique of disputing to be the most typical and often-used
method of his rational-emotive therapy (RET). Disputing means challenging the false
assumptions that you hold about yourself, others, and the world. Take the earlier
example of Leona, the prominent scientist whose personal rule was "I must perform
perfectly well at public speaking at all times." Questions that Leona might ask to
dispute her self-oppressing personal rule include the fo.owing.

"What evidence exists that supports the truth of my personal rule?"
"What evidence exists that reveals the falseness of my personal rule?"
"What are the worst possible things that might happen to me if I gave a less-than-
      perfect public presentation?"
"What, exactly, can't I stand about failing to give a perfect public presentation?"
"Do I demand the same standards of other people as I require of myself in public
      speaking?"
"How, exactly, does giving a less-than-perfect public presentation make me worthless
      as a person?"
"What are the costs and consequences to me of my demand that I always give a per-
      fect public presentation?"

"To what extent does my wanting to give a perfect public presentation represent my
   past learning history rather than the reality of my present situation and wishes?"

You may need to dispute the same self-oppressing personal rule again and again.
This is because you have well-developed habits of reindoctrinating and recontaminating
yourself.

Reformulating

Reformulating means substituting self-supporting for self-oppressing characteristics in
specific personal rules. Some of the main characteristics of self-supporting personal
rules include the following.

- *Expressing preferences rather than demands:* You distinguish clearly between your
  nonabsolutist preferences, wishes, and likes and your absolutist demands, needs, and
  requirements.
- *A coping emphasis:* You manage or cope with situations rather than being a
  perfectionist with regard to them.
- *Being based on your own valuing process:* Your rules are not just rigid internalizations of others' rules.
- *Flexibility:* Where appropriate, you are amenable to change.
- *Absence of self-rating:* Your rules lead to a functional rating of specific characteristics according to their usefulness for survival and fulfillment rather than to a global
  rating of your whole personhood.

Let me illustrate this technique with some possible self-supporting reformulations
for the four earlier examples of Leona, Tricia, Chuck, and Cindy.

Leona

Self-oppressing personal rule: "I must perform perfectly well at public speaking at
all times."

Self-supporting personal rule: "Though my preference is to give a polished talk, I
may not always do so. If I give a less-than-perfect
talk, it is something I can cope with, not a
catastrophe, and I may learn something from it."

Tricia

Self-oppressing personal rule: "There must have been a perfectly correct way for me
to behave that would have prevented the rape."

Self-supporting personal rule: "Nobody's perfect, and there are rarely any perfect
solutions. I did my best under the circumstances, and
just because I have been devalued by another person
is no reason for me to devalue myself."

Chuck

Self-oppressing personal rule: "I must always please my parents."

Self-supporting personal rule: "I would like to please my parents. However, it is more important that I assume responsibility for developing myself as an independent human being, even if this means pursuing a career in music rather than business. I can stand the discomfort of their disapproval."

Cindy

Self-oppressing personal rule: "I must control what my daughter does."

Self-supporting personal rule: "While I would prefer that my daughter did what I wanted, she is an independent person. I can only influence, not control her. If she doesn't do what I want, it does not make me a failure as a person."

The ideal outcome of disputing and reformulating self-oppressing personal rules is that you feel and act better. In the ABC framework, choosing at B to discipline your thinking about A gives you new and better consequences at C. Thinksheet 15 has been designed to help you build your self-help skills of disputing and reformulating self-oppressing personal rules.

--- **THINKSHEET 15** ---

Disputing and Reformulating Your Self-Oppressing Personal Rules

1. Select a problem situation in your life. If it is different from the situation you worked on in Thinksheet 14, you will need to complete that thinksheet again before proceeding.
2. Dispute each of the demands you made in the situation.
3. Reformulate one or more of your important self-oppressing personal rules into a self-supporting personal rule.
4 What effect do you think your new self-supporting rule might have had on your feelings and actions?

Changing Your Actions Along with Your Personal Rules

Changing your personal rules may make it easier for you to act effectively. In turn, acting effectively is a powerful way to generate evidence that helps to dispute self-oppressing personal rules. When integrating changes in your thinking choices with changes in how you act, a basic guideline is *practice, practice, practice.*

Using visualization is one way to bridge changing your personal rules and changing your actions. For instance, Leona might engage in visualized rehearsal. She could visualize herself before, during, and after an upcoming public speaking engagement, and dispute and reformulate any self-oppressing rules she detects. Leona might also choose to use coping self-talk. Altering the underlying personal rules upon which self-talk is based helps enormously to maintain coping self-talk.

Ultimately, however, there is no substitute for real-life practice. Psychologists disagree over whether practice is best approached gradually, from the least to most difficult tasks, or "floodingly," going straight to a difficult assignment. Ellis encourages his clients to do their practice assignments repetitively and floodingly. He believes that, by jumping in at the deep end over and over, clients learn more quickly that their worst fears rarely materialize. For instance, someone afraid of riding on a bus would be encouraged to take bus rides many times a day. Other psychologists advocate taking a more gradual approach. For instance, a person afraid of public speaking might be encouraged to give an easy talk to a few people first, before giving a more difficult one to many people. Some of you do not have much choice, of course. A difficult talk or an important exam is the imminent reality with which you are faced.

The support of a group can be helpful to those wishing to alter personal rules and actions. In recent years, women's groups and groups of disabled persons have tried to alter their members' consciousness concerning self-oppressing rules and behavior so that they think, feel, and act in more self-supporting ways. Earlier I indicated that you may use other thinking skills—for instance, coping self-talk—as you change both your personal rules and the way you act. Additionally, you may need to develop your action skills: for example, projecting your voice better when you speak in public, or using your time better in exams.

THINKSHEET 16

Changing Your Actions Along with Your Personal Rules

1. Select a problem situation in your life, preferably the one you worked on in Thinksheets 14 and 15.
2. Specify realistic goals for changing the way you act in that situation.
3. Visualize yourself acting as you would like to before, during, and after the situation. As you detect any self-oppressing personal rules, dispute and reformulate them.
4. Face the situation in real life and change how you act, as far as possible. As you detect any self-oppressing personal rules, dispute and reformulate them.
5. Practice, Practice, Practice.
6. Use coping self-talk to recognize and reward yourself for any gains you make.

COMBATING YOUR SELF-OPPRESSING DIRECTIVES

There is a lot of overlap between personal rules and directives. I find working with both concepts useful. Some of you may find the concept of self-oppressing directives easier to apply to yourself than that of personal rules.

The term *directives* is derived from Eric Berne's approach to counseling, psychotherapy, and living called transactional analysis. Berne (1972) developed the concept of a person's "script," a preconscious life plan that is the product of parental programming plus the decisions made in response to that programming. In Berne's view, people have an illusion of personal autonomy but are more often than not unthinkingly driven by script directives. Those directives might come from either parent, and might be either consistent or, in varying degrees, contradictory.

Increasing Your Awareness of Self-Oppressing Directives

To adapt from Berne's terms then, self-oppressing directives fall into two major categories: *pressurizers* and *inhibitors*. The difference is that your pressurizers drive you to act against your interests, and your inhibitors block you from acting in your interests.

Some possible self-oppressing pressurizer directives that you may have internalized include the following.

- *Achieve at all costs:* You do not realistically take your interests, abilities, and opportunities into account but rather overstrive. At the worst, this habit can literally be fatal; for example, it might lead to a heart attack.
- *Amass material goods:* Your self-worth as a person is related to the amount of money and goods you accumulate.
- *Be liked:* You need to be liked by people, whether or not you find them likable. Your self-worth is related to the degree that people like you.
- *Be in control:* You must strictly control your own and others' thoughts, feelings, and actions and even your environment.
- *Hurry up:* Time is always to be used rather than enjoyed or—even worse—wasted.
- *Be active:* You are living only if you are actively doing things. There is no room for experiencing people or nature in a reflective and receptive way.
- *Be masculine/feminine:* You clearly act out your gender role. You should be dominant, strong, and assertive if you are male; pretty, gentle, and accommodating if you are female.
- *Be selfish:* Life is basically highly competitive and no one is going to look after you if you do not always "look out for number one."

Inhibitor directives can be the inverse of pressurizer directives. Some possible inhibitor directives are the following.

- *Don't think:* Other people's thoughts are better than your own. Do not take the risk of thinking for yourself.
- *Don't trust:* People are highly untrustworthy. If you trust someone, you are likely to be taken advantage of.
- *Don't feel:* Acknowledging your feelings is a risk for yourself and for others. It is better to anesthetize them.
- *Don't be sensual:* Do not have a relaxed and comfortable attitude toward your own and others' sexuality.

- *Don't enjoy yourself:* This prohibition is summed up by a well-known remark about the Protestant ethic: "You can do anything you want, as long as you don't enjoy it."
- *Don't be different:* Your value lies in what others think of you. Do not risk losing this source of emotional support by deviating from the norm.
- *Don't take risks:* Stick to known and safe ways. You can never tell what the outcomes of change may be.
- *Don't acknowledge death:* The inescapable fact of your death is better avoided than confronted.

Not only do your pressurizers and inhibitors affect you as an individual, you take them along into your relationships. Thus in any partner relationship, each person brings in directives from his or her parents. These different "family of origin" directives may be a source of considerable conflict.

THINKSHEET 17

Identifying Your Self-Oppressing Directives

1. *For your life as a whole*
   a. Take a piece of paper and draw a line down the middle. At the top of the left-hand column, write PRESSURIZER DIRECTIVES; at the top of the right-hand column, write INHIBITOR DIRECTIVES.
   b. In the relevant columns, list your self-oppressing pressurizer and inhibitor directives.
   c. Assess the impact of these directives on the quality of your life.
2. *For a specific problem* Repeat the exercise, but this time focus on one of your specific problem areas: sex, self-disclosing, anger, conflict, and so on. Try to list as many relevant directives that you have internalized as you can.

Choosing to Challenge and to Change Your Self-Oppressing Directives

In a number of ways, you can choose to challenge and change your self-oppressing directives. The three I'll review are disputing, understanding the origin, and giving yourself permission.

Disputing

Disputing your directives is similar to disputing your personal rules. For instance, if you have a pressurizer directive like "hurry up," questions that you might ask to dispute it include the following.

"Where is the evidence that I must always hurry up?"

"What are the costs and consequences to me of always hurrying up?"

"What might happen to me if I did not always hurry up? Would it be so awful?"

"Do I think it realistic to demand that others hurry up, as I demand of myself?"

"In what ways might I approach time other than by pressuring myself to always hurry up?"

The directive "hurry up" is not as innocent as it might seem on the surface. It can contribute to all sorts of stress-related problems, both psychological and physical. For instance, psychologically, it can contribute to your feeling anxious, under pressure, and irritable. Physically, you may suffer ailments such as hypertension, migraines, peptic ulcers, and heart attacks.

Understanding the Origin

Understanding the origin of your pressurizers and inhibitors can help you to realize that, though they may have had a purpose in the past, they have long outlived their usefulness. Take the pressurizer directive "hurry up." While you were growing up, either or both of your parents may have had a similar directive that they applied to themselves as well as to you. Thus not only were you constantly being told to hurry up, but also at least one of them was modeling a hurry-up lifestyle. Because of the potency of your parents, both as examples and as purveyors of rewards to you, your childhood decision to hurry up may have been realistic under the circumstances. Understanding the origin of your hurry-up decision and that you have unthinkingly internalized it since then may make it easier for you *now* to redecide to hurry up only when it suits you. Your changed thinking enables you to behave flexibly rather than compulsively.

Giving Yourself Permission

Giving yourself permission allows you to resist your powerful pressurizers and inhibitors. Permission comes from your Choosing Self, as a way of both relinquishing the negative elements of your Learned Self and of releasing positive elements of your Natural Self. It is a form of self-talk that supports rather than oppresses you. Here are some examples of permission replacing a pressurizer directive.

Pressurizer: Achieve at all costs.
Permission: It's okay to please myself regarding what standards I achieve.

Pressurizer: Hurry up.
Permission: It's okay to go at my own pace and hurry up only when necessary.

Pressurizer: Be masculine/feminine.
Permission: It's okay to express whatever parts of my being I want, regardless of
whether my culture labels them masculine or feminine.

Here are some examples of permission replacing an inhibitor directive.

Inhibitor: Don't think.
Permission: It's okay to use my full mental capacity and to think for myself.

Inhibitor: Don't feel.

Permission: It's okay to listen to my feelings and to act on them if I choose.

Inhibitor: Don't be different.

Permission: It's okay to be myself and to support my development as a unique person.

As with many of your thinking choices, it is one thing to tell yourself that you have permission, and another to integrate it into your daily behavior. This issue will be raised again shortly.

THINKSHEET 18

Challenging and Changing Your Self-Oppressing Directives

1. Select one or more significant *pressurizer* directives in your life. For each one, do the following.
   a. Dispute it.
   b. Try to understand its origin.
   c. Replace it with permission to do otherwise.
2. Select one or more significant *inhibitor* directives in your life. For each one, do the following.
   a. Dispute it.
   b. Try to understand its origin.
   c. Replace it with permission to do otherwise.
3. Ask yourself the following.
   a. To what extent do you restrict yourself through pressurizers and inhibitor directives?
   b. To what extent might you free yourself to be happier and more fulfilled by granting yourself permission?

Changing Your Actions As Well As Your Directives

Your pressurizer and inhibitor directives can be powerful voices in your head. Much of the section on changing your actions along with your personal rules is relevant here. You have to practice, practice, and practice behaving differently. You can use visualization to help you picture and rehearse a different way of being. You may either jump right in at the deep end to change your behavior in a difficult situation, or take gradual steps toward changing. Additionally, the help of a like-minded group may make it easier for you to relinquish self-oppressing directives.

Though self-oppressing directives are frequently difficult to change, certain of them in particular may be policed by anxiety and guilt. For example, exclusively homosexual individuals, female or male, who gradually come to the recognition that they will not have heterosexual lifestyles, must make a choice. Either they must inhibit their sexuality as much as possible or express it homosexually. Though attitudes toward homosexuality are becoming more tolerant, it is still probable that many people are brought up with a strong prohibition against homosexual wishes and behavior. Thus at each stage in the coming-out process—to themselves, to other homosexuals, and to the wider community—homosexual people may experience anxiety and guilt that is a residue of their earlier parental and social programming.

Anxiety and guilt can be associated with the process of relinquishing many other directives. For instance, people with a "Don't enjoy yourself" inhibitor can feel anxious and guilty about spending time and money enjoying themselves. Consequently, when changing your actions along with your directives, you may need to engage in coping self-talk to help manage the associated anxiety. You also need to change your actions at a pace you can handle.

LISTENING TO AND DEVELOPING YOUR CONSCIENCE

Labor to keep alive in your breast that little spark of celestial fire, called conscience.

George Washington

Conscience is the inner voice that warns us somebody may be looking.

H. L. Mencken

To date I have mainly focused on loosening, freeing up, and humanizing your personal rules and directives. Working through and beyond self-oppressing internalizations of others' rules is an important step in developing a self-supporting personal rule book. Another way of viewing your personal rule book is as your conscience. Your conscience is your awareness of what is right and wrong. Or, as existential psychiatrist Rollo May (1953) observed, "Conscience, rather, is one's capacity to tap one's own deeper levels of insight, ethical sensitivity, and awareness, in which tradition and immediate experience are not opposed to each other but interrelated" [p. 215]. When your conscience represents your own valuing process, it is still possible to experience anxiety and guilt—not for failing to live up to others' rules, but for acting in ways that violate your human potential. Consequently, another way to develop a self-supporting rule book is to choose to live up to those rules that protect your happiness and fulfillment.

A further way of viewing your personal rule book takes into account your relationship to the wider human species and community. Fostering a wider social conscience, then, might be viewed as a third way of developing a self-supporting rule book. If your conscience is humane in relation to yourself, you are likely to have more positive energy to direct outside of yourself. You will not be so bogged down in your own negative agendas. Then you may further develop social interests beyond immediate self-interest. The more people who do this, the better are the chances for safeguarding rather than annihilating the human species.

Listening to Your Conscience

There is a body of thought among some psychologists that says that human disturbance results less from trying to live up to others' unrealistic rules than from failing to live up to internal, realistic rules (Mowrer, 1964). For instance, if you want to be respected by other people you need to behave in ways that generate respect. If you want to be happy, you need to choose not to engage in escapist behaviors like drug and alcohol abuse. In short, you may already have self-supporting rules, but fail to support yourself by living up to them.

From this viewpoint, anxiety and guilt are not negative emotions telling you that you have self-oppressing personal rules. Rather they are appropriate or positive emotions signaling that you need to alter your behavior to live up to your self-supporting rules. Guilt then is what Maslow (1962) terms "intrinsic guilt," resulting from the betrayal of one's own inner nature. Such self-disapproval is justified. Therefore, you are responsible for disciplining your thinking and behavior.

Though there are numerous reasons for extramarital affairs, "cheating" on your spouse may be a typical instance of damaging yourself by not listening to your conscience and living up to your rules.

> Brian is a married man with three children, 5, 9, and 13 years of age. He is managing director of a ceramics company and a lay preacher in his church. Over the past 2 years he has worked very hard, often staying late at the office. During this period he has had an affair with Debbie, his secretary. He realizes that there is no long-term future in the affair, also that there is a good chance of saving his marriage and family life if he works on it. This is what he says he wants, both in a positive sense and to ease the anxiety and guilt he feels from not living up to his own freely chosen standards. However, he is in considerable turmoil, since he still has strong feelings for Debbie.

I assume that Brian had a humane conscience. He did not have a punitive attitude toward his affair because of an unthinking internalization of others' values. Rather, his conscience impelled him to live up to a particular standard, that was applicable to his situation and that *he* valued.

Thinksheet 19 is designed to make the point that listening to and living up to your conscience may benefit you in many instances. I do not mean to imply that this is always easy. Sometimes it involves a lot of inner conflict and pain. It may also require skilled outside support.

THINKSHEET 19

Listening to and Living Up to Your Conscience

1. Select one or more areas in your life in which you think you experience anxiety and guilt for not living up to your conscience or personal rule book.
2. State your relevant self-supporting personal rules as clearly as possible.
3. Make a case for why these rules are self-supporting. State the costs and conse-

quences to yourself and to others of not living up to your self-supporting personal rules.
4. Develop a step-by-step plan for bringing your actions more into line with your self-supporting personal rules.
5. Work hard to implement your plan.

Developing Your Social Conscience

Men are rewarded and punished not for what they do, but for
how their acts are defined. This is why men are more interested in better justifying
themselves than in better behaving themselves.

Thomas Szasz

Since the focus of this book is on applying thinking skills to personal rather than to social or species-wide problems, this section is a brief postscript to the chapter. Earlier I mentioned developing a social interest that goes beyond immediate self-interest as a third element of a self-supporting rule book. My position is based on a number of assumptions. First, that higher levels of human development entail listening to and building on the prosocial elements of your human nature. Self-oppressing personal rules may be egocentric ones that restrict you from an awareness of your full humanity. In his famous study of self-actualizing people, Maslow (1970) observed that they "...have for human beings in general a deep feeling of identification...Because of this they have a genuine desire to help the human race" [p. 165]. Second, you may feel more fulfilled if, some of the time at least, you can live up to personal rules that transcend narrow self-interest. Third, enlightened self-interest may help you to develop a more caring attitude toward others who share the same planet. The risk of either conventional or nuclear war is ever present.

All people are likely to have their own rationales for their balance (or imbalance) between self-interest and social interest. Here are a few illustrative self-oppressing rules that people use as a defense against assuming a wider social interest.

- *I must be appreciated:* My acts are not worth doing in themselves, but only for the public approval they bring.
- *I must not be taken advantage of:* In helping others I run the risk of being taken advantage of. This would be terrible.
- *I must help everyone:* Because I cannot do everything, doing anything is useless.
- *I must wait for others:* If it becomes the customary thing among my friends and associates to share a wider social interest, then—but not until then—I will do so, too.
- *Others must help themselves:* Other people are responsible for looking after themselves, and I may only weaken their resolve if I help them.

You can dispute and reformulate any personal rules that block enlightened social interest on your part. You may also try changing your behavior to accord with your changed rules. That may mean starting with small steps, but not necessarily so.

Visualizing the outcomes of your changed behavior might strengthen your resolve. For instance, if you give money to a charity, you can find out and then visualize how it is being used to benefit others. Additionally, mixing with like-minded people, either in religious or lay groups, may further help you to develop your social conscience.

CHAPTER HIGHLIGHTS

Personal rules are your guides for the conduct of yourself, others, and the environment: they can be either self-oppressing or self-supporting.

Inappropriate feelings and actions signal that you may have underlying self-oppressing personal rules.

Self-oppressing personal rules frequently contain absolutist "musts," "oughts," and "shoulds," facetiously termed "mustabation."

A major skill of changing self-oppressing personal rules is that of disputing their irrational assumptions.

Self-oppressing personal rules also need to be reformulated into language that is self-supporting.

Changing your actions along with your personal rules can be difficult and involve significant personal struggle.

Changing your actions is helped by practice, visualized rehearsal, and group support.

Directives are closely allied to personal rules and are the orders or commands that you give to yourself.

Two major categories of self-oppressing directives are pressurizers and inhibitors.

Ways of changing self-oppressing directives include disputing them, understanding their origins, and granting yourself permission to do otherwise.

Changing your actions along with your directives can be difficult and require working through anxiety and guilt.

Your existing personal rules can be self-supporting, in which case you support yourself best by listening to and living up to them.

Developing your social conscience may help you attain more of your human potential; it can also ultimately benefit the human species as a whole.

CHAPTER 6

Choosing How You Perceive

People see only what they are prepared to see.
Ralph Waldo Emerson

Castles in the air—they're so easy to take refuge in.
So easy to build, too.

Henrik Ibsen

Think of yourself as an information processing machine. During all your waking hours, you are bombarded with internal and external stimuli. This bombardment goes on even when you are asleep and dreaming. However, unlike sleep, your waking hours allow you to choose how to perceive those stimuli. If you perceive them accurately, you have a better information base for living effectively. If you distort, deny, or misinterpret significant information, you are susceptible to inappropriate feelings and actions.

That you can often perceive the same event in different ways may be less obvious. Take the example of someone stepping on your toe. Among many different perceptions from which you might choose are that it was accidental, careless, done in anger, done because the other person was pushed, or done because your foot was in the way. You may choose the first perception to cross your mind rather than say to yourself "Stop...think...what are my perceptual choices?" and then choose the most appropriate one for the context. Your reaction is also likely to be influenced by your personal rules. For instance, if you have a rule that says "No one must ever invade my personal space," you may react the same way whether your toe was stepped on by accident or in anger.

In this chapter, we'll explore how you may be choosing to perceive some if not much of the time in self-oppressing rather than self-supporting ways. Useful skills we'll examine are influencing your feelings, perceiving yourself more positively, letting go of defensiveness, and perceiving others more realistically.

INFLUENCING YOUR FEELINGS

Since the early 1960s, Aaron Beck of the University of Pennsylvania has been a key figure in the area of helping people influence their feelings by choosing more realistic perceptions (Beck, 1976; Beck, Rush, Shaw, & Emery, 1979; Beck & Emery, 1985; Beck, 1987). In particular, he has focused on the thoughts that precede depression, anxiety disorders, and phobias. However, you needn't be seriously disturbed to benefit from an ability to influence your feelings by challenging and altering your distorted perceptions and perceptual processes. Faulty perception is unfortunately widespread!

Becoming Aware of the Influence of Perception on Your Feelings

Imagine that you are awakened in the night by the noise of a window banging. If you perceive that the window was banging because a burglar entered your home, you may feel very frightened. If, on the other hand, you remember that earlier you were looking out of the open window, got distracted by a phone call, and then forgot to close it, you may feel irritation and annoyance, but probably not fear. In each case, your feelings are influenced by your perceptions.

Of course, to reason through the preceding example, you must be aware of what you are thinking. However, Beck (1976) observes that frequently you are unaware of the thoughts and perceptions that influence your emotions; that instead you have what he terms *automatic thoughts*. Either you are not fully conscious of those thoughts and images or it does not occur to you that they warrant special scrutiny. Beck collaborates with his patients in the scientific or detective work of exploring and identifying these self-defeating perceptions, or "what you tell yourself."

Below are a few simple examples based on the ABC framework.

A. Kathryn's boyfriend, Abe, is 15 minutes late.
B. Kathryn perceives this as a demonstration of Abe's disrespect for her.
C. She sulks and gets angry with him when he arrives.

But imagine that at B Kathryn had thought "Abe isn't usually late. Why don't I ask him what happened?" At C, then, she could have inquired nonaggressively and learned that he was unavoidably held up by a car accident. She would thereby have escaped her negative feelings and behavior. Here's another example.

A. Enrico is sitting with a group of friends; his best friend, Ron, is deep in conversation with Carolyn.
B. Enrico perceives that Ron is bored with him.
C. Enrico feels lonely and depressed.

If at B Enrico had perceived that Ron's attraction to Carolyn had no negative implications for their own relationship, he might even have been happy for his friend.

There is a connection between self-oppressing perceptions and self-oppressing personal rules. For example, Enrico may have had this personal rule: "I must always receive approval from my friends." This personal rule may have predisposed him to look for anything negative in Ron's behavior. Similarly, Kathryn may have had a rigid personal rule about being on time that led her to self-disparagement when the rule was broken.

How do you monitor the upsetting or self-oppressing perceptions that influence your feelings? Ideally, they should be monitored as they happen. To do so, however, you need to develop the skill of listening to the self-talk that accompanies your inappropriate feelings. Setting aside some time each day to build up the skill of monitoring and recording your upsetting perceptions is another approach. Thinksheet 20 is designed to help you do this.

THINKSHEET 20

Monitoring and Recording Your Upsetting Perceptions

A. The situations (include date and time)	B. Your perceptions	C. Your feelings

1. Make a thinksheet similar to the sample. For the next 24 hours, monitor and record the ABCs of a single category of negative feelings or of any variety of significant negative feelings. In particular, focus on identifying at B the thoughts and perceptions that immediately precede and accompany your inappropriate negative feelings at C.
2. What have you learned about the relationship between your perceptions and your feelings by completing this thinksheet?
3. Repeat the exercise until you feel you have developed some lasting self-help skills to recognize self-oppressing perceptions that contribute to inappropriate negative feelings.

Common Perceptual Errors

Facts or Inferences?

Your perceptions of the world are your subjective "facts." They are the stars by which you steer your course through life. However, subjective facts do not necessarily correspond to the objective facts of reality. Your perceptions may be based on inference rather than fact. To borrow a favorite illustration of this point from one of my Stanford

University professors, "All Indians walk in single file; at least the one I saw did." That one Indian was seen is fact; that they all walk in single file is inference. Facts are the true data of experience; inferences are deductions and conclusions drawn from that data. Inferences are useful so long as the assumptions on which they are based are recognized and accurately evaluated. All too often, however, inferences are mistaken for facts. This deprives you of accurate information on which to base further thoughts, feelings, and actions.

You can make inferences about yourself, others, or the environment. They can be positive or negative, and of varying degrees of accuracy in relation to the factual data on which they are based. Below are some examples of the difference between facts and perceptual inferences. The speakers may be utterly unaware of the leap in logic that has taken them from fact to inference.

Fact	Inference
This evening I left home briefly a couple of times to run errands.	I didn't hear from my mother; she therefore did not phone me this evening.
I do not immediately understand the first question on an exam paper.	This is a very difficult exam, which I am bound to fail.
I get feedback from a couple of students on how my teaching could be improved.	I am a lousy teacher.
I get a high grade on an essay.	The teacher did not read it properly.
I win at gambling after a series of losses.	I will be lucky in the future, too.

I stress the distinction between fact and inference because it underlies most perceptual errors. You may jump to conclusions and also be unaware that you have made the leap. Illusion then becomes your reality, in whole or in part.

Specific Perceptual Errors

Below are some specific perceptual errors that may contribute to your having inappropriate negative feelings.

- *Negativeness:* Overemphasizing the negative aspects of yourself, others, and the environment and minimizing the positive aspects.
- *Personalizing:* A tendency to perceive yourself as being the center of attention more than is warranted. For instance, "If I go to a dance, everyone will stare at me and realize that I am a poor dancer."
- *Overgeneralizing:* Drawing a broad conclusion from a specific observation. For example, "The fact that Pat turned me down for a date means that all other girls will, too."

- *Magnifying and minimizing:* Distorting the significance of events when there is no basis for such gross errors of perception.
- *Black-and-white thinking:* Perceiving in either/or terms. For example, "Either Stan is crazy about me or he does not love me at all."
- *Self-rating:* Going beyond a functional rating of a specific characteristic to devaluing yourself as a whole person as well as your competence to live effectively.
- *Misattributing:* Failing to accurately assign cause and responsibility for your own and others' behavior. For instance, Eve is separated from her husband, Eric, and thinks, "If Eric does not admit how badly he has treated me, I'll be unable to break loose from him emotionally."
- *Tunnel vision:* Focusing on only a portion of the available information in a situation rather than taking into account all significant data.

In addition to these perceptual errors, many others come under the category of perceiving defensively. These will be explained and listed later in the chapter.

Choosing to Question Your Perceptions by Logical Analysis

The goal here is to achieve an appropriate flexibility in how you perceive, rather than to oppress yourself needlessly with automatic and rigid perceptual patterns. When you become aware that you are either feeling and acting or at risk of feeling and acting in inappropriate ways, it is a good idea to check out the accuracy of your information base. The computer maxim "garbage in, garbage out" applies to human thinking as well.

Choosing to question your perceptions by logical analysis requires self-talk that tries to answer the following questions.

"Stop . . . think . . . what are my perceptual choices?"

"Are my perceptions based on fact or inference?"

"If they are based on inference, are there other ways of perceiving the situation that are more closely related to the factual evidence?"

"What further information might I need to collect?"

"Does my way of perceiving this situation reflect any of my characteristic perceptual errors?"

"What perception can I choose that represents the best fit with the factual evidence?"

When questioning your perceptions, you conduct a logical analysis of the accuracy with which you construe your experiences. This process requires both analytical and creative skills. The latter now become our focus.

Generating Different Perceptions

One of the ways in which you may disturb yourself is by being a "stick-in-the-mud." In this context, this means unnecessarily sticking in the mud of the first perception that you have rather than being more creative and flexible. Many people lack the skill of generating different perceptions to better understand the reality of the situations they face. You can be much more effective if you sharpen your inferences to correspond more closely to the available facts. Here's an example of how to generate different perceptions, taken from my private practice.

A. Katie's 16-year-old daughter, Sandra, has decided to live with Katie's estranged husband, Peter, and has not contacted her for a couple of weeks.
B. Katie's perception of Sandra is that "She is selfish and hard." Katie's perception of herself is that "I am a failure as a mother."
C. Katie makes no effort to contact Sandra, and she feels angry, anxious, depressed, confused, and powerless.

When I first asked Katie whether there were other ways of perceiving Sandra's behavior, she could not think of any. Using a whiteboard, a useful adjunct to this kind of work, either in counseling or on your own, Katie and I set about generating alternative perceptions. Here are a few of them.

"Sandra has her year-end exams coming up. She is anxious about them and finds it easier to study at Peter's place, without the distracting interruptions of her three younger siblings."

"Sandra currently has a lot of conflict with her 13-year-old sister, Betsy; by living with her dad she can avoid that conflict."

"Sandra is confused and upset over Peter's and my separation and needs time to think things through."

"I tend to come on strong with Sandra. For instance, the other day she went home in the school lunch hour with her boyfriend, Rick, when nobody was in the house. I was furious with her."

"Sandra was never that fond of her dad and may be unhappy there."

These were just some of the different perceptions that we generated. Each of them contained some truth helpful in explaining Sandra's behavior. Also, they helped Katie stop labeling Sandra as "selfish" and "hard" and move toward seeing her as a three-dimensional teenager with strengths and vulnerabilities. Furthermore, Katie had the insight that Sandra felt threatened by her "coming on strong." This helped Katie change her own behavior to attain her goals.

Soon after her exams, Sandra came home to have a good talk with her mom. Instead of scolding her for how she had behaved, Katie listened sympathetically and said how glad she was to have her home. Sandra now gives Katie support: for instance, she takes on some of the domestic load when Katie is tired. This brainstorming process helped Katie not only to perceive her way through one particular problem, but also to develop her self-help skills of generating different perceptions.

Evaluating Different Perceptions

Perceptions, once generated, require evaluation to see which ones best fit the factual evidence. In the preceding example, Katie evaluated each of the different perceptions generated as having some validity. She based that evaluation on her knowledge, itself partly based on facts, of how Sandra thought about and coped with her world.

Here is another example in which Louise, a former prostitute and manager of an escort agency, generated and evaluated new perceptions.

A. At the end of a social gathering, Louise walks past Karl and Anna, who are talking in the parking lot. Karl sees her, but goes on talking to Anna.
B. Louise perceives "Karl does not like me."
C. Louise feels depressed and unattractive.

With encouragement, Louise generated new perceptions, one of which was "Karl has the hots for me but is afraid to show it." She laughed about this, but concluded that there was no evidence in her previous contact with Karl to justify that happy thought. A further perception was "Karl was deeply engrossed in his conversation with Anna, and his returning his gaze to her did not reflect negatively on me." She evaluated this as a realistic perception based on the evidence of their contact together.

Thinksheet 21 gives you practice in identifying your perceptual errors and generating and evaluating new perceptions.

———————————— THINKSHEET 21 ————————————

Identifying Your Perceptual Errors
and Generating and Evaluating New Perceptions

A. The situation	B. Your feelings (before and during)	C. Your perceptions (before and during)	D. New perceptions you generate

1. Make a thinksheet similar to the sample.
2. Think of a situation in which you think a stick-in-the-mud perception may have

(continued)

THINKSHEET 1 (continued)

contributed to your inappropriate negative feelings. Describe the situation in column A, the inappropriate feelings in column B, and your faulty perceptions in column C. Add to column C any perceptual errors, such as overgeneralizing, that you feel distorted your perceptions.

3. In column D, generate at least five new perceptions of the situation. Evaluate each one to assess how closely it corresponds with the available facts. Then put a star by those you think best fit the facts.

4. Repeat this exercise until you feel you have developed some lasting self-help skills to identify your perceptual errors and generate and evaluate new perceptions.

Choosing to Question
Your Perceptions Through Personal Experiments

Sometimes the sequence for improved perception is that you change your perceptions through logical analysis, behave differently, and then get feedback that confirms your changed perceptions. For instance, Katie not only changed her perceptions about Sandra, but also improved her listening skills. Consequently, when Sandra came home Katie was much more rewarding for Sandra, which in turn made it easier for Sandra to behave in ways that were not "selfish" and "hard."

On other occasions, changes in perception may follow from personal experiments. For instance, even if Katie remained convinced that Sandra was "selfish" and "hard," she might have chosen to behave differently to see what happened. Katie could be encouraged to view this as an experiment to test a hypothesis: *if* she behaved differently in specified ways toward Sandra, *then* Sandra would be more caring toward her. Assuming that Sandra became more caring, Katie's perception of Sandra would alter in light of this feedback. In short, instead of logically analyzing *existing* evidence, you can change your behavior to see if it generates *new* evidence to test the accuracy of your perceptions.

The following are some perceptions that might lend themselves to hypothesis testing through appropriately designed personal experiments.

"I'm too shy to smile and initiate conversations with people I don't know well."

"I'm too nervous to phone and ask for information."

"I cannot speak in public without making a fool of myself."

"I can't change the tire on my car."

"I might not enjoy myself if I joined a karate club."

"Now that I am separated, my friends won't enjoy being entertained by me as a single person."

"I cannot go on a vacation by myself."

"He or she is an unfriendly person."

"People will reject me if they find out I failed a test last year."

Keep a number of considerations in mind when designing, carrying out, and evaluating personal experiments.

- State your "If...then..." hypothesis as clearly as possible. You may phrase it as a positive ("If I join a karate club, then I will enjoy myself") or as a negative ("If I join a karate club, then I will not enjoy myself").
- Set clear and realistic goals. Do not try to take on too much.
- Consider a gradual approach, using intermediate-step experiments, if attaining your ultimate goal is difficult.
- Avoid self-rating: the object of the exercise is to collect information that confirms or discredits your hypothesis.
- Give yourself ample opportunity to implement your new behavior.
- Use coping self-talk as necessary.
- Use and develop other skills as appropriate.
- Endeavor to evaluate accurately the information generated from your experiment by being sensitive both to the difference between fact and inference and to specific perceptual errors.
- Make sure that you change your perceptions to account for any new evidence from your experiment, and that you remain open to future new evidence.

THINKSHEET 22

Testing the Accuracy of Your Perceptions Through a Personal Experiment

Think of a situation in which you perceive you are currently unable to act effectively to meet your needs. Conduct a personal experiment to test the accuracy of your perception. Go through the following steps.

1. Clearly state your hypothesis in "If...then..." terms.
2. Make a careful plan of how you intend to go about changing your behavior.
3. Implement your plan.
4. Assess the consequences of your changed behavior for yourself and for others. Do they merit altering your perceptions?
5. Clearly state any changed perceptions resulting from your personal experiment's findings.
6. Practice the self-help skills of using personal experiments to test the accuracy of your perceptions in other situations in which your perceptions may be oppressing rather than supporting you.

PERCEIVING YOURSELF MORE POSITIVELY

Possibly the world's best-known self-help book is Norman Vincent Peale's *The Power of Positive Thinking* (1953). Peale's message is simple: negative thinking produces negative results; positive thinking produces positive results. Your perceptions of yourself are a crucial area in which you may be choosing to oppress rather than to support yourself. For example, you may be using labels to devalue yourself and lower your confidence. Negative self-labeling is a symptom, cause, and effect of severe depression. It is also associated with both moderate and mild feelings of depression and with more minor "lows." In varying degrees, negative self-labeling is a characteristic of virtually all humans. It is paradoxical that, despite their desire for others' approval, many people are extremely reluctant to approve of themselves. At different levels of awareness, you may be engaging in harsh self-criticism that interferes with your happiness and fulfillment.

Becoming Aware of Your Negative Self-Labels

Negative self-labels are unrealistically negative perceptions either of your specific characteristics or of yourself as a person. They are overgeneralized perceptions rather than functional ratings that help you attain your goals. Negative self-labels that you might apply to your intelligence include "stupid, dumb, idiot, fool, klutz, moron." You may apply negative self-labels to other areas, such as your body, your sexuality, your social skills, your feelings and emotions, your tastes and preferences, your leisure pursuits, and your study or work habits.

You may also perceive yourself as having global negative traits. This allows you to negatively rate yourself as a total person. In a study of vulnerability to depression, British researchers Teasdale and Dent (1987) selected the following self-devaluing adjectives from a list of words associated with depression:

deficient	incompetent	stupid	useless
failure	inferior	unloved	weak
inadequate	pathetic	unwanted	worthless

Negative self-labeling allows you to construct a picture or personification of yourself, which becomes your subjective reality. However, as we've seen, subjective and objective reality do not always correspond. You may be making inferences about yourself that do you less than justice. My experience as a practicing psychologist has shown me that most clients' personifications are unrealistically negative. They are much better at listing what is wrong than what is right with themselves. This perceptual habit of ignoring resources and focusing on deficits perpetuates feelings of anxiety, depression, and diminished confidence and vitality. Thinksheet 23 encourages you to become more aware of your negative self-labels so that you may challenge and change them.

——————————— THINKSHEET 23 ———————————

Becoming Aware of Your Negative Self-Labels

1. *Monitoring your self-labeling*
   a. Take a small notepad and, for a 24-hour period, jot down the negative and positive

perceptions of yourself that enter your consciousness. The emphasis is on *your* perceptions, so include feedback from others only if you agree with it.

    b. At the end of the 24-hour period, transfer your perceptions onto a master sheet with NEGATIVE SELF-PERCEPTIONS over one column and POSITIVE SELF-PERCEPTIONS over the other.

    c. Star each self-perception that you think may be a negative self-label rather than a realistic assessment of yourself.

    d. Evaluate what you have learned about yourself.

2. *Becoming aware of your negative self-labeling in different areas*

    a. Write down your negative self-perceptions in whichever of the following areas are relevant to you.
- your body
- your sexuality
- your intelligence
- your study habits
- your occupational life
- your leisure life
- your social life
- your marital life
- your parenting
- your global view of yourself as a person

    b. Star each self-perception that you think might be a negative self-label rather than a realistic assessment of yourself.

    c. Evaluate what you have learned about yourself.

Choosing More Positive Self-Perceptions

A number of the skills discussed thus far in this book will help you change negative self-labels to more positive perceptions. You can use questioning, logical analysis, understanding the origin, and reality testing through personal experiments. You can also use coping self-talk to deal with specific situations. Additionally, you may develop specific skills—for instance, study or relationship skills—that help you counteract your negative self-labels.

Reducing Negative Self-Labeling

Below are some more skills that may curb your tendencies toward negative self-labeling.

    • **Thought stopping:** When you catch yourself in an unproductive, negative train of thought, silently shout to yourself "Stop!" Try to stifle your negative self-labels as soon as you become aware of them. The thoughts are likely to return, but just repeat the procedure as needed.

- **Mental vacuuming:** This is a visualization skill advocated by Kassorla (1984). She gets her clients to visualize a tiny toy vacuum cleaner sweeping across their foreheads and vacuuming up all their negative words and images.

- **Thought switching:** When you find yourself ruminating on negative self-labels, replace them with positive perceptions and an appreciation of positive experiences. For instance, if you feel lonely and inadequate, switch to thinking of your friends and possibly even contact one. If you perceive that you rarely achieve anything, switch to thinking of an achievement that had personal meaning for you. If you are dwelling on something unpleasant in the future, switch to thinking of a positive future event. Thought switching can be combined with thought stopping and mental vacuuming. When negative self-labels intrude into consciousness, (1) instruct yourself to "Stop!", (2) mentally vacuum the negative self-label away, and (3) switch to a positive self-label or appreciation of a positive experience.

Increasing Positive Self-Perceptions

Why wait for negative thoughts before switching to positive thoughts? Be ready to own your positive attributes. If anything, the insecurity that leads to apparent conceit comes from unrealistic negative self-labeling rather than from owning realistic positive perceptions. For some of my underconfident clients, I prescribe a simple homework assignment: for a week they face a mirror for 5 minutes each day and affirm their worth as a person by saying, "I'm Joe/Jane Doe and what I think and feel is of value." Some of you with confidence problems may wish to try this for yourself. It may seem artificial, but some clients find that it starts getting the message across.

You may need to search for ways of perceiving yourself positively. Leading counseling psychologist Allen Ivey and his colleagues consider the positive asset search an important and sometimes neglected aspect of counseling and psychotherapy (Ivey, Ivey & Simek-Downing, 1987). It is also an important and frequently neglected aspect of living.

Here is a vignette to demonstrate a counseling session search for resources.

> Ben, age 16, told his life story with dignity despite the considerable psychological abuse he had suffered, especially from his alcoholic father. His mind went blank when I asked him to state something positive about himself. In one of our early sessions I used a whiteboard, and together we searched for and listed his perceived strengths. These included the following.

Relationships

I am caring.
I like helping others.
I get on well with my age group.
I am attractive to some girls.
I am strongly heterosexual.
I have a girlfriend.

Work

I'm willing to learn.
I'm good with colleagues and customers in the store where I work.
I like practical as well as thinking tasks.

Leisure

I like disco dancing.
I like going out with my friends.
I like listening to soft rock music.

Ben required the emotional and practical support of long-term counseling to gain more control over his life and his thinking. Nevertheless, he did much of the work for himself. He managed increasingly to own his positive attributes and, with that growing success, to discard much of his negative self-labeling.

Thinksheet 24 encourages you to identify and own your resources. Remember that habits of negative self-labeling tend to be deeply ingrained, so you may have to work hard to learn and maintain the skill of supporting yourself with honest self-affirmations.

THINKSHEET 24

Searching for and Affirming Your Resources

1. Search for and make a list of what you genuinely consider to be your strengths or resources as a person. Start each item with the words "I am..." or "I like..." Looking at the list of Ben's perceived resources may help you to get started. Add to your list each day for the next week, if not longer.
2. Each day for a week stand before a mirror and, in a confident voice, read aloud your list of resources at least once.
3. During the day when you label yourself negatively, instruct yourself to "Stop!" and switch to affirming your resources.
4. Practice, practice, and practice to build up the discipline of supporting and affirming yourself with honest positive perceptions of your resources.

LETTING GO OF DEFENSIVENESS

There is an old British saying "There's nowt so queer as folk." Perhaps this refers to the human animal's vast capacity for perceiving defensively. *Defense mechanisms, defenses,* and *security operations* are other terms for the ways in which people "operate" on incoming information to reduce high anxiety. Their objective is to maintain consistency in their personifications of themselves and others. All of you, in varying degrees, have vestiges of childish ways of handling reality that have now become habits that oppress rather than support you. Those defensive processes and perceptions reflect your lower level of mental development when, as a child, you needed to protect yourself against a stronger and sometimes frightening world. Since defensive processes and perceptions distance you from reality, they may have serious consequences for yourself and others. The greater your deficits in this area, the less likely you will perceive your defensive processes. You do it to yourself and then forget that you have done it.

Ways of Perceiving Defensively

The following are some ways in which you may be protecting your picture of yourself by perceiving defensively. All of them involve diminishing your awareness to make your life more psychologically comfortable in the short term.

- *Denial:* Totally warding off from conscious awareness a fact or concept regarded as too frightening or threatening: for instance, some socially stigmatized or undesirable aspect of yourself, such as homosexual tendencies or hypocrisy.
- *Distortion:* All the ways in which you operate on incoming information to maintain your picture of yourself. You may distort positive feedback to maintain a negative self-picture, negative feedback to maintain a positive self-picture, or both.
- *Misattribution:* All the ways in which you attribute cause to protect yourself from assuming full responsibility for your life: for example, by blaming others needlessly.
- *Rationalization:* Ways of excusing behavior that causes anxiety. Rationalization differs from excuses in that you do not have full insight into what you do: in short, you deceive yourself as well as others.
- *Projection:* Externalizing something internal: for example, having difficulty controlling your sexual urges, yet setting yourself up as a guardian of public morality.
- *Reaction formation:* Forming reactions that are the opposite of what you really feel: for instance, apparent repulsion masking a sexual attraction, or apparent love masking intense anger.
- *Avoidance:* A common manifestation of denial: for example, being unaware that you repeatedly avoid a difficult person or situation.
- *Defenses against the good:* Blocking off or diluting your awareness and manifestation of positive qualities such as generosity and concern for others.
- *Attack:* Attacking and intimidating others who provide or might provide unwelcome feedback: going for their jugular veins.
- *Defensive lying:* Making up stories about yourself and others with the goal of placing yourself in the right and the other person in the wrong. Giving way to the Nelson-Jones Reality Principle: "If you cannot accept reality, create it!" Defensive lying differs from deliberate lying in that you actually believe the distortions of reality entailed in your dishonesty.

Choosing to Give Up Your Defensive Processes

Relinquishing your defensive processes can be difficult. You may want to hold on tenaciously to your version of reality. There is a joke about a psychiatrist who worked unsuccessfully for 3 months with a patient who thought he was dead. Finally, in frustration, the psychiatrist asked the patient, "Do dead men bleed?" The patient replied "No." The psychiatrist then pulled out a scalpel, slashed the patient's forefinger, and held it up to his face. In amazement the patient observed, "Well, hang me, Doc, dead men *do* bleed!"

Letting go of childish ways of thinking can be hard for a number of reasons. You may have an illusion of rationality. Or you may not know what thinking processes to look for. Those processes may be partially or totally submerged beneath your awareness. Relinquishing defensive perceptions reveals a different you, which may be highly threatening even if the new information is positive.

The first step in giving up defensive processes is to realize that they exist in almost all people, including yourself. The second step is to know what the various processes are. The third step is to review and monitor your behavior to see if you can spot any of those processes. Since they are rarely fully conscious, you may only get glimpses of them. For instance, if you catch yourself reacting aggressively to criticism, you may question the justification for your reaction. When you calm down, you may realize the criticism was accurate, though you did not wish to hear it. You may then become aware that attack is one of your defensive ways of maintaining your picture of yourself. Likewise, if you catch yourself always criticizing others for characteristics you dislike in yourself, you may suspect that projection is one of your defensive processes.

Once you become aware of a defensive process, tell yourself "I can get by without this childish way of thinking." Then work hard to identify what triggers your defensiveness and to block it early on. For instance, if you know that you tend to get defensive when someone questions whether you behave consistently, calm down, acknowledge your tendency to overreact, and think of the most appropriate response, given the available evidence. Use your skills of distinguishing inference from fact and of evaluating how realistic your inferences are. Additionally, it is much easier for you to acknowledge and fight against your defensive processes if you can overcome certain self-oppressing personal rules. These mustabatory rules include "I *must* be rational at all times," "I *must* be perfect," "I *must* never make mistakes," "Others *must* think me rational at all times," and "Others *must* agree with my picture of myself."

Defensive processes, once identified, require constant vigilance; they represent well-established ways of distorting reality. Sometimes they perform a benign self-protective function in allowing you to put off acknowledging information until a time and at a rate that you feel able to process it. More often, though, your defensive processes are self-oppressing. Additionally, they can be incredibly painful for others: for instance, you may act dishonestly toward them and then attack them for noticing you have done so; you may then further attack them for reacting negatively to your attack. Identifying and overcoming a defensive process once does not mean you are immune to its recurrence. The probability is that you will have to work and practice to keep on top of it.

Thinksheet 25 has been designed to help you start exploring your defensive processes in the hope that you will choose, and keep choosing, to resist them and to think more rationally.

THINKSHEET 25

Letting Go of Your Defensive Processes

1. On a piece of paper, list the following defensive processes in the left-hand margin. Leave writing space under each one.
   a. denial
   b. distortion
   c. misattribution
   d. rationalization
   e. projection
   f. reaction formation
   g. avoidance
   h. defenses against the good
   i. attack
   j. defensive lying
2. Write out your assessment of the extent to which you engage in each of these defensive processes. Where possible, cite specific examples of how you do so.
3. Spend some time each day for the next week reviewing your thoughts and behavior that day to see if you can add information to your thinksheet.
4. Develop and implement a plan to let go of each of your defensive processes.
5. Work hard to relinquish your defensive processes in your daily life, both current and future.

PERCEIVING OTHERS MORE REALISTICALLY

Two-thirds of what we see is behind our eyes.

Chinese proverb

The way you choose to perceive others can support or oppress them as well as yourself. You may negatively label others in ways that have unwanted repercussions for both of you. Close relationships tend to go through cycles of alienation and affection, but persistently labeling your partner negatively is a sure way of decreasing affection and increasing alienation, possibly to the breaking point. Here we'll briefly look at ways in which you may bring perceptual distortions to your dealings with others. Though the focus is on close personal relationships, the discussion has relevance for less intimate professional and personal contacts.

Becoming Aware of Your Perceptual Distortions of Others

When you develop a close relationship, each of you brings to it a learning history of perceptual strengths and weaknesses. When you first meet, you may have little information about each other; then gradually you each develop a fuller picture. However, "the course of true love never did run smooth," as others than Shakespeare have noted. There are many perceptual roadblocks to genuine intimacy; we'll look at three of them.

Personifying Your Partner Inaccurately

Two people in a relationship are actually relating to their personifications of each other and of themselves. Those personifications are of varying degrees of accuracy, of course. You may think that because you're living with your partner all the time, you know him or her like the back of your hand. However, this is frequently not the case. Two main contributors to an inaccurate picture of your partner are a lack of information and your own perceptual errors.

Lack of information As people get acquainted they discover more about one another, in both breadth and depth. Breadth knowledge is gained from the number of topics you discuss: for instance, sports, money, and sex. Depth knowledge is gained according to the intimacy level of your disclosures and the degree to which each of you will risk being esteemed less by the other because of those disclosures. Many relationships get stuck at a level of self-disclosure that falls short of genuine intimacy. The fact that partners tend to match each other's behaviors consolidates the "stuckness."

There are many explanations for why you may know less than you think about your partner. Your partner may lack "talking-about-myself" skills. You, too, may lack disclosing skills, which in turn makes it more difficult for your partner to open up. Additionally, you may have skills weaknesses in listening, understanding, and showing understanding. Thus, rather than encouraging disclosure by being safe to talk to, you may be perceived as threatening and unsafe.

Perceptual errors You may use many of the perceptual errors with which you oppress yourself to oppress others as well. To rephrase those errors, you may be overemphasizing your partner's negative aspects; overgeneralizing by drawing broad conclusions from specific observations; engaging in black-and-white thinking (for instance, your partner either cares for you or does not care at all); and rating him or her as a whole person (for instance, "If my partner does not remember our anniversary he or she is a rotten person"). Additionally, your defensive processes may interfere with the accuracy of your vision. "My view of me" needs to be sustained by your fulfilling "my view of you," however inaccurate both of these personifications may be.

Misperceiving Your Partner's Power to Control You

Realistically, the balance of power in any relationship may be unequal. For instance, a husband may have more power over financial resources than his wife, thus putting her at a disadvantage. However, it is easy to misperceive a partner's power. In particular, there is a perceptual tendency to misperceive the extent of a partner's power over how you think, feel, and act. Your partner may influence you, but cannot control you. The need to accurately attribute responsibility for your choices and to own your thoughts, feelings, and actions has already been mentioned.

Here is an example of not owning responsibility for feelings, thoughts, and actions. At an American Psychological Association Convention, a family therapist showed a video of his work with a rigid American-Greek husband who was justifying battering his wife "because her behavior makes me so angry." Eventually, the therapist confronted and visibly stunned him with this question: "You're not going to let her keep controlling your behavior like that, are you?" There was applause in the audience. It was an "aha" experience for the husband to start realizing how he had misperceived his wife's power to control his behavior. Instead of seeing himself as having no choice, he now had the opportunity to accept responsibility for his behavior.

Misperceiving Your Partner's Behavior and Intentions

A number of studies have found that people in distressed marriages are more likely to perceive their partner's negative attributes as causing their marital problems than are people in stable marriages (for instance, Jacobson, McDonald, Follette, & Berley, 1985). For example, distressed couples are quicker to ascribe malicious intent to each other. Other negative attributions often made are that their partner neither loves nor cares for them and that their partner's personality is flawed. In some instances, the negative attributions may have been accurate all along. In others, the negative attributions are self-fulfilling prophecies: they were initially inaccurate, but generated responses that made them accurate. In still other instances, they are consistently inaccurate.

Here is an example of a wife who oppresses both herself and her husband by wrongly inferring a lack of caring from his relationship skills deficit.

> Connie thought that Angelo did not care for her. She wanted him to verbalize and demonstrate his positive feelings for her more openly and often. When she did not get the desired demonstrations of love, she became increasingly demanding and aggressive, saying that Angelo "just did not understand women." The reality was that Angelo had grown up in a strict family in which demonstrations of feeling were discouraged and sometimes punished. He cared for Connie but lacked the confidence and skills to show it. Connie's misperception of his behavior and her aggressive demands were only making matters worse for both of them.

Imputing negative characteristics to your partner is more likely if you have certain self-oppressing personal rules. Rules that lay the groundwork for marital dissatisfaction include "I *must* always win in a conflict," "My partner *must* always fulfill my demands," and "My partner *must* never challenge my image of myself."

Choosing to Change Your Perceptions of Others

How can you introduce greater accuracy into your perceptions of others? People can blossom and be much more cooperative if they feel appreciated. Consequently, you can support yourself and others by working hard to counteract your destructive negative perceptions of them that are not based on reality. Though the focus here is on close personal relationships, these skills can be extrapolated to revise your perceptions of others in many contexts.

- *Collecting more information:* Use good listening and self-disclosing skills to make it safe for your partner to reveal more. Are you leading unnecessarily secret lives with each other? If so, try to be more open and mutually supportive.
- *Understanding the origin of your partner's behavior:* Get to know the influences that have shaped your partner. What rules and directives were received from her or his family, background, and other sources? What struggles and disappointments has your partner had, and how well has she or he coped with them? A fuller knowledge of your partner's background may make it easier for you to forgive perceived transgressions.
- *Correcting your specific perceptual errors:* Try to identify what they are and then choose not to let them interfere with the quality of your relationship.
- *Owning more responsibility for your problems:* Do not erroneously attribute to others the power to control your thoughts, feelings, and actions. You are responsible for choosing how you perceive others and yourself.
- *Using logical analysis:* When you start having persistent negative feelings about your partner, say to yourself, "Stop . . . think . . . what are my perceptual choices?" Use your skills of distinguishing fact from inference and of assessing the validity of your inferences.
- *Conducting personal experiments:* Try altering your behavior to see if your negative perceptions of your partner are as much a function of your behavior as they are of hers or his. Just as partners tend to match negative behaviors, they also tend to match positive behaviors. There may be realistic opportunities for you both to behave differently and thereby lessen your negative perceptions of each other.
- *Altering oppressing personal rules:* Try to become aware of the mustabatory demands you make on others. Question those oppressing rules and reformulate them into rules more supportive of others. Work hard to stop "laying trips" on others in terms of how you expect them to behave.
- *Improving specific relationship skills:* You may need to develop further relationship skills: for instance, of managing anger and conflict.

There are no easy ways to clear up inaccurate perceptions of your partner. Some people's negative perceptions reflect their own deep insecurities, for which they may require professional counseling. Even if you are not deeply anxious, you still have to work hard to discipline your thinking. This is especially true when you are in conflict or under stress.

THINKSHEET 26

Choosing to Perceive Others More Realistically

Answer the following questions.

1. With regard to your partner or to some other person of your choice, assess the extent and ways in which you do the following:
   a. personify him or her
   b. misperceive his or her power to control you

(continued)

THINKSHEET 26 (continued)

    c. misperceive his or her behavior and intentions

2. If you believe that some of your perceptions are inaccurate, assess the extent to which each of the following might help you to perceive the other more realistically.
   a. collecting more information
   b. understanding the origin of their behavior
   c. correcting your specific perceptual errors
   d. owning more responsibility for controlling your behavior
   e. using logical analysis
   f. conducting personal experiments
   g. altering oppressing personal rules
   h. improving specific relationship skills
3. Set yourself clear and achievable goals for perceiving the other more realistically; then develop and implement a plan to meet those goals.
4. Assess the costs and consequences to you of choosing to work to discard your unrealistic perceptions of the other.

CHAPTER HIGHLIGHTS

You have a choice about how you perceive yourself and others.

How you perceive influences how you feel and act.

Facts are the true data of experience; inferences are deductions and conclusions drawn from that data.

You can learn to regulate your feelings by becoming more aware of your unrealistic perceptions and perceptual errors; you can also alter them, using the skills of logical analysis and conducting personal experiments.

By labeling yourself negatively, you oppress rather than support yourself.

You can learn to become more aware of your unrealistic negative perceptions—both of your specific characteristics and of yourself as a person.

Skills to reduce negative self-labeling include thought stopping, mental vacuuming, and thought switching.

Skills to increase positive self-perceptions include searching for and affirming your resources.

Defensive processes and perceptions are ways of maintaining your self-picture by changing and distorting discrepant feedback.

You may choose to let go of the childish ways of thinking entailed in defensive processes, but it requires awareness, work, and practice.

Three ways in which you may misperceive others are by (1) personifying them inaccurately; (2) misperceiving their power to control how you think, feel, and act; and (3) misperceiving their behavior and intentions.

Relevant skills for perceiving others more realistically include collecting more information, understanding the origin of their behavior, correcting your specific perceptual errors, owning more responsibility for controlling your behavior, using logical analysis, conducting personal experiments, altering oppressing personal rules, and improving specific relationship skills.

CHAPTER 7

Attributing Cause

*It is the act of an ill-instructed man to blame others for
his own bad condition; it is the act of one who has begun to be instructed
to lay the blame on himself; and of one whose instruction has been
completed, neither to blame another, nor himself.*

Epictetus

In Chapter 3 I introduced the notion of attributing responsibility accurately, both for the authorship of your life and for your everyday problems and decisions. I'll now elaborate on the relationship between your motivation and how you attribute cause for what happens in your life. Attributions are the explanations, interpretations, or reasons you give yourself for what happens. They influence how you think about the future as well as how you feel and act. The theory is that you always seek explanations of what happens to you so that you can accurately understand and predict your world. This then enables you to act more effectively. In practice, you may proceed somewhat differently. You may make numerous explanatory errors that interfere with your motivation and effectiveness. Let's examine potential attributional errors in three areas for which you seek cause: your problems, positive and negative events, and academic success and failure.

ATTRIBUTING CAUSE FOR YOUR PROBLEMS
Failing to Acknowledge Problems

When attributing cause for your problems, it is important to be able to separate fact from inference and to make realistic inferences where facts are limited. However, before you can attribute causes for your problems you must acknowledge their existence. Denial is one way of dealing with problems. In the immediate aftermath, people may deny the deaths of their loved ones. With more everyday problems, they may say "I'm not anxious" or "I'm not depressed" rather than accept the challenge to their self-images posed by those feelings. Also, in relationships it may be psychologically more comfortable to deny anger and conflict rather than to acknowledge their existence. However, the risk is that those negative emotions will fester. Then they may either come out sideways, in activities like gossip, or directly, in aggressive outbursts.

Not locating problems in yourself is another way of distancing yourself from their existence. For instance, in the case of a misbehaving child, neither the child nor the parents may own the problem. The child thinks his or her parents' reaction to the misbehavior is their problem; the parents consider the problem to be located in the child. The parents may fail to acknowledge that they, too, have a problem of how to deal with the child's misbehavior if it bothers them. The child may thoroughly enjoy misbehaving but be worried about parental reactions to it. Consequently, the child may need to own the problem of how to cope with negative parental reactions.

Another way of not locating problems in yourself is to project them defensively onto others. Thus, if you are unconsciously concerned about your own aggressive tendencies, you may become very aware of aggression in others, even when it is not present.

Misattributing Causes of Problems

Once you have acknowledged the existence of a problem, many misattributions can help you to remain unnecessarily stuck with it. These explanations are often partial truths that, because they are incorrectly treated as whole truths, weaken your motivation to change. They lead to self-defeating predictions: either that you will be unsuccessful in changing or that you will be unable to change unless others do so first. Below is a list of possible misattributions about the causes of your problems.

• *It's my genes.* Undoubtedly your genetic endowment has limited your physical characteristics—for instance, height—and abilities—for instance, intellectual or musical prowess. However, many people's work and study problems are compounded—if not caused—by lack of effort rather than by lack of ability. Also, saying that you are "naturally" an angry person or that it is "natural" to feel angry obscures the role of your own choice in generating and sustaining your anger.

• *It's my mental illness.* The medical profession has done the public a huge disservice by fostering the concept of mental illness. It has overemphasized the roles of heredity and physical factors in human problems and underemphasized the roles of learning and choice. Fortunately, many physicians and, probably, most psychologists recognize that the concept of mental illness is largely a myth, except for a few—albeit important—biologically influenced conditions such as schizophrenia. That mental illness can block change is demonstrated by the depressed person who thinks, "I am mentally ill," rather than, "I can develop skills for better meeting my needs."

• *It's my unfortunate past.* Your unfortunate past, or what others did to you, may have contributed to the skills weaknesses that make you prone to problems. However, you sustain your skills weaknesses mainly by what you do to yourself. Some people with unfortunate pasts require counseling to give them the nurturing and healing they never received from their natural parents. Many people, with or without professional help, have learned to overcome the skills deficiencies caused by past psychic wounds.

- *It's my bad luck.* Undoubtedly, luck does play a part in life. But you either wait for your luck to change, which may be forever, or you make your luck. As one very successful golfer put it, "The more and more I practice, the luckier and luckier I get."

- *It's my poor environment.* As we saw in Chapter 3, adverse social and economic conditions may make it more difficult for you to fulfill yourself. However, as in Viktor Frankl's example of Nazi concentration camp triumphs, you still have a choice about how you cope with those deprivations.

- *It's all their fault.* Here, at least, you acknowledge that you have a problem, but attribute its cause entirely to another or others. Instead of looking from the inside to the outside, you look from the outside to the inside. Because you do not like what you see outside, it provides a convenient excuse for not looking at your own behavior. Also, since it is all their fault, others must change before you can. Thus you allow others' behavior to control your life.

- *It's all my fault.* This is often a misattribution of very depressed people. All negative events in their lives are their fault. Consequently, by overgeneralizing they weaken their confidence and motivation to deal with the realistic difficulties in their lives.

- *The future is hopeless.* You may feel overwhelmed and not know where to start. The future may seem hopeless; you may feel helpless to influence events. The fact that you have many problems does not mean that you have to work on them all right away. Instead, you may choose to work on one or a few and then move on to others when you are ready. Your perception of the number and difficulty of your problems may alter, too, as you start having your first and then subsequent successes.

- *I've tried before.* You may have tried to overcome your problems before and been unsuccessful. However, that need not affect the future. For instance, this time you may try harder, have more skills for coping with your problems and with setbacks, and be better at enlisting the support of others. Previous "failure" does not mean that you cannot now learn new and better skills to help you succeed.

- *I can't stand setbacks.* Setbacks are a part of learning any new skill, just as problems are a part of living. Unrealistic expectations about the ease of the learning process and smoothness of life will make you vulnerable to setbacks. However, you can develop the skills of learning to handle stressful situations better and of being able to support rather than to oppress yourself when faced with setbacks.

Changing Misattributions About the Causes of Problems

Changing any misattributions you have made about the causes of your problems involves awareness, choice, and action.

Awareness   You need to be aware in two ways. First, you need to acknowledge that *you* have a problem. Second, you need to become aware of what your specific misattributions are. Whenever you find yourself unable or unwilling to work on a problem, ask yourself whether you are eroding your motivation and confidence through unproductive misattributions. Then try to identify which ones you use.

Choice   If you think your misattributions may be helping you to stay stuck rather than to work on your problems, you can challenge them by logical analysis, gathering additional information, and conducting personal experiments. Some techniques for challenging your misattributions through logical analysis are implied in the preceding list of misattributions. For instance, the misattribution "It's my unfortunate past" might be disputed by giving examples of people who have overcome unfortunate pasts by learning new and better skills, hopefully in more benign environments.

Misattributions like "It's my genes" and "It's my mental illness" may be challenged by collecting additional information. For instance, a math aptitude tests might provide more realistic information for people attributing their math problems to a biologically based disability. They might discover that their aptitude is higher than they realized. This in turn would raise the issue of whether they were underachieving for other reasons, such as lack of effort, poor teaching, or high anxiety. People who think they are mentally ill can check it out with a competent helping professional. They can be screened for biologically influenced mental disorders; if none show up, they might be given information that helps them conceptualize their problems in learning terms.

Misattributions like "The future is hopeless" and "I can't stand setbacks" can be tested by personal experiments. Here you approach working on your problems by seeking new information.

Whenever you successfully challenge a misattribution, make sure to reformulate it in appropriate self-talk. For instance, the misattribution "The future is hopeless" might be reformulated as "I've started to work on my problems, and, though I still have to develop a lot more skills, I have made progress in doing so. I now think I can cope with the future." In brief, "The future is hopeless" becomes "I can cope with the future."

Action   When you carry out personal experiments to challenge misattributions, you are already engaged in action. However, when you have convinced yourself through logical analysis or collecting additional information that you are misattributing the cause or causes of your problem, you still need to act on that insight. The only way to do so is to start working to change your behavior in the problem area. Hopefully, now you will be free from misattributions that interfere with your motivation to change.

--- **THINKSHEET 27** ---

Changing Misattributions About the Causes of Your Problems

1. Either for a particular problem or in regard to your approach to your personal problems in general, note the extent to which you make or have made each of the attributional errors listed below. Use the following scale:

never   0
sometimes   1
frequently   2

Your Rating	**Misattribution**
_____	It's in my genes.
_____	It's my mental illness.
_____	It's my unfortunate past.
_____	It's my bad luck.
_____	It's my poor environment.
_____	It's all their fault.
_____	It's all my fault.
_____	The future is hopeless.
_____	I've tried before.
_____	I can't stand setbacks.

2. Challenge any misattributions with a rating of 1 or 2 by either (a) logical analysis, (b) indicating what additional information you require, (c) formulating an appropriate personal experiment, or (d) a mixture of two or more of the above.
3. Reformulate each misattribution into appropriate self-talk that accurately attributes the cause(s) for your problem(s).
4. Assess the extent to which and manner in which changing self-oppressing misattributions to self-supporting ones will free you to work more effectively on your problem(s).

ATTRIBUTING CAUSE FOR POSITIVE AND NEGATIVE EVENTS

Your attributions of cause for the positive and negative events in your life may be either accurate or inaccurate. They can therefore affect both your motivation and your self-esteem. The importance of making accurate attributions about positive and negative events is illustrated here in relation to depression.

Becoming Aware of Depressive Attributions

People feel depressed for many different reasons. Some of them were covered in previous chapters: the tyranny of self-oppressing personal rules and perceptions, for example. Another contributing factor may be that people who are depressed feel powerless to influence their environments to achieve desired outcomes. This explanation is favored by psychologists Lyn Abramson, Martin Seligman, and John Teasdale (1978). The reason that people feel helpless is they have learned a depressive attributional style when faced with negative events: for instance, an unsuccessful job search.

Three main characteristics typify a depressive attributional style, and the degree of a client's depression can be judged by the extent to which he or she partakes of these assumptions:

1. *Internal attributions:* Negative events are seen as something caused by you as a person, as opposed to something in the situation. For example, at two extremes, an unsuccessful job search might be explained as "totally due to other people or circumstances" (external) or "totally due to me" (internal).

2. *Stable attributions:* Negative events are viewed as caused by stable factors, not transient ones. Thus their effects are permanent. Again at two extremes, the factors in an unsuccessful job search "will never again be present" (unstable) or "will always be present" (stable).

3. *Global attributions:* Negative events are viewed as being caused by factors present in a variety of situations, not factors specific to the situation. At the two extremes, the cause of an unsuccessful job search might be something that "influences just this particular situation" (specific) or "influences all situations in my life" (global).

There is little doubt that you can undermine your effectiveness and mood by misattributing the causes of both negative and positive events in your life. However, research findings on the relationship between depression and internal, stable, and global attributions have been inconsistent. In a survey of the research literature by Peterson, Villanova, and Raps (1985), roughly half the studies supported the link between both internal and stable attributions and depression. Approximately three-quarters of the studies supported the link between global attributions and depression. Problems in measuring attributional style, especially internality, may contribute to these inconsistent findings.

Thinksheet 28 encourages you to explore your attributional style for assessing negative and positive events. It seeks to raise your awareness about how you may be lowering your motivation and mood through attributional errors. Unlike the well-known Attributional Style Questionnaire (Peterson, Semmel, von Baeyer, Abramson, Metalsky, & Seligman, 1982), the thinksheet asks you to focus on real, not hypothetical, events.

THINKSHEET 28

Assessing How You Make Attributions About the Causes of Negative and Positive Events

1. Identify one recent or current event in your life in each of the following categories.
   a. a negative event in one of your relationships, such as a fight with someone
   b. a negative event in your work or study life, such as not getting a promotion or getting a low grade
   c. a positive event in one of your relationships, such as receiving appreciation from someone
   d. a positive event in your work or study life, such as receiving a salary increase or getting a high grade

2. For each of your negative and positive events, do the following.
   a. Write down *one* major cause.
   b. Rate the major cause on each of the following scales.

   - *external-internal attribution*

totally due to other people or circumstances	1 2 3 4 5	totally due to me

   - *unstable-stable attribution*

will never again be present	1 2 3 4 5	will always be present

   - *specific-global attribution*

influences just this particular situation	1 2 3 4 5	influences all situations in my life

3. Assess what doing this thinksheet has suggested to you about the following:
   a. the way in which you attribute cause for negative and positive events in your life
   b. what influence your attributional style has on your motivation and mood
   c. whether (and in what ways) you need to change how you attribute cause for negative and positive events.

Altering Depressive Attributions

Once you become aware that you may have a depressive attributional style in identifying the causes of negative and positive events in your life, you can choose to alter it. The main way to do so is to monitor and question your attributions and then search for alternative explanations. Then you select the attribution that best fits the facts of a particular situation. You should regard internal/external, stable/unstable, and global/specific as potentially useful dimensions for thinking about your attributions. However, make sure that you avoid the trap of black-and-white thinking. What you seek is an accurate or realistic attributional style; frequently this means attributing cause somewhere between the extremes of each dimension. When you have decided on a best-fit attribution, state it in simple, clear language so that you can remember and use it when necessary.

ATTRIBUTING CAUSE FOR ACADEMIC SUCCESS AND FAILURE
Becoming Aware of Your Attributions

If you are a student, your motivation to achieve and hence your achievements can be influenced by how you attribute cause for your academic successes and failures. Say you have a test coming up. The following are four categories of attribution suggested by

Weiner and Kukla (1970) that you may use both before the test and when evaluating the results.

- *Ability:* This is an internal and stable attribution. Ability is something with which you were born. You have varying degrees of ability in different areas. Your levels of ability are basically outside of your control.
- *Effort:* This is an internal and variable attribution. Effort is a matter of choice, not of genetic endowment. It is largely within your control.
- *Task difficulty:* This is generally viewed as an external attribution. It is composed of the realistic difficulty of the task plus any of your perceptual distortions that magnify or minimize it. While the realistic difficulty of the task may be outside your control, your perceptual distortions are potentially within your control. Thus, where perceptual distortions occur, what may first seem to be an external attribution might also be viewed as internal.
- *Luck:* Luck and its opposite, bad luck, are external attributions. Your academic successes and failures are due to chance. As such, they are outside of your control.

You can attribute a specific academic success or failure to all four of these categories in varying degrees. Also, you might make other attributions: for instance, poor teaching or incompetent grading. Additionally, numerous socioeconomic considerations affect how motivated people are to achieve academically and how much effort they can put in. For instance, if you live in a noisy home with few books and no role model who has achieved academically, and in which no one is interested in your academic success, it may be much harder to make the required effort than if you live in the opposite circumstances. Also, if you have to support yourself, you have less time and energy for academic pursuits. Additionally, your gender may either work for or against your academic motivation and achievement.

Considerable research evidence suggests an attributional self-serving bias, in that people are more likely to take responsibility for their successes than for their failures. The results of a series of studies conducted by Herbert Marsh (1986) indicate that this bias is likely to be more pronounced among more able than less able students. A possible explanation is that failure may be harder for more able students to accept, because it is more discrepant with their academic self-perceptions. In the short term the self-serving bias may give students some artificial motivation, in that they are cushioned against discouragement. In the long term they may find they have been living in a fool's paradise, in which they have failed to make realistic connections between their failures and inadequate effort.

Here are some examples to underscore the importance of being able to make accurate attributions for your academic successes and failures.

> Rachel is a second-year psychology major at a university. She is thinking of giving up psychology because she thinks she lacks the ability to do statistics. The reality is that Rachel's numerical ability is above average, but so is her numerical anxiety!

> Juan is a 15-year-old Hispanic-American high school student who is "underachieving." His command of English is still poor because his family immigrated from Mexico 18 months ago and English is a new language for him. He feels despair over his inability to keep up with his classmates. At times he thinks he is stupid.

Lee is an Asian student of mechanical engineering whose parents have sacrificed to educate him overseas. He is currently repeating the first year of his requirements. Even though Lee works all the time, the staff doubts that he has the ability to complete the major. Lee refuses to accept this feedback, because he is terrified of going home a failure.

Sarah is a 15-year-old high school student who just cannot believe her luck. She has received A's in her two most recent history assignments. She tells her friends "I just can't believe this is happening to me." Her parents point out that this is no fluke, as she has finally started to take her homework seriously. They say her A grades are the reward for effort.

In each of these examples, attributions are based on unfounded predictions and will possibly lead to self-defeating actions. Rachel might unnecessarily give up her psychology major. Juan is in danger of ceasing to catch up. Lee may keep bashing his head against a brick wall rather than accept his limited ability in mechanical engineering. Though her parents are doing their best to make the connection between effort and outcome, if Sarah persists in thinking her success is due to luck, she may stop working so hard.

Altering Unrealistic Attributions

Many thinking skills weaknesses contribute to erroneous attributions about academic success and failure. Your personal rules may be such that you set yourself unrealistically high standards and hence feel the need to rationalize your failures. Your manner of perceiving may be such that it is easier for you to notice either your failures or your successes. Additionally, you may talk yourself into failing rather than succeeding.

As in all instances of faulty attribution, first you must become aware of them and then identify specific questionable attributions. Next, question and dispute these seemingly shaky attributions to see to what extent they are supported by facts. When necessary, generate alternative attributions and consider which fit the situation best. If necessary, collect additional information. For instance, if Rachel's previous math record did not give her sufficient information, she could take a numerical aptitude test. She could also talk to someone in her university counseling service about her anxiety over statistics.

You can also conduct personal experiments to test the accuracy of your attributions about academic success and failure. For instance, Juan might keep making an effort to see if he could catch up with his peers. He and his parents might also look into the possibility of tutoring in remedial English. When you finally choose the attribution that best fits the facts, try to verbalize it simply and clearly so that you may then act on it. Just as you can do much to damage yourself by making inaccurate causal attributions about your academic success and failure, you may do much to support yourself by verbalizing accurate attributions.

Thinksheet 29 encourages you to look at the attributions you make for your successes and failures. Though primarily aimed at students, it is also relevant, with some adaptation, to employed persons.

THINKSHEET 29

Accurately Attributing Cause for Your Academic Successes and Failures

1. For this thinksheet, academic successes are defined as results that pleased you and academic failures as results that displeased you. Draw a line down the center of a sheet of paper. At the top of the left-hand column write ACADEMIC SUCCESSES; at the top of the right-hand column write ACADEMIC FAILURES.

2. In regard to a current or recent academic experience, describe in the relevant column the extent to which each of the following causes accounted for academic successes and failures.
   a. ability
   b. effort
   c. anxiety
   d. task difficulty
   e. staff competence
   f. luck
   g. socioeconomic considerations
   h. gender-related considerations

3. Do you detect a self-serving bias, in that you accept more responsibility for your successes than for your failures? If so, how pronounced is it and what do you think about it?

4. Question and dispute any seemingly inaccurate attributions of yours concerning the causes of your successes and failures. Search for alternative attributions that best fit the facts. State your best-fit attributions in clear and simple language.

5. Think of actions you need to take to support the changed attributions you have chosen.

CHAPTER HIGHLIGHTS

Attributions of cause are your explanations of what happens.

Failure to attribute cause accurately for your problems interferes with your motivation to change.

Misattribution about the cause of positive and negative events in your life can adversely influence your feelings and actions.

There is some evidence that depressive attributions are exaggeratedly internal, stable, and global in nature.

Misattributions about the causes of academic success and failure can undermine both your motivation and achievement.

Thinking skills for correcting a misattribution of cause include logical analysis and designing personal experiments.

CHAPTER 8

Predicting
and Creating Your Future

As a scientist, man [sic] seeks to predict, and thus control, the course of events.
George A. Kelly

The future: anxiety about living in the context of anxiety about dying

Humans lead their lives well into the future—the focus of most of their desires, hopes, and fears. Sometimes their view of the future is bleak. George Orwell had a character in *1984* say, "If you want a picture of the future, imagine a boot stamping on the human face—forever." Sometimes their view is rosy, perhaps unjustifiably so. Eighteenth-century British wit Samuel Johnson said, of a man who remarried immediately after the death of a wife with whom he had been very unhappy, that it was "the triumph of hope over experience."

What is your future? One way of looking at it is as a collection of what actually happens, or the objective reality of future events when they happen. This includes future events that you can influence as well as those you cannot. Another way of looking at your future is as a mental construct based on your subjective reality: the words and pictures in your head about what is to come. You have no facts about the future, as it has not happened. However, it is a fertile breeding ground for inferences of varying degrees of accuracy. Also, you can formulate goals and make plans to shape what is to come.

The way you view your future reflects your attitude toward time. Time is an objective reality in the sense of seconds, minutes, and hours. However, it is also subjective. You may either contemplatively savor time or feel under constant pressure to use time for achievement. The latter attitude has been termed "hurry sickness" by Friedman and Rosenman (1974) in their book analyzing predictors of heart disease, *Type A Behavior and Your Heart*. This constant time urgency affects people's attitudes toward their present and future and also their life expectancy. Expressions like "wasting time" place a subjective value—wasting—on an objective concept—time as expressed in seconds, minutes, and hours. Another way of viewing both time and the future is in terms of quantity and quality. Neither presupposes the other. For instance, you may have a long and miserable life, or be dying yet still experiencing high-quality living.

In this chapter, we'll examine two ways in which you may influence your future: by making predictions of risk and reward and by setting goals.

PREDICTING RISK AND REWARD

*Let me assert my firm belief that
the only thing we have to fear is fear itself.*

Franklin D. Roosevelt

Fortune aids the brave.

Terence

As you lead your life into the future, you constantly assess the probable outcomes of your actions. You also make predictions concerning others' actions and larger events in the environment. George Kelly (1955b) took a rational approach to prediction when he wrote "The two factors from which predictions are made are the number of replications already observed and the amount of similarity which can be abstracted among the replications" (p. 53). However, predictions can also contain perceptual distortions. For instance, a pessimist might predict that it is always going to rain, an optimist that it is always going to be sunny, and a realist something in between. Since your predictions can either help you—by being accurate inferences—or oppress you—by being perceptual distortions—they are very important. Though you make predictions about others' actions and the environment, we'll focus on making predictions about the risks and rewards of your own actions. In this context, risks may be defined as the chances of bad consequences, rewards as the chances of good consequences. You may either overestimate or underestimate the probability of both bad and good consequences.

Predicting Risk Inaccurately

Predicting risks and predicting rewards are interrelated. However, here they are first treated separately before being treated together in the section titled Choosing to Predict Risk and Reward More Accurately.

Underestimating Bad Consequences

You may deny or minimize the chances of bad consequences arising from your actions. Such perceptual distortions are particularly relevant to taking preventive health measures. The research in this area suggests that people demonstrate a pervasive tendency to underestimate their own, relative to other people's, risk for various illnesses and negative life events (Weinstein, 1980, 1984). For some people, "It is less likely to happen to me" may extend to total denial: "It can't happen to me." The result of these unrealistic predictions is that people may fail to take proper care of their health and so become more rather than less at risk. Some of the underestimation of risk in health matters may be attributed to ignorance, some to negligence, and some possibly to death anxiety. Money is another area in which many people underestimate the chances of bad consequences. In fact, many money problems are the direct result of distorted prediction, be it in the stock market, the racetrack, or grandiose business ventures. Matrimony is yet another area in which a realistic assessment of negative consequences may not be made prior to the event.

Overestimating Bad Consequences

Fear of change, failure, and success are powerful motivators that help you overestimate the negative consequences of your actions.

Fear of change   You may have built up a way of dealing with the world based on the assumption that "the known ways are safest and best." Change means moving beyond the safety of the known. Therefore, you may see it as a bad consequence in its own right. Here is a vignette illustrating this point.

> Sean is a 30-year-old bachelor who still lives at home. He struggles with a number of decisions: moving away from home, changing his job, and starting to go out with women. Over the years Sean has chosen consistently to make the safety rather than the growth choice. He is now terrified of change.

Fear of failure   Failure can be defined in many ways, depending on the context and your subjective standards. It often consists of two elements: fear of negative consequences and doubts about your ability to cope with them if they occur. The negative consequences of failure can be imaginatively magnified to the point of becoming catastrophes (Argyle, 1988). You can also unrealistically view failure as a reflection on your whole person.

Fear of failure and rejection is part of all relationships. In fact, for many it is present at every utterance. For instance, most people are extremely sensitive about how their revelations of what they dislike and like about themselves will be received. In varying degrees they lead unnecessarily secret lives and may have a double standard by which they judge themselves more harshly than others. Of course, sometimes your prediction that you will be rejected for your disclosure is entirely accurate. Highly anxious people commonly both overestimate the bad consequences of failure and underestimate their ability to cope with them (Lucock & Salkovskis, 1988). One way of viewing high anxiety is as a prediction disorder involving unrealistically negative estimates of risk and failure.

Fear of success   Success can be a two-edged sword. As Oscar Wilde observed, "In this world, there are only two tragedies. One is not getting what one wants, and the other is getting it." If you succeed in getting the desirable partner, the promotion, or the high grades, you are forced to handle the consequences. You may also have to resolve the inconsistency with your previous negative self-perceptions.

Success, then, has negative as well as positive consequences. There are demands inherent in the role of being a successful person. You may feel that the higher you rise, the greater will be your fall; or you may simply not feel ready for success.

> Robin is a 23-year-old clerk in a municipal office. He is extremely sensitive about a blushing problem and prefers to work on his own. However, he is proficient at his job and has received a promotion that requires him to supervise three other people. While delighted to be offered the promotion, Robin is now very worried that his subordinates will notice him blushing when he gives them instructions.

How others may react to your success can provide further anxiety. Your success may challenge their perceptions of their own adequacy and engender hostility and envy. For some, *Schadenfreude*—the German word for malicious joy at another's discomfort —may be a more congenial feeling than genuine joy at another's success. Additionally, you may fear social ostracism: for example, academically successful females may worry that they are less socially attractive to males.

Fears of change, failure, and success often have some basis in reality. However, when they involve distortions that overemphasize risk, they can lead to passivity, inhibition, and a failure to take realistic opportunities to improve and enjoy your life.

Predicting Reward Inaccurately
Overestimating Good Consequences

Overestimating good consequences frequently accompanies underestimating bad consequences. Your predictions go askew in a rosy glow of money, success, love, domestic bliss, or other delights. Disastrous consequences can ensue for your health, happiness, independence, and financial security if you engage in rash actions based on false positive predictions. Overgeneralization, drawing a broad conclusion from a specific observation, can lead to fatal overestimations of reward. For instance, if the first horse you back wins a race, that does not mean that all other horses you back will win, too. Another thinking skills deficit that contributes to overestimating reward is selectively perceiving only the positive in a situation or relationship at the expense of a more balanced appraisal.

Underestimating Good Consequences

Probably far more people who see counselors and psychotherapists underestimate good than overestimate bad consequences. They have a predictive style that focuses on risk far more than on reward. They often oppress themselves with the double negative of overemphasizing risk and underemphasizing reward.

Two trends are common in underestimating reward. First, you may be poor at perceiving the potential rewards of your proposed courses of action. You may be much better at thinking up risks. Second, even when rewards are identified, you may not give them the weight they deserve.

Thinking Errors and Prediction

Some thinking errors already mentioned influence the accuracy of your predictions. They include the following.

- *Overgeneralizing:* Drawing a broad conclusion from a specific observation. For instance, "I am alone and unhappy now; therefore I will always be alone and unhappy."
- *Black-and-white thinking:* Thinking in either/or terms. For example, "If I go to the interview, they are either going to love me or hate me."
- *Catastrophizing:* Believing that the negative consequences of not achieving your desired outcomes will be much worse than is justified.
- *Personalizing:* Predicting that you will be the center of attention more than is warranted.
- *Self-rating:* Predicting that the outcomes of events are not only positive or negative in themselves, but have global implications for your worth as a person.
- *Misattributing:* Failing to own responsibility for what happens in your life, which increases the chances of self-fulfilling prophecies. For example, you may predict "Things aren't going to go well in our relationship." Then you wait for the other person to make the first move, and "things do not go well."

Thinksheet 30 encourages you to explore how you make predictions of risk and reward. Are you making realistic inferences about the future, so that your actions are soundly grounded? If not, are you viewing the future more bleakly or more optimistically than is justified?

─────────────── **THINKSHEET 30** ───────────────

Exploring How Accurately You Predict Risk and Reward

1. When you predict the consequences of your actions, you can do any of the following:
   a. underestimate the bad consequences (risks)
   b. overestimate the bad consequences (risks)
   c. overestimate the good consequences (rewards)
   d. underestimate the good consequences (rewards)
   Write down the extent to which you feel each of these describes how you make predictions. When possible, give specific illustrations.
2. Select an aspect of your life for which you feel you may have been making self-oppressing rather than self-supporting predictions. Possibilities include looking after your health, meeting new people, being a more open person, looking after your money, relating to a partner or family member, coping with work or study, and taking examinations or completing reports.
   a. Using the fourfold classification for overestimating or underestimating risk and reward, write out how you think you have been making inaccurate predictions in the area you selected.

(continued)

THINKSHEET 30 (continued)

   b. To what extent have your inaccurate predictions contained the following thinking errors?
- overgeneralizing
- black-and-white thinking
- catastrophizing
- personalizing
- self-rating
- misattributing

   c. What have been the consequences of your inaccurate predictions, for yourself and for others?

Choosing to Predict Risk and Reward More Accurately

How you approach changing the way you predict risk and reward depends on your awareness and ability to pinpoint your weaknesses. Four approaches to improving your predictions are discussed here.

Assessing Probability

Assessing probability requires reviewing your assumptions about the likelihood of risks or rewards occurring. You may erroneously assign high probability to low-probability events or low probability to high-probability events. For instance, you may be very afraid of dying in an airline crash. However, the chances of your doing so have been figured at 1 in 1 million years of life expectancy (Emery, 1982). Actuarial tables are not available for most events about which you make predictions. Nevertheless, you can use your skills of distinguishing fact from inference and verifying that your inferences have as much factual basis as possible.

    Questions that you might ask yourself in assessing probability fall into two categories. First, what *rational* basis do I have for making a particular prediction? In mathematics, probability is the likelihood of an event as measured by the ratio of favorable cases to the whole number of cases possible. You will rarely have sufficient information to achieve such predictive precision. Nevertheless, you can assess the number and similarity of previous events as a basis for predicting future events. And you can collect additional information to help this process. The second category of question is what *irrational* considerations might interfere with the accuracy of my prediction? The thinking errors mentioned earlier, your state of emotional arousal, and your physical condition might each interfere with your ability to predict.

Assessing Your Coping Capacity

Your predictions may be based on an inaccurate assessment of your skills at coping with a particular situation. You may have been engaging in negative self-labeling and need to counteract this with a search for your resources. Additionally, you may have many supportive factors that you have inadequately taken into account: for example, someone who can help you prepare for an upcoming task, friends and relatives who can support you emotionally, or second chances to repeat tasks that you failed at the first time. Acknowledge your support factors. One approach that places both the situation and your coping capacities in better perspective is to visualize the worst possibility occurring. If you can see yourself managing to cope in such dire circumstances, it may give you the courage to cope with your current, less dire circumstances.

Generating and Evaluating Additional Risks or Rewards

If your predictive errors lean toward overestimating the potential for reward and underestimating the potential for risk, you may need to develop the skill of generating what other risks there might be. However, more of you are likely to overestimate the risks, and hence may need to develop the skill of generating and evaluating rewards. Let's return to Sean, the 30-year-old bachelor mentioned earlier in the chapter, to see how to do this.

> Despite his age and heterosexuality, Sean had little experience of dating women; his longest experience had lasted three dates. In his church group, Sean was on a committee with Suzanne, who had been friendly to him. Sean wondered if he should ask her out, but worried "Why bother to take the risk of seeking the reward?" With his counselor, Sean generated both the potential risks and rewards of taking this initiative. He was already expert at acknowledging risks, but needed to learn that it was in his interest to look at rewards as well as risks when making decisions. His list of potential rewards for asking Suzanne out included the following:

"I might have a chance of a strong relationship."

"I might gain more experience in developing relationships."

"This might contribute to helping me become happier."

"I might gain confidence and a more positive self-image."

"I might develop my ability to express my feelings more."

"I might give myself the opportunity to let Suzanne take some of the initiative, too."

> Sean decided the rewards of asking Suzanne out outweighed the risks. She later became his first steady girlfriend.

Reality Testing Through Personal Experiments

The most conclusive way to ensure the accuracy of your predictions is to reality-test them. This is similar to carrying out personal experiments to test the accuracy of your perceptions, mentioned in Chapter 6. Here are some examples of people who need to reality-test their predictions.

Debbie, at 19, wants to move away from home. She predicts "I'll never find an apartment that I like."

Maureen, age 27, is afraid to tell her husband how she would like him to make love to her. She predicts "If I tell him, he'll be furious."

Amy, age 33, did not learn to swim as a child. She predicts "I will never overcome my fear of the water."

In each of these examples, the individual needs to set herself a specific goal. Debbie's goal might be to find an apartment within 3 months, Maureen's to tell and show her husband what she likes within the next month, and Amy's to be able to swim by the end of the year. Then each one needs to think through how best to attain her goal. If necessary, each should write out a plan that specifically outlines how she intends to change her behavior. They can experiment, or test their predictions by changing their behavior and seeing what happens. The information gained from the experiments requires accurate assessment, and, when necessary, separating inference from fact. The original predictions are then either confirmed, discredited, or modified. More realistic reformulations should be stated clearly and simply. For instance, Debbie might tell herself, "Though I had to spend a lot of time on it, I did succeed in finding a nice apartment and can probably do so again if I have to."

Reality-testing your negative predictions may become easier if you carefully break tasks down, take small steps before larger ones, rehearse what you are going to do, and, when appropriate, enlist the support of other people. Anyone whose unrealistic predictions are deeply embedded in his or her style of relating to the world might consider seeking professional help.

THINKSHEET 31

Correcting Your Inaccurate Predictions of Risk and Reward

1. Think of a situation in which your negative predictions may block you from achieving a goal important to you.
2. Review the accuracy of your predictions in the following ways:
   a. assessing probability
   b. assessing your coping capacity
   c. generating and evaluating additional rewards
3. Design a personal experiment that tests the accuracy of your previous negative predictions. If possible, carry out and evaluate your experiment and then correct your predictions in light of this additional information.
4. Repeat these steps for other situations in which possibly inaccurate negative predictions block you from attaining your goals.

SETTING YOURSELF GOALS

People often say that this or that person has not yet found himself.
But the self is not something one finds; it is something one creates.

Thomas Szasz

In addition to making accurate attributions and predictions, a third way that you can beneficially influence your future is to set yourself realistic goals. Though the grave is your ultimate destination, the quality of your living will meanwhile be enhanced through improving your skills at setting goals. Some of the *rewards* to be gained from setting realistic goals include the following:

- *Authorship of your life:* Setting your own goals enables you to create your future rather than to either drift aimlessly or attempt others' goals under the guise of attempting your own.
- *Clarity of focus:* Well-stated goals clearly identify the directions in which you want to go. What may previously have been ignored or only partially sensed now becomes articulated in full awareness.
- *Increased meaning:* Well-thought-through goals give meaning to your existence. They can give you hope and a sense of purpose, and can help you avoid feelings of emptiness, boredom, and existential despair.
- *Increased motivation:* Because goals provide you with something tangible to work for, they can increase your motivation and persistence. Goals require implementation, which creates a pressure to plan the appropriate steps to attain them.

There are also risks to setting yourself goals. Such risks usually stem from goals set in the wrong way or at the wrong time; it is rarely wrong to set any goals at all. Some *risks* of setting yourself goals include the following:

- *Self-alienation:* Your goals may represent other people's ideas and values rather than your own. They may be based on self-oppressing rather than on self-supporting personal rules.
- *Doing rather than being:* Your goals may involve you in constant activity. You may have no time to become attuned to the flow of your own being and that of nature. Your goals may be overly focused on achieving, excluding more contemplative and responsive values.
- *Too much pressure:* Your goals may be unrealistically high and place you under constant pressure. Friedman and Rosenman's (1974) Type A Behavior Pattern illustrates the danger of overstriving: "Type A Behavior Pattern is an action-emotion complex that can be observed in any person who is *aggressively* involved in a *chronic, incessant* struggle to achieve more and more in less and less time, and, if required to do so, against the opposing efforts of other things or other persons" [p. 67]. This kind of achievement orientation has negative psychological consequences for yourself and others, not the least of which is that you may be less likely to achieve your personal goals.
- *Health risks:* Unrealistic goals can contribute to your having stress-related physical problems such as heart disease and hypertension. They can also contribute to unhealthy attempts to cope with stress; for instance, by eating, smoking, or drinking too much.

Values and Goals

A man who knows the price of everything, and the value of nothing.
Oscar Wilde's definition of a cynic

What are the values by which you choose to live your life? What, ultimately, is of worth to you? While your goals are your objectives, your values are the underlying principles and priorities on which they are based. Another way of viewing your values is that they represent your philosophy of life. This should not be something static, but rather a process reflecting your development and increasing experience of life. Wilde's cynic appears to have had a materialistic philosophy of life, centered on economic values.

The following are some of the values people consider, consciously or otherwise, when forming a philosophy of life.

- *Survival:* the primary instinctual value, though other values sometimes override it: for example, patriotism or religious belief
- *Love:* loving and being loved; appreciating others for who they are and not just for what they do
- *Friendship:* being joined to others outside your family by mutual intimacy and interests
- *Family life:* having and being part of a family; valuing parenthood
- *Religion:* acknowledging the need for connectedness to some ultimate and superhuman power
- *Materialism:* valuing the accumulation and control of money
- *Aesthetics:* appreciating beauty and good taste, with special reference to arts such as music, literature, and painting
- *Intellect:* valuing analytical and rational pursuits
- *Social consciousness:* helping others; showing social concern
- *Hedonism:* valuing fun, pleasure, and having a good time
- *Career:* valuing the work you do
- *Practical orientation:* valuing practical pursuits and, where practical matters are concerned, self-reliance
- *Nature:* appreciating and valuing being outdoors and in communion with nature
- *Autonomy:* valuing independence, thinking for yourself, and personal enterprise
- *Convention:* appreciating tradition; valuing obedience and conformity to the status quo
- *Self-actualization:* being committed to personal growth and development

This list of values is far from exhaustive. At any given time, whether you know it or not, you have a profile of values. This profile is composed of your values and the weight you attach to them. Sometimes your values will conflict. For instance, women especially may experience a conflict between family life and career values.

Your Philosophy of Life

One approach to creating your future is to clarify your values or philosophy of life. Thinksheet 32 asks you to write out such a statement. But first read the following two philosophy-of-life statements: one for an older and one for a younger person. The younger person's statement is more tentative, because of her limited life experience: she is still in the earlier stages of defining her philosophy.

My name is John. I am a 46-year-old married man with three children. My Catholic faith is my most fundamental value. I attend church regularly with my family and strive to be an honest and caring person, both within and outside of the family. Family life is also a very high priority for me, though at times I find this value comes into conflict with my job as a social worker, in which I try to meet the needs of the senile elderly and their relatives. Other values and activities that give meaning to my life are friendship, being able to spend time in nature, listening to music, and playing my guitar. I'm not particularly materialistic, though as a family we seem to manage all right. I'm deeply committed to a more equal distribution of wealth and of educational and health resources.

My name is Susan. I'm 18 and in the first year of an accounting major in college. Right now I want to have fun and live my life to the full. I enjoy going to parties, meeting people, and having friends. I want to be successful in my career. Money is very important to me, though it is not everything. I'm uncertain whether I want to be my own boss or work for a large firm. I would like to get married, but not until my late twenties. Part of me would like to have a family, but I'm concerned about the effect that this will have on my career and independence. I was brought up in a religious home. Frankly, I'm not that interested in helping others, though I wish them no harm. I don't go to church and can't make up my mind whether there is a God. Apart from my boyfriend, the main things that I enjoy at the moment are my car, going sailing, and partying. I'm not academically inclined, but am smart in a practical way.

THINKSHEET 32

Choosing Your Philosophy of Life

1. Below is a list of values. Rate each one in terms of its importance for you on the following scale:

very important	3
important	2
slightly important	1
of no importance	0

Your Rating	**List of Values**
_____	survival
_____	love
_____	friendship
_____	family life
_____	religion
_____	economics
_____	aesthetics
_____	intellect
_____	social consciousness
_____	hedonism
_____	career

(continued)

THINKSHEET 32

(continued)

_____	practical orientation
_____	nature
_____	autonomy
_____	convention
_____	self-actualization

Are there values not included in this list that are important for you? If so, what are they? Add them to the list and rate them.

2. At the top of a piece of paper write MY PHILOSOPHY OF LIFE. Then write out a statement of your philosophy, using the two examples as models. This statement should incorporate the values you rated as most important for you.

Stating Your Goals

If your goals are going to help you, they must be stated clearly and cogently. Below are some things to consider when you set and state goals for yourself.

- *Do they reflect your values?* Your goals should reflect what you consider to be worthwhile in life. This is not necessarily a straightforward task. You may have to think, listen to your inner valuing process, and debate with others long and hard to discover what goals truly reflect your values. Some of this information may come from trial-and-error life experiences, too.
- *Are they realistic?* Your goals are realistic when they adequately acknowledge the constraints of your own emotional resources and personal skills. These constraints should be neither overestimated nor underestimated. Your goals should reflect realistic and potentially attainable standards.
- *Are they specific?* State your goals as specifically as you can. Ideally they should be stated so that you can easily measure the success of your attempts to attain them. For instance, ''I want to be happier'' is too vague. You need to state specific goals for making yourself a happier person.
- *Do you have a time frame?* Goals can be short-term, medium-term, or long-term. State whether you wish to attain each goal within a week, a month, a year, or some other time frame. Vague intentions are insufficient.

Thinksheet 33 asks you to state your goals in five broad areas: relationships, work or study, recreation, health, and finances. Joe, a 21-year-old college student, intended to attain all his goals within one month.

Relationships

I will ask Laura for a date.
I will tell my father how much I appreciate his support.
I will stand up to my roommate and not agree with him all the time.

Study

I will study a minimum of 2 hours outside of class each weekday.
I will ask my biology teacher how I can get extra tutoring in the subject.
I will verbally participate at least once in every seminar that I attend.

Recreation

I will join the college swimming club.

Health

I will cut down my smoking to five cigarettes a day.

Finances

I will pay off the short-term loan I have from the college.

Some of you are already reasonably good at setting realistic goals for yourselves. Others of you may assume much more control over your future by developing this skill.

THINKSHEET 33

Choosing and Stating Your Goals

1. State at least one goal for yourself in each of the areas listed below. Your statement of each goal should reflect your values, be realistic, be specific, and give a time frame.
   a. relationships
   b. study or work
   c. recreation
   d. health
   e. finances
2. Think of other areas of your life in which you would like to assume more responsibility for creating your future. Articulate your goals in each of those areas.
3. Take a piece of paper and write at the top MY FIVE-YEAR GOALS. List the most important goals you want to attain during that period.

CHAPTER HIGHLIGHTS

The future is both what is to come and what you tell yourself about it.
Predictions estimate the probability of future events and can contain perceptual
   distortions.
In predicting risk and reward you may err in four directions: overestimating or underestimating good or bad consequences.
Thinking skills for improving your predictions include assessing probability more
   systematically, assessing your coping capacity, generating and evaluating potential

risks and rewards, and reality-testing your predictions through personal experiments.

Setting realistic goals for yourself can help you to become the author of your life.

Your values are your choices about what is worthwhile to you, and these principles and priorities constitute your philosophy of life.

Helpful goal statements reflect your values and are realistic, specific, and give a time frame for their attainment.

CHAPTER 9

Visualizing with Your Mind's Eye

Imagine all the people, living life in peace.

John Lennon

I have a dream that one day this nation will rise up,
live out the true meaning of its creed: we hold these truths to be self-evident,
that all men are created equal.

Rev. Martin Luther King, Jr.

The opening quotations of this chapter use words to convey a visual or mental picture of how the speakers would like people to behave. They are appropriate to a chapter on visual, rather than verbal, thinking. There are a number of colorful phrases to describe visual thinking, such as "the pictures in your head," "the movies in your mind," and the "videos in your brain." All of them are oversimplifications. Visual thinking, or visualizing, is often accompanied by verbal thinking: for instance, Lennon and King used words to conjure up images. Additionally, visual images interact with feelings: in one research study, some 90 percent of anxious patients reported visual images prior to and concurrent with their anxiety attacks (Beck, Laude, & Bohnert, 1974).

You think in pictures before you think in words, of course. Babies' visual capacities are not fully developed at birth; however, from the first days of life they create internal visual representations of experience called schemata. By their first birthday, infants are entering the world of verbal thinking and beginning to apply language labels to familiar phenomena. I stress the visual foundations of your thinking because even for adults, much thinking remains visual. In fact, William Glasser (1984) asserts that 80 percent of the perceptions people store in their memory albums are visual. Consequently, the ABC framework used earlier requires elaboration:

A. the activating event
B. your thoughts and *visual images*
C. your feelings and actions

At B you have a choice of what you see as well as of what you say to yourself.

The Language of Visualization

A number of terms are used to describe different aspects of visualizing. Some of them are as follows:

- *Daydreams:* pleasant, dreamy visual images and thoughts
- *Dreams:* sequences of images and thoughts that pass through your mind while you sleep; also, your conscious hopes for the future
- *Fantasies:* fanciful speculations and reveries
- *Illusions:* false rather than real images and thoughts, hallucinations—seeing and hearing imaginary sights and voices—being an extreme example
- *Images:* visual and verbal representations of people or things
- *Imaginings:* mental images of what is not present; the creation of visual and verbal ideas
- *Memories:* visual as well as verbal recollections
- *Symbols:* visual objects used to represent something else; for instance, the eagle, the lion, or the cross
- *Vision:* something seen in a dream or in the imagination
- *Visualizing:* forming mental pictures and visual representations of people, things, and ideas

The cornerstone of Sigmund Freud's psychoanalytic theory was the interpretation of dreams. However, my emphasis here will be on the conscious use of visualizing as a self-help skill.

DEVELOPING AN AWARENESS OF VISUALIZING

Some of you may be unaware of the extent to which visualizing forms a part of your daily thinking. Sexual reveries are an excellent example. You may conjure up past pleasures and anticipate future ones in your mind's eye. You may experience in your imagination what is currently unattainable. The following limerick about a virgin illustrates this.

> *There was a young virgin from Wye*
> *Who wanted to have a good try*
> *To find out about love*
> *From below and above,*
> *Not just visualizing it in the mind's eye.*

Visualizing enables you to go on mental journeys. These journeys may be into your past or into your future, into reality or into fantasy, into scenes that make you feel either good or bad, and into scenes that involve other senses such as touch and smell. Thinksheet 34 is designed to increase your awareness of different kinds of visualization.

THINKSHEET 34

Becoming More Aware of Visualization

For each of the following exercises, you should be in a quiet room with soft lighting and no interruptions. Relax and sit in a comfortable chair. After reading the instructions for each exercise or exercise segment, put the book down and close your eyes. Take your time. If you have difficulty visualizing, say out loud what you're trying to see.

1. *Photographic visualization:*   Visualize someone with whom you are intimate. Focusing on his or her face, try to visualize every detail as if you are recreating a good photograph of it.
2. *Visualizing your past, present, and future*
   a. *Your past:* Picture the childhood home that has the most meaning for you. Visit its various rooms and conjure up its atmosphere.
   b. *Your present:* Visualize your current home. Pay special attention to the room you feel most comfortable in. What are its sights? What are its textures? What are its smells?
   c. *Your future:* Visit a home that you would like to live in five years from now. Picture it and the lifestyle that would go with it.
3. *Visualizing images associated with other senses*
   a. *Taste:* Visualize yourself eating a favorite food, such as chocolate ice cream.
   b. *Touch:* Visualize yourself taking a hot shower or bath; concentrate on the sensation of the water on your skin.
   c. *Smell:* Visualize yourself looking at and smelling a rose.
   d. *Sound:* Visualize a thunderstorm.
4. *Visualizing images associated with feelings*
   a. Visualize something or someone that "makes" you feel *happy*. Stay with the image and reflect on what it is that produces this happy feeling.
   b. Visualize something or someone that "makes" you feel *angry*. Stay with the image and reflect on what it is that produces this angry feeling.
   c. Visualize something or someone that "makes" you feel *afraid*. Stay with the image and reflect on what it is that produces this feeling of fear.
   d. Visualize some place where you feel *calm* and *relaxed*. Stay with the image and reflect on what it is that produces these feelings of calmness and relaxation.
5. *Using your imagination:*   Think of as many visual symbols to represent as you can in 5 minutes. Then decide which symbol best suits you.

People's ability to visualize varies. Some of you have well-developed powers of imagery. Others of you may experience great difficulty in visualizing and may need to emphasize other ways of controlling your thinking. In general, the more you can experience the senses and feelings attached to your images, the better you can use visualizing as a self-help skill.

For the remainder of this chapter, we'll look at how you can use visualizing skills in five different, though somewhat overlapping, areas.

MANAGING YOUR FEELINGS

Visualizing skills may help you manage a variety of feelings better. They may be helpful in their own right or as adjuncts to other thinking and action skills.

Becoming More Relaxed

I deal with relaxation first because when you visualize, it is best that you be relaxed. Additionally, relaxation can be a useful skill to master for those of you with problems such as tension headaches, hypertension, and feelings of excessive stress. The most common approach to relaxation in counseling is probably the Jacobson progressive muscular relaxation technique (Jacobson, 1938). In this technique, clients are encouraged to tense and then relax various muscle groups throughout their body sequentially. For instance, an abbreviated version of progressive muscular relaxation might require tensing and relaxing in turn the muscles in your face, your arms, the trunk of your body, and your legs and feet. Progressive muscular relaxation requires regular practice for maximum benefit. It is best done in a quiet environment, without distractions, while you either sit in a comfortable chair or lie down with your eyes closed. Your clothing should be loosened to increase your sense of freedom.

Visual imagery can be used to enhance progressive muscular relaxation. For instance, as you tense and relax your various muscle groups, you can use the metaphor of switching lights off in the rooms of a house until the whole house is completely dark. Also, you can mentally picture tight muscles and the tension flowing away when you relax them. When you complete your muscular relaxation you may visualize a restful, calming scene.

Visual relaxation may be used independently of as well as in conjunction with muscular relaxation. Each of you probably has one or more favorite scenes that make you feel relaxed. Some of you can think of one of these right away; others may require more time. The following is an example of a visual relaxation scene.

> I'm lying on an uncrowded beach on a pleasant, sunny day, enjoying the sensations of warmth on my body. There is a gentle breeze. I can hear the peaceful noise of the sea lapping against the shore nearby. I haven't a care in the world, and enjoy my feelings of peace, calm, relaxation, and well-being.

There are many other scenes that people find conducive to relaxation. They include looking at a valley with lush green meadows and sitting in a favorite comfortable chair at home. Thinksheet 35 will help you to use visualizing to relax. Some of you may wish to add progressive muscular relaxation to the exercise.

Many of the other thinking skills in this book are relevant to becoming more relaxed. For example, if you overcome perfectionist personal rules you will place yourself under less stress; if you perceive yourself, people, and situations accurately you are more likely to avoid unnecessary troubles; and if you use coping rather than negative self-talk you will feel more like a human being.

THINKSHEET 35

Using Visualizing to Relax

Allow plenty of time to complete the following steps. The first time you do the exercise, you may need to open your eyes to check on the next step. Later you should complete the entire exercise with your eyes closed.

1. Go to a quiet room with soft lighting and no distractions. Sit in a comfortable chair and loosen any clothing that feels tight.
2. Become aware of your breathing. Take a few deep breaths, and as you let out each breath say the word "relax."
3. Now complete the following sequence:
   a. Focus on your face. Visualize the tension leaving your face and your face feeling more and more relaxed.
   b. Focus on your arms. Visualize the tension leaving your arms and your arms feeling more and more relaxed.
   c. Focus on the trunk of your body. Visualize the tension leaving the trunk of your body and your trunk feeling more and more relaxed.
   d. Focus on your legs. Visualize the tension leaving your legs and your legs feeling more and more relaxed.
   e. Focus on the whole of your body. Visualize the tension leaving the whole of your body as the whole of your body feels more and more relaxed.
4. As you sit there feeling relaxed, visualize a restful and relaxing scene. Evoke not only the sights, but the sounds, smells, and other sensations that make this such a calm and peaceful scene for you. Stay in the scene for 2 to 5 minutes as you enjoy your feelings of relaxation and well-being.
5. Let the muscles in your eyelids loosen up as you get ready to open your eyes and become aware of your surroundings. Open your eyes and carry on with your activities feeling refreshed.
6. Practice this exercise daily for a week as you build up your skills of visualizing and relaxing.

The exercise in Thinksheet 35 can be used as a prelude to other visualization activities. The quality of your visualizing is likely to be better if you are relaxed rather than tense. Also, remember that all visualizing skills require practice if they are to be properly learned and maintained.

Self-Desensitization

The technique of self-desensitization allows you to imagine yourself coping with anxiety-evoking situations while relaxed (Lazarus, 1977; Wolpe, 1982). It has three main steps. First, learn to relax yourself. Include muscular relaxation along with visual relaxation. Second, draw up a hierarchy of anxiety-evoking scenes that you can visualize. These scenes should cluster around a theme that you find problematic: for instance, test-taking, public speaking, or dating. Third, when you are relaxed, visualize coping with each scene from the least to the most anxiety evoking.

Constructing Hierarchies

A hierarchy, in this context, is a list of thematically related scenes rated according to the amount of anxiety they evoke.

> Barb, 26, is a Ph.D. student in biology. Her moment of truth has come: her departmental chairperson wants her to give a seminar to the staff and other doctoral students on her research. Barb is so terrified at this prospect that she seriously thinks of abandoning her dissertation. Her hierarchy comprises progressively more difficult scenes on the theme of her fear of public speaking.

A common way of assessing the anxiety-evoking potential of a scene is to say that 0 is a feeling of no anxiety of all, and 100 is the maximum anxiety you can feel in relation to a particular theme. You then rate individual scenes according to their positions on your subjective anxiety scale. One way to generate scenes for your hierarchy is to make a list of all those situations that evoke anxiety. Another way is to keep a journal for a week or more in which you log anxiety-evoking situations.

When you feel you have enough scenes, arrange them in a hierarchy. Each scene should include sufficient details to trigger your imagination. So that you take a gradual approach, try not to have gaps of more than 10 to 15 units of anxiety in your hierarchy. For instance, Nate, 19, constructed the following hierarchy for an important economics test.

1. (rated 10) Thinking about the test while studying at my desk one month before it.
2. (rated 20) Thinking about the test while studying at my desk one week before it.
3. (rated 30) Thinking about the test while studying at my desk the night before.
4. (rated 40) Traveling by train on the way to the test.
5. (rated 50) Waiting outside the test room.
6. (rated 60) Going into the test room.
7. (rated 70) Sitting down and waiting to see the test.
8. (rated 80) Looking at the test paper for the first time.
9. (rated 90) Feeling that I have insufficient time from the start.
10. (rated 95) Feeling that I have made a mess of an answer.
11. (rated 100) Struggling to complete the test 10 minutes before the time runs out.

Visualizing Scenes from Your Hierarchy

The following are some points to remember when visualizing scenes from your hierarchy.

- *Become relaxed.* Use muscular and/or visual exercises.
- *Emphasize coping rather than mastery.* Your aim is to manage your anxiety rather than be completely anxiety-free.

- *Strive for a clear image.* Verbalize the details of the image if you have difficulty visualizing it.
- *Take a step-by-step approach.* Visualize the less anxiety-evoking scenes before moving on to the more anxiety-evoking scenes.
- *Use coping self-talk.* Use coping self-talk, with its coaching and calming dimensions, to help you manage anxiety evoked by your visualizations.
- *Use repetition.* Anxiety reactions may become considerably less intense with repeated visualizations of the scene.
- *Intersperse relaxation.* When you find yourself getting too tense, be prepared to relax yourself again.
- *Move on when you feel comfortable.* When you feel that you have coped adequately with a scene and can comfortably manage the anxiety attached to it, move on to the next scene.
- *Be flexible.* If you get stuck with a scene after repeated visualizations, consider placing one or more less anxiety-evoking scenes before it.
- *Don't do too much in a single session.* Continue with a session only as long as you feel that your relaxation, visualization, and concentration are good. If necessary, you can return to the task later.

Self desensitization is not the only way to deal with fears such as test anxiety. Many test-anxious people have to work on their personal rules that demand unrealistic standards of achievement. Some require better review and test-taking skills. Still others are anxious because tests confront them with the fact that they have not done much work throughout the semester. They need to prepare better.

THINKSHEET 36

Self-Desensitization

1. Construct a hierarchy for an area in which your fears interfere with your effectiveness. Rate the anxiety-evoking potential of each scene in your hierarchy. Your hierarchy should contain a minimum of five scenes.
2. Relax.
3. Once you are relaxed, take your time and visualize the scenes in your hierarchy. Follow the guidelines for visualizing scenes mentioned earlier.
4. Try out the behaviors you feared in real life, using your self-desensitization skills to help you cope with anticipatory anxiety.

An alternative for visualizing hierarchy scenes is to record them on a cassette and then play them back, switching off the cassette recorder after each presentation of a scene.

Visualizing the Worst Possibility

Self-desensitization is a process requiring gradual steps. Another, one-step, approach to overcoming your fears is to visualize the worst-case scenario. Ask yourself "*So what if* the worst were to happen?'' and then visualize it happening. Spell out the worst in detail.

> Tammy, 16, had great difficulty saying ''no'' when she was asked out on a date. On one level she feared hurting the boy's feelings if she said ''no.'' On another she was terrified that if she said ''no'' she would be subjected to a torrent of abuse in which she would be angrily told how hard, ugly, selfish, and insensitive she was and asked why anyone would want to ask out such a wimpy, unattractive, unintelligent, and inferior slob.

When Tammy visualized her worst fears being realized she first experienced some anxiety. However, as she stayed with the scene she began to realize that, though she might not like being ridiculed, it would not be the end of the world for her. Even better, she realized that she had the inner resources to cope with her worst predictions. Also, she acknowledged that this kind of feedback was highly unlikely. Visualizing the worst helped her to acknowledge her faulty perception of her own vulnerability and her inaccurate prediction of a highly hostile response to her saying ''no.'' Tammy still felt her nervousness might cause her to say ''no'' more sharply than she wanted to. Consequently, she decided to add to her repertoire the skill of saying ''no'' in a calm and supportive way.

There are numerous situations in which visualizing the worst possibility can help you to put feared situations in better perspective. However, you need to stay with the visualization long enough to work through the initial increase in anxiety that you may experience. By actually spelling out your catastrophic fears you may decatastrophize them. For instance, if you are afraid of losing your job, it may help you to visualize the actual consequences. Confronting your worst fears may rid them of much of their power. Also, you may identify the sources of support available to you; for instance, your family, friends, and others.

Some therapists, among them Albert Ellis (1980), actively encourage their clients to engage in shame-attacking exercises. Here clients go beyond visualization to carrying out personal experiments in which they reality-test their dire predictions about social disapproval. For instance, try shouting out the names of the subway stops, or going to a pharmacy and discussing in a loud voice the merits and demerits of different condoms!

THINKSHEET 37

Visualizing the Worst Possibility

1. Think of a situation in your life that causes you anxiety.
2. Spell out in some detail what you imagine to be the worst that could happen.
3. Visualize the worst happening and stay with the visualization.
4. If the worst were to happen, could you cope with it? What strategies would you adopt and what sources of support would you have?
5. Review the original situation. Has visualizing the worst helped you to put it in perspective and also freed you to think of more effective ways of coping with it?

Visualizing Positive Images

The happiness habit is developed simply by practicing happy thinking.
Norman Vincent Peale

I do not advocate happy thinking when the circumstances do not warrant it. Nevertheless, as mentioned in Chapter 6, many people choose to oppress themselves through negative self-labeling. Below are some ways that you can use positive visualizing both to counteract tendencies to self-denigration and to acknowledge realistic sources of happiness and strength.

Listing Positive Images

Make a list of positive images that you can pass through your mind. The giving and receiving of love and friendship is a rich source of positive images. List visual images of people you love and of your friends. List images of your making others happy as well as of receiving affection. Other sources of positive images include achievements by you or others of which you are proud; favorite leisure pastimes; scenes from nature; and, if you are religious, religious images. You can actively choose to focus on these positive images at various times during the day. It may help if you write out each image on a 3-by-5 card.

You can also list positive images as ways of both anticipating and counting your blessings. For instance, before you get up in the morning, you can visualize positive things that may happen that day. Before you go to sleep, you can visualize the positive things that have happened. Visualizing your blessings either in advance or retrospectively can cover any time period you wish.

Stopping and Switching

In Chapter 6 I mentioned thought stopping, mental vacuuming, and thought switching. The thoughts from which and to which you switch can be visual as well as verbal. When you become aware that you are oppressing yourself with negative thoughts and images, you can (1) instruct yourself to "Stop!"; (2) mentally vacuum away the negative thoughts and images; and (3) switch to more positive thoughts and images.

Visualizing Rewards

In predicting the future, some people have a tendency to overemphasize risk and to underemphasize reward. If this is a problem of yours, you can develop the skill of visualizing the rewards or benefits that might flow from taking specific actions. You still realistically evaluate your positive visualizations; however, you now give yourself a vision of what good might come from your actions instead of dwelling on negative— even catastrophic—thoughts and images.

Bud and Frances are a couple in their mid-twenties who had reservations about having a baby because of the possible negative effects on their time and their emotional and financial independence. They found it easy to list the negative aspects of parenthood. However, when they visualized what it would actually be like living with their first child, they were able to get in touch with the love, joy, and feelings of fulfillment that also might come from parenthood.

Visualizing Mastery

You may be able to counteract feelings that you are good for nothing by visualizing yourself accomplishing something that you can manage. Depressed people often have feelings of helplessness that make it hard for them to feel able to influence their environments positively. If you are feeling low, identify some activity, however mundane, that you accomplish to your satisfaction. This may be cooking a meal, driving a car, playing a game, gardening, going for a walk, writing a letter, talking to a friend, and so on. If you relax and visualize yourself carrying out your accomplishment, you achieve at least two important things. First, you have successfully challenged your perception of being good for nothing. Second, by acknowledging that mastery of a task is possible for you, you are in a better position to try this and other tasks.

Arnold Lazarus (1977) gives the example of a 54-year-old woman who had excelled at golf and skiing but became depressed when she was forced to give up these activities after a stroke. She looked for other sources of mastery in her life. Finally, she came up with making a fancy cake using a special recipe. Then she identified other things that she was good at, including canasta, poker, and amateur photography. Lazarus had her visualize and get in touch with her subjective feelings of mastery in each of these areas in turn. As a consequence, her gloomy and depressed feelings started to lift.

--- **THINKSHEET 38** ---

Visualizing Positive Images

1. Search for and write out a list of positive images that may help you to feel happier and more fulfilled. Try to get at least ten images on your list.
2. At least once a day for a week, relax in a comfortable chair, close your eyes, and visualize the positive images on your list. Each time you finish, assess whether you feel any different.
3. During the day when you get unwanted negative thoughts and images, instruct yourself to "Stop!" and switch to visualizing your positive images.
4. Practice, practice, and practice to build up your skills of using positive visual as well as verbal thinking.

Time Projection

Time projection or "time tripping" is a useful skill to help you cope with negative feelings related to transient difficulties. These difficulties may seem huge, even overwhelming, at the time they occur. The ways that you may use time tripping to get matters in perspective are as follows.

• *Visualizing looking back on the present:* If you visualize many difficulties from a vantage point 3, 6, or 12 months down the road, it may be easier for you to see their true significance. This may help you to manage negative feelings like depression as well as to act more constructively. For instance, you may be reeling from someone's breaking off a relationship with you. However, if you take a trip into the future 6 months from now and look back on this situation, you will probably realize that you have the resources to cope with it. Also, you may realize that there are many other fish in the sea to whom you can relate.

• *Visualizing looking into the future:* The ability to visualize how your life might be different at some point in the future is also a useful skill for managing difficult periods. For example, rejected lovers might imagine what their lives might be like a year from now. They may need to fight against catastrophic predictions to visualize a more realistic view of how their lives might be different. Other times in which this technique might help include when you are bedridden for some weeks, have an awkward colleague who will leave within 6 months, receive a letter of rejection in response to a job application, go through messy divorce proceedings, or are renovating a house.

PERFORMING BETTER

Some of the visualization skills already described—for example, self-desensitization—may help you perform better. Here I'll focus on visualizing the processes and outcomes of skilled performance. Sports professionals are increasingly using visualization to improve their performance, from Chris Evert and Jack Nicklaus to the U.S. National Olympic Ski Team. However, you do not have to be a top sportsperson to use these skills.

Visualized Rehearsal and Practice

Say you are anxious about an upcoming public speaking task. Many of you will have limited opportunity to rehearse and practice your skills, other than by performing in front of the bathroom mirror. However, you have virtually unlimited opportunity for visualized rehearsal and practice. I do not propose you substitute it for the real thing; nevertheless, visualized rehearsal and practice can help you in the following ways.

• It can provide a method of rehearsal and practice when there is no easy opportunity for real-life practice; for example, visualizing an important interview.
• It can provide a method of rehearsal and practice in addition to existing ones; for instance, as well as working on your assertion skills with a friend, you can visually rehearse them on your own.

- It can help you to break tasks down and to focus on the processes of skilled performance.
- It can help you to identify potential setbacks and to develop ways of coping with them; for example, before a match Chris Evert visualizes herself countering her opponent's tactics.
- It can provide you with an opportunity to rehearse and practice your coping self-talk along with your visualizing skills.
- It may allow you the chance to get sufficient practice so that aspects of your performance that you want to be virtually automatic are more likely to become so.

Here is an example of using visualized rehearsal and practice to help attain a personal goal.

> Todd, 27, had worked for a consulting engineering company for 15 months. When he was taken on, he was promised a salary review after a year. That review never took place. Todd decided to take the initiative and ask his supervisor for the salary review. He thought over the best ways to do so, focusing on his vocal and body messages as well as his words. He also thought of approaches to handling the different ways his supervisor might respond. Todd acknowledged his anxiety over what he was about to do. However, he engaged in repeated visualized rehearsal and practice until he felt confident that he could handle himself well. He asked for the review, then during it he calmly stated the contribution he thought he was making to the company. Todd received his hoped-for salary increase. Even if he had not gotten what he wanted, Todd had visualized how to handle that possibility.

Visualizing Attaining Goals

Visualized rehearsal and practice focuses on the *processes* of skilled performance. However, you may also enhance your performance if you visualize yourself being successful in attaining your goals. For example, if you rehearse hard and then visualize that you are going to perform as a great actress, you are more likely to do so than if you visualize a lack of success. Again, if you have practiced hard, you may be more likely to play a better game of tennis if you think of yourself as a champion like Steffi Graf or Ivan Lendl than if you think of yourself as a tennis incompetent.

Some research evidence suggests the power of positive visualizing immediately prior to a performance to enhance that performance. Scholars studied the effect of different visualizing instructions on the ability of subjects to putt a golf ball accurately (Woolfolk, Parish, & Murphy, 1985). Thirty college students were randomly assigned to one of three experimental conditions: (1) positive visualizing, (2) negative visualizing, and (3) a control group. Subjects in the positive-visualizing group imagined the ball "rolling, rolling, right into the cup"; subjects using negative visualizing imagined the ball "rolling, rolling, toward the cup, but at the last second narrowly missing"; subjects in the control group received no visualizing instructions. Each subject tried ten putts on each of the six consecutive days. Over this period, the positive-visualizing group improved by 30 percent over its initial score per ten putts; the negative-visualizing group showed a decline in accuracy of 21 percent; and the control group showed an increase in accuracy of 10 percent. No wonder Jack Nicklaus believes in positive visualizing!

THINKSHEET 39

Visualizing for Better Performance

1. Think of a specific situation that is not too difficult but that you would like to handle better: something like Todd's request for a salary review.
2. Think through how you would like to behave in the situation by breaking the task down into its component parts. Also think through how you might cope with setbacks.
3. Every day for the next week, spend some time relaxing and then visually rehearsing and practicing managing the situation. Adjust your performance if you get better ideas for how to handle it. As appropriate, use coping self-talk along with visualizing. During this period you may also engage in live rehearsal and practice.
4. Perform your changed behavior in the real-life situation; visualize yourself attaining your realistic goals immediately prior to your performance.
5. Assess whether and how much visualizing helped you to perform better.

VISUALIZING GOALS AND ROLES

Where there is no vision, the people perish.

Proverbs, 29:18

Clarifying Your Goals

Though the thinking skills involved in making decisions are covered more fully in the next chapter, I'll mention some ways here in which you can use visualizing to clarify your goals and make better decisions.

Tapping into your daydreams   Your daydreams about your future can be a rich source of data for planning your life. The question "What have been your occupational daydreams and how do you feel about them now?" is relevant for such varied groups as high school and college students thinking about their first job, women returning to the work force after raising a family, and people who contemplate midlife career moves. You may also gather useful information from your daydreams and fantasies in numerous other areas: what sort of lifestyle you want, whether or not you want marriage and a family, possible leisure interests, educational aspirations, retirement activities, and sexual behaviors.

Visualizing what you want in life   Visualizing can help you to achieve a clear picture of the sort of person you want to be and the sort of life you want to have at various stages in the future: "How would I like to see myself develop as a person over the next 5 years?" "What sort of work and leisure interest would I like to have 5 years from now?" "What sort of financial position?" "What sort of home would I like to live in?" "What sorts of relationships would I like to have?" Visualizing your answers to these and other questions is a process during which you are likely to clarify and refine your goals. Clarifying your goals does not mean that they have to be rigid. You can still change them in light of new information and fantasies. Like those of John Lennon and Martin Luther King, Jr., some of your dreams may reach beyond self-interest to social interest. You may visualize answers to the questions "What sort of district, state, country, or world would I like to see?" and "What actions am I prepared to take to bring this about?"

Visualizing what it would be like   Another use of visualizing is to try to imagine in detail what a contemplated activity would actually be like. Here you attempt to "flesh out" and visually reality-test your daydreams and visions of the future. Thomas Skovolt and Ronald Hoenninger (1974) developed a script in which people in a career exploration group were asked to imagine events throughout a typical workday in their lives 6 years later. The script covered being at home before going to work, traveling to work, what sort of workplace and what sort of work, what you do for lunch, what your fellow workers are like, what is it like when you get home, what sort of home you have, and what do you do in the evening. Visualizing what it *would be* like is not a substitute for collecting on-the-spot information about what it *is* like. For instance, someone contemplating a career as a dentist may profitably spend a day in a dentist's practice (though not in the chair!). However, sometimes collecting on-the-spot information is either difficult or impossible and visualizing may be the next-best thing.

In sum, your daydreams and visual images are a precious part of your existence. The poet W. B. Yeats wrote "Tread softly because you tread on my dreams." If you can develop your skills of freeing yourself to dream and then of fashioning your dreams into realistic goals, your life will be the richer.

Changing Your Role

Earlier I mentioned visualized rehearsal and practice as an approach to changing your behavior. Another approach to changing your behavior is based on George Kelly's (1955a) idea of fixed-role therapy. Here I adopt the term *changed-role visualization* for a modification of Kelly's approach. Changed-role visualization consists of the following five steps.

1. *Write out a self-characterization.* Draw up a description of yourself as though it were written by a friend who knows you intimately. Write this description in the third person: for example, "John/Jane Doe is . . ."

2. *Develop a changed-role sketch.* Use your self-characterization as the basis for a sketch of a different role that you will portray as an experiment for the next 1, 2, or 3 weeks. Visualize yourself as you would like to be and incorporate some realistic changes so that your role sketch depicts a different, yet plausible, person. You deliberately use your sketch to try out new behaviors to see whether they suit you. After the trial period, you have no commitment to adopt any aspect of your changed role that does not suit you.

3. *Visually rehearse and practice your role sketch.* Visual rehearsal and practice develops your confidence and the skills to enact your changed-role sketch. In your mind's eye, work through how you are going to implement it, including handling others' reactions to your changed behaviors.

4. *Enact your changed role.* Enact your new changed role for the period of time you decide is appropriate. Throughout this trial period, keep your vision of your role in mind to guide your action.

5. *Evaluate your experience.* Inevitably you will evaluate your experience during your role enactment. However, at the end be sure to evaluate which parts of your changed role you wish to incorporate in your future self-perception and behavior. You should have gained more insight into your freedom to choose what sort of person to become. George Kelly (1955b) advocated a philosophical position he termed "constructive alternativism." He wrote "We assume that all of our present interpretations of the universe are subject to revision or replacement" [p. 15].

——————————————— **THINKSHEET 40** ———————————————

Visualizing Goals and Roles

1. *Visualizing goals:* Picture the kind of life you would like to be living 5 years from now. (Be prepared to tap into your daydreams; however, keep your goals within the bounds of reality.) Cover the following areas, plus any others you consider relevant.
   a. "How would I like to see myself develop as a person?"
   b. "What sort of work would I do?"
   c. "What sort of leisure interests would I have?"
   d. "What sort of intimate and family relationships?"
   e. "What sort of friendships?"
   f. "What sort of home?"
   g. "What sort of financial position?"
   h. "What sort of health and physical condition?"
2. *Visualizing a role:* Do one of the following.
   a. Carry out the five-step changed-role visualization procedure described in the text.
   b. Develop a one-page changed-role sketch for yourself that includes new behaviors that you are prepared to try out for a week. Visually rehearse your sketch; then enact and evaluate it.

ENHANCING YOUR RELATIONSHIPS

Developing your visualizing skills may improve your relationships. I'll demonstrate this by suggesting some ways in which you can use visualizing skills in four areas: understanding others, managing anger and resentment, positive assertion, and sharing sexual fantasies.

Understanding Others

Visualizing can be an important skill for understanding others. Visual words and phrases are often used to describe this process: for example, understanding their "viewpoint" or how they "see" things. The ways in which visualizing can help you to understand others include the following.

- *Keeping in touch:* Probably many of you already use visualizing to help you understand and keep in touch with others. For instance, if you are parted from a loved one you evoke a mental picture of him or her. If you phone or write to loved ones you may visualize them as you do so. Each of you may try to visualize what the other's life is like so that you can better understand what the other experiences.
- *Listening:* Good listening requires you to be empathic. Empathy means understanding other people on their own terms. It means overcoming egocentric thinking to get into their frame of reference. People vary in the degree to which they use graphic images in their speech. Nevertheless, you may relate to people better if you try to understand the pictures in their minds as well as the words that they speak.
- *Comprehending another's world:* In caring relationships, partners develop a good understanding of what it is like to be the other person, with his or her hopes, fears and activities. They collect information that enables them to create pictures of what the other's life is like from his or her viewpoint. They create a three-dimensional model of each other's lives. If these models are reasonably accurate, they provide a good information base for each partner to feel loved and understood.
- *Role-taking:* You can visualize to improve your understanding of different experiences that people go through: for instance, unemployment and dying. Additionally, you can visualize to deepen your understanding of differences between yourself and others: for instance, being of a different gender, sexual preference, age, or ethnic identity. Visual role-taking is a skill that may help you develop and demonstrate social concern. You may visually project yourself into the plights of those less fortunate: for instance, the homeless and starving in Third World countries.

Managing Anger and Resentment

Some ways in which you can use visualizing skills to prevent and manage destructive anger include the following.

- *Visualizing another's position:* In conflict, it usually helps to understand the other person's position as well as your own. Another's position may be easier to grasp if you visualize how your behavior is perceived by her or him. Having a visual picture of how you behave may also give you insight into whether your behavior matches your intentions.
- *Taking a balanced view of another:* Just as you may perceive yourself too negatively, so you may perceive others the same way. You may help to manage your anger better if, instead of dwelling on negative thoughts and images about another person, you balance your view by visualizing positive incidents in your relationship together and things that you like about the other.

• *Overcoming resentment:* Resentments tend to be pain held over from the past. The Simontons, who run a Cancer Counseling and Research Center in Dallas, Texas, believe that holding on to resentment is a restressing experience that contributes to cancer. They have developed a visualization procedure that they claim has helped many patients to let go of their resentments (Simonton, Matthews-Simonton, & Creighton, 1978). Briefly, it consists of relaxing, getting a clear image of the person you resent, visualizing good things happening to that person and her or his reactions to this, being aware of your own reactions to this visualization, reviewing the original situation in terms of your own role and how it looked from the other person's point of view, acknowledging that you now feel more relaxed and less resentful, and resuming your normal activities. This visualization procedure may need to be repeated a number of times. Often, as people get greater insight into their own behavior, they feel a need to forgive themselves as well as the other person.

Positive Assertion

In this context, positive assertion means being able to state positive thoughts and feelings and take positive actions toward others.

> Dorothy and Clifford, both in their late teens, had been going steady for a year. However, their relationship was becoming increasingly problematic and was "heading toward the rocks." Each felt the other was no longer appreciative and was continually finding fault. They were replacing their positive mental images of each other and their relationship with negative ones.

As the section in Chapter 6 on perceiving others realistically showed, it is very easy for relationships to enter downward spirals when partners engage in matching negative comments about each other. Often people are blocked in their capacity to express affection and appreciation for each other. Also, they often find it difficult to do "the little things that mean a lot" for others, let alone the larger things.

Visualizing can be a useful tool for overcoming blocks to positive assertion. First, you can visualize some or all of the people toward whom you would like to be more positive. Second, you can think of all the different ways in which you could be more positive toward them. These include smiling, expressing appreciation, paying compliments, touching, making a phone call, writing a letter, extending an invitation, giving a present, making a visit, or a number of other possibilities. Third, visualize yourself being positive toward one or more people in ways that they will appreciate. Picture how it makes them feel and acknowledge your reactions. Fourth, you may wish to take the next step of implementing your positive assertions and seeing what happens. A simple, if not invariable, rule of thumb is that the more positive you are toward others the more positively they will reciprocate.

Sharing Sexual Fantasies

Sex can be a matter of routine coupling or it can involve tenderness, fun, variety, imagination, and play. You may have difficulty owning and acknowledging your sexual fantasies. You may expect your partner to read your mind and know instinctively what you desire. You may make it difficult for your partner to share his or her sexual fantasies. All of these characteristics interfere with your sex life. Most if not all partners have ideas about how they would like their lover to act, what variations they would like introduced into their lovemaking, what they would like their lover to do to or for them, when and where. Take the time to get in touch with and visualize your own fantasies. Do not feel you have to edit them. There is a difference between the image and the deed. Imagine what it would be like to play the opposite gender in your lovemaking. Visualize different ways of mentioning to your partner fantasies that you have not already shared. Visualize his or her reactions. Visualize asking your partner to share more of his or her sexual fantasies with you. How might you go about this? Think about and visualize the risk and rewards of having a more open sex life with your partner. If you think the rewards outweigh the risks, you may wish to take the risk of obtaining the reward.

THINKSHEET 41

Visualizing for Enhanced Relationships

Complete those parts of this thinksheet that you consider relevant for you.

1. *Understanding others:* Visualize what it would be like to be someone of the opposite sex, about your own age, from the time you wake up in the morning to the time you go to sleep at night.
2. *Managing anger and resentment*
   a. Use visualizing skills in relation to someone with whom you either are angry or have been recently angry, to achieve the following:
      • understand their position, including how they see your behavior
      • take a balanced view of them in which you acknowledge their positive and not just their negative qualities
   b. Use visualizing skills in relation to someone toward whom you feel a long-standing resentment, both to imagine good things happening to her or him and also to explore your own role in the situation that caused the resentment.
3. *Positive assertion:* Using visualizing, draw up a plan for increasing your positive assertion with at least one person. Visually rehearse and then implement your changed behavior.
4. *Sharing sexual fantasies:* Acknowledge and own your sexual fantasies in relation to your partner. Visualize ways of sharing them more with your partner and of encouraging him or her to do likewise. Visualize the likely outcomes of an increased mutual sharing of your sexual fantasies.

AVOIDING NEGATIVE CONSEQUENCES

I couldn't help it. I can resist everything except temptation.

Oscar Wilde

Ah, the sweet delights of giving way to temptation! However, sometimes you may not want to face the negative consequences of giving way. You may wish to strengthen your willpower in relation to such things as chocolate fudge sundaes, high-speed driving, snorting cocaine, heavy alcohol consumption, chain-smoking, and various pleasures of the flesh. Though virtue may have its rewards, they may be insufficient to curb your cravings. This section focuses on visualizing the negative consequences of unwanted behaviors. The objective is to decrease significantly your motivation for engaging in them.

Visualizing Realistic Negative Consequences

In discussing prediction in Chapter 8, I mentioned that though some people had difficulty perceiving potential rewards, others failed to predict and give sufficient weight to potential risks. As we saw, preventive health is an area in which many people inadequately assess the risk factors. If you wish to give up bad habits, it may pay you to collect actively visual images of their potential negative consequences. These you can use in two ways. First, by being able to visualize clearly these negative consequences you may be less inclined to experience the temptation. Second, when you do experience temptation, you have a self-help strategy at your disposal. You can instruct yourself to "Stop!" and then intensely visualize the negative consequences of giving in to the temptation. You may also choose to engage in a substitute rewarding activity that involves little or no risk.

> Bernie, 33, enjoyed having casual sex with other males. He had read a lot about AIDS in the papers, but still found it difficult to change his behavior. However, as time went by, he developed a number of negative images about promiscuous and unsafe sex. He saw a video of a counseling group in which AIDS sufferers openly shared their psychological and physical pain. He collected a number of graphic colored medical photographs that depicted AIDS-related symptoms such as Kaposi's sarcoma and malignant lymphomas. Additionally, he spent a few hours a week in volunteer work with AIDS sufferers, including attending the funeral of one. With this store of negative images, he found it much easier to resist the temptation to cruise.

Lazarus (1977) equates the difference in people's levels of willpower to the extent to which they are able to construct well-defined images of negative consequences. He observes that weak-willed people, instead of dwelling on negative consequences, often switch to dwelling on the short-term rewards. If you sincerely wish to break a bad habit, the time to reward yourself is when you have resisted temptation, *not* when you have given in to it.

Visualizing Exaggerated Negative Consequences

Joseph Cautela (1967) of Boston College developed what he termed a "covert sensitization" approach to undermining and resisting temptations. You visualize exaggerated negative consequences whenever an unwanted temptation is experienced. For instance, if the habit you wish to break is overeating, and you have targeted rich cakes as a food to avoid, you might visualize the following sequence when relaxed.

> You are at home, sitting around the table at dinner, and a rich cake is being served. As you see it you start getting a nauseous feeling in your stomach. You accept a piece. As you take your first bite, you vomit all over the table and your clothes. You keep puking as the food you have previously eaten comes out in a disgusting, smelly mess. Seeing and smelling your vomit makes you retch even more violently. You feel very weak and faint. Everybody looks at you in disgust. As you get up from the table, having made up your mind to eat no more, you feel much better. You wash, change, and feel great.

Visualizing exaggerated negative consequences is obviously not for the squeamish. You need to rehearse and practice the negative imagery until it becomes a virtually automatic response to the real-life temptation. My preference is for visualizing realistic rather than exaggeratedly negative consequences. The realistic consequences can be horrific enough in their own right. However, some of you may find that the exaggeration increases the power of your negative imagery, with a beneficial effect on your willpower.

THINKSHEET 42

Visualizing Negative Consequences

1. Think of a bad habit you wish to break.
2. What graphic images of the realistic negative consequences of your bad habit might serve as a turn-off for you?
3. Make a systematic effort to collect graphic images of the consequences of your bad habit, similar to Bernie's medical photographs of AIDS-related symptoms.
4. Play the negative images through your mind for 10 to 15 minutes daily for at least a week, whether or not you feel tempted that day. Additionally, at any other time you experience temptation, instruct yourself to "Stop!" and switch to visualizing your negative images. If you find it helps you to exaggerate visually the negative consequences of your bad habit, then do so.
5. Practice, practice, and practice visualizing the negative consequences of your bad habit until you become able to resist the temptation.

Visualizing skills are often most helpful when used in conjunction with other thinking and action skills. However, it is probable that most people, including most professional helpers, underestimate rather than overestimate the power of visual thinking.

CHAPTER HIGHLIGHTS

Much of your thinking is visual.

Visual imagery can help you become more relaxed, both independently of and in conjunction with progressive muscular relaxation.

Self-desensitization has three steps: (1) relaxing, (2) compiling a hierarchy of anxiety-evoking scenes for a given theme, and (3) presenting the scenes to yourself when relaxed.

Visualizing your reactions to the worst-case scenario may help you obtain a better perspective on your ability to cope with an existing problem.

Visualizing positive images can counteract tendencies to self-depreciation, help you envision realistic rewards, and put you in touch with feelings of mastery.

Time projection can help you put present difficulties in better perspective by (1) visualizing the present from a vantage point in the future, and (2) seeing the future from the vantage point of the present.

Visualized rehearsal and practice as well as visualizing attaining your goals may help you to perform better.

Visualizing can help you clarify your goals by tapping into your daydreams, visualizing what you want, and seeing what achieving your goals would actually be like.

Visualizing can help you formulate, try out, and evaluate a new role for yourself.

Visualizing skills may help you understand others better, manage anger and resentment, assert yourself positively, and own and share your sexual fantasies.

Visualizing may help you break bad habits by collecting images of both realistic and exaggerated negative consequences.

CHAPTER 10

Making Decisions

Life is the art of drawing sufficient conclusions from insufficient premises.

Samuel Butler

This chapter is about making those "little" decisions that may have major implications for your happiness and fulfillment. Such decisions include making choices about jobs and career, your major area of study, college and graduate school, getting married, getting divorced, having a family, your recreational activities, where you live, what you do with your money, and how you look after your health. It has been said that "Life is just one darned decision after another." Each decision defines your existence and is an act of renunciation: every "yes" implies a "no."

Decisions produce varying degrees of conflict and anxiety. Sometimes the most appropriate way to act is unclear. You may fear the consequences of making the wrong decision. Additionally, you may be under stress at the time of the decision: for instance, when contemplating divorce. Decisions also imply commitment. For example, if you have decided "yes" but act on "no," you have not decided at a very fundamental level. Commitment means being prepared to carry through your decision, though you can still take further realistic feedback into account.

This chapter is divided into three sections. First, you are encouraged to explore your decision-making style. Second, a framework for and some skills of rational decision making are presented. Third, based on the thinking skills described in this book, some suggestions are made for improving your decision making.

YOUR DECISION-MAKING STYLE

He who hesitates is sometimes saved.

James Thurber

Your style of decision making is how you approach and make decisions. It is the pattern of your information-processing and deciding behavior. Your decision-making style should not be viewed as rigid and immutable, because you may make different decisions in different ways. Additionally, you may possess a profile of different decision-making styles rather than a single, strongly predominant style. Also, your style may alter when you make decisions in conjunction with other people.

Styles of Individual Decision Making

When you are faced with a decision, are there any characteristic patterns in your behavior? Below are seven styles that describe how you may make decisions. Of course, your own style may be a blend of one or more of these.

• *Rational:* In a rational style of decision making, you dispassionately and logically appraise all of the important information pertinent to your decision. You then select the best option in light of your objectives. When you experience decisional conflict, your aim is to resolve the conflict by obtaining the best solution under the circumstances.

• *Feelings-based:* The basis for your choice is what intuitively feels right. This does not mean that you are in a state of heightened emotionality that may impair decision making. Rather, the emphasis is on getting in touch with what you truly feel, with your subjective preferences, and with your inner valuing process. In the feelings-based style, you may generate and appraise different options; however, the final criterion of choice is how you feel rather that what you think.

• *Hypervigilant:* You try too hard. You become so anxious and aroused by the conflict and stress triggered by the decision that your decision-making efficiency decreases. For instance, you may engage in a lengthy and frantic search and appraisal process for the "right" decision. In this process you may fail to take into account or to weigh adequately relevant information. You may get bogged down in so much detail that, losing perspective, you fail to see the forest for the trees.

• *Avoidant:* You cope with decisions by refusing to acknowledge them or hoping they will go away, and/or by engaging in delay tactics like procrastination. You may also defensively avoid information pertinent to the decision. Your objective is to maintain your short-term psychological comfort whatever the long-term costs.

• *Impulsive:* You make decisions rapidly, based on sudden impulses rather than on a cool and rational appraisal of the facts. The impulsive style differs from the feelings-based style in that you act on initial or surface feelings rather than explore and evaluate options by getting in touch with your deeper feelings.

• *Compliant:* You conform to what others expect of you. You depend on them to signal how you should decide. The outstanding feature of this style is passivity. You allow your decisions to be influenced, if not made, by others rather than actively make them yourself.

• *Ethical:* the basis for your choice is a code of ethics. For instance, if you are a devout Catholic you make your decisions with reference to Catholic teachings. If you are not religious, you may still make your decisions on what you consider to be moral principles of right and wrong. Your decisions take into account the good of humanity and reflect social concern as well as self-interest.

Styles of Joint Decision Making

In your relationships many decisions are best made jointly. Much of the preceding section on styles of individual decision making still applies, however: for instance, joint decisions can be made rationally or can be avoided by both parties. Joint decisions may subject you to the same stresses and inner conflicts that individual decisions do. But you may experience further conflict if you have different interests, wishes, and needs than the other person.

> Raúl and Nora are an engaged couple in their final year of college. Nora wants to go on to a top graduate school, but if they then wish to live together, this limits where Raúl can get a job. Raúl has already been offered an excellent job where there are no top graduate schools in Nora's field.

In situations such as the above you are confronted with a potential conflict of interest with your partner. Assuming you confront the need for a decision, there are three main joint decision-making styles you can adopt: the competitive, the compliant, and the collaborative.

• *Competitive:* You view the decision as a competition for scarce resources; consequently, there has to be a winner and a loser. The loser is not going to be you. You adopt an "I win, you lose" approach to the decision and do all in your power to get your way. Some risks of such an approach are that you may not necessarily arrive at the best solution and that your partner may feel violated.

• *Compliant:* You are unassertive and go along with or give in to your partner. You may deceive yourself about your motivation for complying, but basically this is an "I lose, you win" decision-making style. Some risks are not finding the best solution and your feeling violated.

• *Collaborative:* You both search for the solution that best meets each partner's needs. You work together to find an "I win, you win" solution that is freely entered into by each of you. Neither of you attempts to impose your wishes on the other. As well as acknowledging and stating your individual wishes, you each have a sincere commitment to the welfare of your partner and of the relationship.

Thinksheet 43 is designed to help you explore your decision-making style. Do you always make decisions rationally, or do you use one or more other styles?

─────────────── **THINKSHEET 43** ───────────────

Exploring Your Decision-Making Style

1. *Personal decisions*
   a. Write out the extent to which you adopt each of the following decision-making styles when you have personal decisions to make.

- rational
- feelings-based
- hypervigilant
- avoidant
- impulsive
- compliant
- ethical

   b. Assess the extent to which your current profile of decision-making styles supports or oppresses you.

2. *Joint decisions*

   a. Write out the extent to which you and your partner, when making decisions that affect both your interests, use each of the following decision-making styles.

- competitive
- compliant
- collaborative

   b. Assess the extent to which your and your partner's current style or styles of making joint decisions supports or oppresses your relationship.

RATIONAL DECISION MAKING

Rational decision making can be viewed as taking place in two main stages: first, confronting and making the decision; second, implementing and evaluating it. Following is a seven-step framework for rational decision making within the context of these two main stages.

Stage One: Confronting and Making the Decision

Step One: *Confront* the decision.
Step Two: *Generate* options and *gather information* about them.
Step Three: *Assess* the predicted consequences of options.
Step Four: *Commit* yourself to a decision.

Stage Two: Implementing and Evaluating the Decision

Step Five: *Plan* how to implement the decision.
Step Six: *Implement* the decision.
Step Seven: *Assess* the actual consequences of implementation.

This is a simplified version of the decision-making process. Sometimes the steps overlap. Sometimes you need to backtrack from a later step to an earlier one. Nevertheless, if you are to make major decisions—and even some minor ones—effectively, you need to consider each of these steps.

Step One: Confront the Decision

Rational decision makers do not avoid decisions. Confronting decisions ideally requires a number of different attitudes from you.

• *Being open to external information:* Many of your decisions are stimulated by your environment. For example, you see an interesting job advertised and then have to decide whether or not to apply. Or you learn more about the hazards of smoking and are then forced to decide whether or not to give up smoking. If you are a rational person, you are open to information from external sources.

• *Being open to internal information:* The stimulus for a decision may be more proactive than reactive. You become attuned to changes in your wants and wishes: for instance, the desire for an intimate relationship or a more rewarding leisure life. These inner changes stimulate you to make decisions about how to attain what you want. If you are out of touch with your feelings, you may fail to confront the need for some decisions.

• *Having a clear focus:* Decisions need to be clearly identified and stated. For instance, if you are very unhappy in your job, you need to go beyond a vague statement of feelings to a specific statement about the decision you face. This decision is either to stay with and if possible improve your job or to seek a better one.

Step Two: Generate Options and Gather Information about Them

Generating options   Decisions frequently do not involve black-or-white choices. You may need to generate and consider different options.

> Fred, 22, wondered what to do when he did not get into any of the clinical psychology degree programs he wanted. His first reaction was to consider joining his father's timber business. But he saw a career counselor, who encouraged him to explore other opportunities in the helping professions. Fred ended up enrolling in a social work program. He was thankful that he had been encouraged to explore further options rather than going into the timber business "on the rebound."

Coming up with different options is a creative process. The objective is to generate a range of choices, among which may be effective ones. Sometimes it can be helpful to brainstorm. Brainstorming originally developed as a procedure for idea finding in groups. Nevertheless, you can apply some of its rules on your own: criticism of ideas is ruled out, freewheeling is welcomed, and quantity is desirable. The quantity rule is particularly important. Several research reports have supported the value of brainstorming, indicating that it is more likely to generate effective ideas than are attempts to produce *only* good-quality options (D'Zurilla & Goldfried, 1971).

Gathering information   Good decisions depend on good information. Sometimes further options emerge from your information gathering. Rational decision makers aim to gather as much information as they need to make a successful decision. This requires a disciplined approach, both to searching out and surveying sources of information and to knowing when to stop.

> Frank, 28, worked as a computer operator for the telephone company. He decided to explore whether or not he could get a better job. His approach was to gather as much relevant information as he could. He divided his information search into two main areas: jobs within and jobs outside of the telephone company. He set himself a deadline of 2 months to collect this information. His approach to investigating jobs within the company included finding out more about how his own section operated and the opportunities within it, looking at notice boards where in-house jobs were advertised, and having a discussion with the personnel office. His approach to investigating jobs outside of the company included discussions with contacts, combing advertisements in the papers, going to the library and surveying newspaper ads for relevant jobs in the past 3 months, and registering with an employment agency specializing in his area. As Frank gathered this information he became clearer not only about what jobs were available but also about what his own occupational goals were.

THINKSHEET 44

Generating Options and Gathering Information

1. *Confronting a decision:* Think of a current decision in your life on which you want to work. State it as clearly as you can.
2. *Generating options:* Is your decision a simple black-or-white one, or are there other possible options? Spend 10 minutes brainstorming as many options for your decision as possible. Adopt the following rules: criticism of ideas is ruled out, freewheeling is welcomed, and quantity is desirable. At the end of your brainstorming period, put a star by each option that you wish to consider further.
3. *Gathering information:* What, if any, further information do you need to collect to increase the probability of making the best decision? Follow these steps:
   a. Specify the information needed.
   b. Develop a plan for gathering the information.
   c. Implement your plan.
4. *Evaluation:* Do you see your decision differently in the light of your work with this thinksheet? Has it helped you to take a more rational approach to the decision than you might otherwise have done?

Step Three: Assess the Predicted Consequences of Options

Decision making entails assessing the consequences of your options to choose the best course of action. Your choices are likely to be guided by considerations of *probability* and *utility*; that is, how likely it seems that different options will achieve your desired outcomes, and your subjective estimations of the value of various outcomes.

Psychologists Irving Janis and Leon Mann (1977) have advocated the use of a balance sheet to assess the consequences of decisions. They write, ''The more errors

Table 10.1. A Balance Sheet for Assessing the Consequences of a Decision Option

Description of option:

Consequences of option

For Myself

	Positive	Negative
Short-term		
Long-term		

For Others

	Positive	Negative
Short-term		
Long-term		

of omission and commission in the decision maker's balance sheet at the time of becoming committed to a new course of action, the greater will be his or her vulnerability to negative feedback when the decision subsequently is implemented'' [p. 148]. Janis and Mann's balance sheet procedure requires that you take into account a series of considerations in four areas: gains and losses for self, gains and losses for others, self-approval or self-disapproval, and the approval or disapproval of others.

Table 10.1 is a balance sheet for assessing the consequences of one of the major options available to you. Thus, for any decision you will need as many balance sheets as there are options under serious consideration.

The consequences you need to consider vary with the decision. For example, if you are choosing a job, relevant consequences for yourself may be location, travel time, income, amount of work, difficulty of work, interest, degree of autonomy, security, status, superannuation, chances of advancement, chances to develop skills, physical environment, social considerations, perceived competence of management, and so on. The relevant consequences for others also depend on the nature of the decision. For instance Dave, a married man considering whether to accept on out-of-state promotion, takes into account his family's thoughts and feelings about the disruption this would entail. Debbie, a separated woman seeking a divorce, takes into account the impact it would have on her children. Frequently, the best way to assess the consequences of your decisions for others is to let those concerned speak for themselves rather than trying to read their minds.

THINKSHEET 45

Assessing the Consequences of Decision Options

1. Select a decision on which you wish to work. It can be the decision you used for Thinksheet 44 or another one.
2. What are the major options from which you can make your decision?
3. Make out balance sheets for assessing the consequences of each of the above options.
4. Do you perceive your decision differently after completing this thinksheet? Has it helped you to take a more rational approach to the decision than you might otherwise have done?

Step Four: Commit Yourself to a Decision

There is no more miserable human being
than one in whom nothing is habitual but indecision.

William James

Assuming that you have gone systematically through the previous steps, you are now ready to make your decision. However, it is one thing to rationally make a decision and another to commit yourself to carrying it through and doing your best to make it work. Making major decisions confronts you with your existential isolation. Ultimately, nobody else can make them for you. Especially if the options have come close to balancing, you may have regrets about those you have renounced as well as doubts about the one you chose.

How can you strengthen your resolve to carry out a difficult decision? First, you can endeavor to see that the decision is in accord with your key values. Second, you can be thorough in generating options, gathering information about them, and assessing them. Third, you can state your goal or goals clearly and list the specific rewards and payoffs for yourself and others for attaining those goals. The balance sheet for your preferred option should provide this information. Fourth, you can carefully plan how best to implement your decision, including how to handle setbacks and negative reactions from others. Fifth, you can adopt a flexible attitude and adjust both the decision and how you implement it in response to feedback. Being flexible does not necessarily mean weakening your resolve. You may choose to reaffirm your original decision at the same time as you adopt different tactics to carry it out, for example. However, if the evidence truly warrants it, you may choose to modify or even totally reject your original decision. Sixth, you can acknowledge and keep in mind the rewards of your decision as they appear. Your decisional balance sheet can be completed *during* the implementation of a decision as well as *before* it. This may help you gain more perspective as you experience the effort and frustration of implementing it.

Step Five: Plan How to Implement the Decision

Plans are outlines of how to proceed. You may need to engage in planning as part of your decision-making process and not just when you are about to implement your final decision. For example, Frank, the telephone company employee, developed a plan to gather information about different job possibilities.

Once you have arrived at a decision—to obtain a divorce, move to a new location, take up a new recreational activity, give up smoking, engage in some form of community service—you are still faced with planning how best to act. Some of the skills of planning include the following.

• *State your goals and subgoals clearly.* In Chapter 8 it was suggested that adequate statements of goals should not only reflect your values but be realistic, specific, and given a time frame. In planning you may need clear statements of your subgoals as well as of your overall goal. Subgoals are the steps you need to take to obtain your overall goal. For instance, Sally and Mike are a young couple who have decided to buy a house and start a family. One of their subgoals is to save a stipulated sum for a down payment on a house within 12 months. Peggy has just moved to a new city and has decided to join a physical fitness club, both for exercise and to meet some new people. One of her subgoals is to gather information about all physical fitness clubs within a certain distance of where she lives by the end of the month.

• *Break down tasks.* The concept of subgoals implies that you often need to break down tasks. You do not have to do everything at once. For instance, Edna decides to divorce Jack, from whom she has been separated for nearly 2 years. She breaks down the implementation of this decision into a number of different parts: how best to handle the legal aspects of divorce; how to relate to Jack; how to inform and relate to her children; what to say to her family, in-laws, and friends; how to handle her own feelings about divorce; and how to build a more independent life for herself.

• *Generate and assess alternative courses of action.* For each of your subgoals, ask yourself "How can I best achieve this subgoal?" You'll need to use your skills of brainstorming, to generate different courses of action and of assessment, to decide which courses of action are most likely to help you achieve your goals and subgoals.

• *Anticipate difficulties and setbacks.* When possible, take realistic difficulties and setbacks into account. For instance, Lynne knows that her decision to go overseas for a year is not going to please her boyfriend, Sam. In advance, she thinks through how she can break the news to him in an assertive yet caring way.

• *Identify sources of support.* Difficult decisions can often be best adhered to in the context of an adequate support system. For example, Brad realizes that he is much more likely to adhere to his decision to give up drinking if he is part of a support group rather than trying to break the habit on his own. Consequently, he has joined Alcoholics Anonymous. Brad thinks it will also help him if he establishes better relationships with his wife and family, as well as with friends who do not encourage his drinking.

• *Write out your plan.* If your plan is at all complex, it may help you to write it out. You may be able to commit yourself better to implementing its steps if they are clearly set out. A written plan can act as a reminder if it is put in a readily visible place. When writing out your plan, do not get lost in its detail. Your plan is an outline or map of how to get from A to B. You do not have to fill in every building, field, and tree along the way. Write it out with a clear structure to support attaining your central goal and its related subgoals.

THINKSHEET 46

Planning to Implement a Decision

1. Select a decision that you wish to implement. It may be the one you worked on in Thinksheets 44 and 45, or another one.
2. Write out a realistic plan to implement your decision, adhering to the following guidelines:
   a. State your goals and subgoals clearly.
   b. Break down tasks.
   c. Generate and assess alternative courses of action.
   d. Anticipate difficulties and setbacks.
   e. Identify sources of support.
   As you write out your plan, remember to avoid the twin pitfalls of giving insufficient or too much detail. Ensure that your plan is easy for you to understand and follow.

(continued)

3. Assess your skills, in your daily life, of making and implementing plans that help you attain goals.

Step Six: Implement the Decision

The time has come for you to implement your decision. This may be a straightforward matter, in which both your decision and how to proceed are clear to you. Some guidelines for implementing decisions include the following:

- *Consider timing.* You can often choose the best time to implement a decision, if you have worked out how to proceed and feel reasonably confident that you can carry out your plan. Sometimes, however, the timing of when to implement your decision will be heavily influenced by others' needs; for instance, if you are a parent, you may not wish to change location during your son's senior year of high school.

- *Be prepared for postdecisional conflicts.* There are many reasons why you may have conflicting feelings about implementing a decision. You may be sad about some of the trade-offs and compromises you are making to get what you want. You may still feel you lack the confidence to implement your decision. You may have realistic reservations about the wisdom of your original decision and wish to reconsider it. You may become highly anxious at having to act, and then engage in avoidance behavior. Postdecisional conflict may be especially intense as you start to implement a decision, but become less so as you carry on and gain confidence in the wisdom of your decision. However, if you experience persistent conflict in implementing a decision, you may choose to reconsider it.

- *Accept no excuses.* This guideline is another way of underlining the importance of assuming responsibility for implementing your decision. When you face setbacks you need to ask yourself questions like "Stop...think...what do I need to do to handle this situation?" and "How is my behavior helping me?" rather than indulge in a litany of excuses.

- *Be open to feedback.* As you implement your decision you may get feedback from many sources: yourself, others, and your environment. You need sensitivity and good judgment to sort out helpful from harmful feedback. If appropriate, you may decide to modify your plan to help you better obtain your goals. Flexibility in the light of realistic assessment of feedback is desirable. You can be strong and flexible at the same time.

- *Use positive self-reward.* Implementing some decisions can be a reward in its own right. In other cases, you may use rewards to strengthen your motivation. For instance, you may use positive self-talk like "That's great," or "Well done," or "I'm glad I made it" that clearly acknowledges your satisfaction at performing desired behavior. Another method of positive self-reward is to make a contract with yourself in which there is a clear connection between specific achievements and self-administered rewards. These rewards can fall into two categories: (1) rewards that are outside your everyday life, such as a new item of clothing or some special entertainment; and (2) withholding some pleasant everyday experience until you've achieved what your contract stipulates.

• *Be ready to handle guilt.* Guilt may be one of the feelings you need to work through when you make your decision. However, I refer here to the guilt you may feel if you do not live up to your decision. You can handle feelings of guilt in ways that weaken or strengthen your resolve. If you engage in a lot of self-disparagement, it may lower your self-esteem to the point at which your self-talk may go something like this: "I'm worthless anyway, so why bother?" "I've made a mess of it once, so it's obvious that I'm not going to succeed." A more rational approach is to try to understand why you did not live up to your decision and to make plans to prevent a repeated occurrence. Furthermore, you may need to tell yourself that setbacks are often part of the process of implementing difficult decisions or giving up bad habits. You need to have the courage to persist and not think yourself into giving up.

Step Seven:
Assess the Actual Consequences of Implementation

You need to assess both how you have implemented your plan and the consequences of having attained or not attained your goals. Do not stay stuck with decisions and plans that do not work for you. You may decide to review your original decision, in which case this seven-step model comes full circle, and you start off with step one again. Rational decision making requires an accurate perception of feedback and a willingness to act on it. Efficient information processing helps you to both make and assess decisions.

IMPROVING THE QUALITY OF YOUR DECISION MAKING

How can you increase the probability of making decisions that work for rather than against you? How can you increase the self-supporting and decrease the self-oppressing elements of your decision making? In this section I'll demonstrate how many of the skills discussed earlier can improve the quality of your decisions. Let's start with the example of Grace, who is coming to terms with a poor decision.

> Grace, 33, was a salesperson with a bedding company. She was becoming bored with the job, wanted more money, and had begun to have conflict with Ed, her sales manager. For instance, she resented his asking her to make him coffee. However, Ed had been promoted and was not going to be around much longer. Within 3 weeks of seriously considering a switch, Grace had landed a new job as a sales representative for an entrepreneur marketing a special kind of display plant to hotels, offices, and retailers. It was the only job Grace considered, and she rushed into it. During her first week on the new job she started getting anxious, depressed, and "worried sick that I have made the wrong decision." Additionally, she suffered from insomnia. Her reservations about her new job included the product's limitations; her new boss's egotism; a

company car inferior to that of her previous job; a heavier workload; and a low-percentage sales commission that could nullify her goal of making more money.

In this example, Grace is paying for her impulsive decision-making style. She says that gaining more self-esteem is one of her main goals in life, but she has behaved in a way that it makes it harder for her to see herself as a successful person than if she had adopted a more systematic decision-making approach. She suffers not only physical symptoms and an unsatisfactory work environment, but also a probable loss of money. Had she taken a more rational approach she might well have found a higher-paying job or, failing that, been able to negotiate a more competitive commission rate in the job she took.

Many of the skills discussed earlier might have helped Grace. For instance, if she had used coping self-talk in relation to Ed she might not have been in such a desperate hurry to change jobs. If she had more realistic personal rules for tolerating boredom and not getting her own way immediately, she might have looked around more. Her self-perception was also negative. Instead of thinking "I'm a good salesperson with valuable skills to offer and need to find a place where I can use my skills to best effect," she jumped at the first opportunity. Additionally, in her emotional state Grace failed to perceive her position in the bedding company accurately, since she insufficiently took into account Ed's imminent departure. If Grace had collected more information, too, she would have made more accurate predictions about her new job: for instance, since it was an important criterion for her she could have found out in advance what sort of car she would have. Neither did Grace use visualization skills. She could have developed a clear picture of what sort of life she wanted and imagined what it would actually be like doing the job she chose *before* she accepted it.

Table 10.2 is a decision-making checklist that may help you improve the quality of your decision making if, like Grace, you find this problematic. It begins by checking whether you are engaging in the steps of rational decision making, and then asks a series of questions about your use of the thinking skills discussed earlier in this book to support your decision making. The steps of rational decision making have already been presented. Consequently, the remainder of this chapter reviews the other nine questions on the checklist. I do not suggest you use the checklist for every little decision: life is too short. However, if you have an important decision to make and are afraid you may make a mistake, that is a good time to use the checklist.

Am I Owning Responsibility for the Authorship of My Life?

You may fail to own responsibility for the authorship of your life in many ways. You may not be fully aware of your capacity to make your life through your choices. You may lack full existential awareness of the transitory nature of life. You may expect others to be responsible for what happens to you.

Decisions are often fraught with anxiety. You may bring your ongoing anxieties to your decision making. And some decisions, of course, evoke more anxiety and inner conflict than others do. This may be because the stakes are high, the decision is

---

Table 10.2. A Decision-Making Checklist

1. Am I engaging in the steps of rational decision making?
2. Am I owning responsibility for the authorship of my life?
3. Am I in touch with my underlying feelings?
4. Am I using self-talk constructively?
5. Are my personal rules and directives helping rather than harming me?
6. Are my perceptions of myself and others accurate?
7. Are my attributions of cause accurate?
8. Are my predictions realistic?
9. Am I articulating my goals clearly, and do they reflect my values?
10. Am I using visualizing to best effect?

---

complex, a value conflict is involved, or there is no clearly best option. You may handle your anxiety about decisions in some of the styles mentioned earlier: avoidance, impulsiveness, and hypervigilance.

Decision making can require courage. Some of you may be passive rather than active in your decision making. You may have become used to depending on others, such as your parents, for advice about how you should act. You may be hypersensitive to the conventions of your peer group and afraid to lose its esteem. You may feel the need to obey authority figures and to cede responsibility for decision making to them. Thus, you may gain external approval at the expense of integrity and possibly self-esteem.

Here are some simple questions relevant to assuming authorship of your life: "Am I too passive in my approach to life; do I wait for things to happen?" "Do I take the easy way out by avoiding decisions?" "Do I get so anxious that I am afraid to make up my mind?" "Do I lack the courage of my convictions and become too dependent on others for my decisions?"

Am I in Touch with My Underlying Feelings?

As you make decisions, you define and create yourself. In general, good decisions rely on skills not only of reasoning but also of instinct: of getting in touch with your underlying feelings. In Grace's case, she was almost too aware of her short-term feelings of boredom, annoyance with Ed, and impatience to leave. However, she lacked the capacity to get more deeply centered by listening to her own valuing process. Because she listened to her superficial rather than to her deeper feelings, she made a poor decision. Put another way, Grace had problems of self-esteem and identity, which, along with being out of touch with her feelings, contributed to her making decisions too quickly. Others of you may be out of touch with your wants and wishes and be in a state of indecision, as contrasted with too-ready decision making.

There are a number of approaches to getting in touch with your feelings. They include the following:

• *Taking more time:* "Sleeping on it" is a common approach to making important decisions. Hopefully, this does not entail sleepless nights. The idea is that a night's sleep helps you put matters in perspective, lessens the risk of making hasty decisions, and allows you to decide when you're refreshed. Issues of timing and pacing are very important in decision making. Sometimes when given more time you may find the confidence to make a previously difficult decision.

• *Gathering external information:* Again, this affects your readiness to make a decision. Making decisions is a process. You may find that as you collect more relevant information you are able to understand what you really want. Attention to the process has then produced a decision with which you feel comfortable.

• *Listening to your inner voice:* A vital source of information comes from within. You may need to develop your skills of inner focusing and of giving yourself a chance to listen to your feelings (Gendlin, 1981). If you always rush around you may not allow yourself time for creative contemplation. Part of Thinksheet 7 (Chapter 3) focused on inner listening when you had a decision to make that was bothering you. The skills and steps of inner listening include: (1) physically and psychologically clearing a space; (2) setting aside periods of "quiet time," possibly after relaxing yourself; (3) with your eyes shut, trying not to analyze or think through the decision but rather experience your flow of feelings in relation to it; and (4) at the end of the quiet time asking yourself if you feel any differently about the problem.

• *Asserting yourself:* You may particularly need to assert yourself, because the "noise" from outside may be so great that it blocks your inner listening. I'll deal with assertion more thoroughly in the final chapter. For now, suffice it to say that numerous other people may have vested interests in the outcomes of your decisions. Even if they do not, they may still be overly ready to offer advice rather than help you to your own conclusions.

• *Using anxiety management skills:* Anxiety can be a devastating anesthetic. Many of the thinking skills listed in Table 10.2, such as using coping self-talk and having realistic personal rules, may help you to lower debilitating anxiety. This in turn allows you to become more in touch with your wants, wishes, and feelings.

Am I Using Self-Talk Constructively?

There are a number of ways that you can use self-talk to help in your decision making.

• *Using "I" self-talk:* You can use "I" self-talk constructively. For example it is much more self-supporting to say "I can't make up my mind" rather than "You fool! Why can't you make up your mind?"

• *Using calming self-talk:* As you learned earlier, coping self-talk consists of two elements: *calming* self-talk and *coaching* self-talk. When you experience anxiety over a decision you can use calming self-talk: "Keep calm." "Relax." "I can cope."

• *Using coaching self-talk:* You can consciously coach yourself through the steps of a rational decision-making process. For example, you can ask yourself questions about each of the steps: "Am I adequately confronting the decision?" "The next thing I need to do is to generate options and gather information; how do I go about this?" "What do I predict the consequences of my options to be, and what are my criteria for assessing them?" "What seems to be the best option, and am I prepared to commit myself to implementing it?"

• *Engaging in a self-talk dialogue:* One approach to resolving a decision-making conflict is to conduct a dialogue. The part of you that is in favor of an option can hold a dialogue with the part of you that is against it. You tend to weigh the pros and cons when you make any decision, but some of you may find it helpful to externalize these existing self-talk processes, even to the extent of moving from chair to chair as you alternate roles. Given privacy, you can hold your self-talk dialogue aloud.

Are My Personal Rules and Directives Helping Rather Than Harming Me?

You may have mustabatory personal rules in regard to the way you make decisions and to the content of your decisions. Self-oppressing personal rules about the decision-making *process* include the following:

"I *must* always make the right decision."

"I *must* always make decisions quickly and easily."

"The information I need to make a decision *must* always be available immediately."

"In decisions shared with other people, I *must* always get what I want."

Mustabatory rules concerning the *content* of your decisions vary according to the area under consideration. If you make a career decision, possible self-oppressing personal rules include the following:

"I *must* get into the most prestigious career possible."

"I *must* make more money than my peers."

"I *must* choose a career that will please my parents."

"I *must* be accepted by every company and agency to which I apply."

"When I go to interviews I *must* be liked by everyone."

As corollaries to your mustabatory personal rules, you may have pressurizer and inhibitor directives that impair your decision making. Possible pressurizer directives include "Hurry up" and "Be in control." Possible inhibitor directives include "Don't think," "Don't feel," and "Don't take risks."

If you become aware of your self-opposing rules, you can dispute them and reformulate them into language that is more self-supporting. If you become aware of pressurizer and inhibitor directives you can dispute them, understand their origins, and grant yourself permission to think and act differently. You may have to struggle hard to counteract your self-defeating "voices in the head," internalized from others, with your own rational rules and directives.

Are My Perceptions of Myself and Others Accurate?

You may need to verify whether you are making the distinction between facts and inferences and, when facts are limited, keeping your inferences as realistic as possible.

• *Self-perceptions:* Are you evaluating yourself realistically, or do you attach false negative or positive labels to yourself? For instance, when Grace made her decision to leave the bedding company, she undervalued not only her specific characteristics as a salesperson but also her worth as a human being. She would have done much better to have taken a more balanced approach, acknowledging and listing her resources and realistically perceiving her limitations. Focusing on your weaknesses and unnecessarily putting yourself down can cause you to be overanxious and hence to miss good opportunities. Similarly, being defensive and not acknowledging realistic weaknesses prevents you from having a sound information base for your decisions.

• *Perceptions of others:* Many decisions require you to perceive other people accurately. If you have a tendency to focus on other people's weaknesses rather than on their strengths, you may find yourself making decisions to end relationships and jobs when it might have been in your interest to stay with them. Other perceptual errors that may contribute to your perceiving others unrealistically include black-and-white thinking ("He/she is either all for me or all against me") and overgeneralizing ("Because he/she ignored me once, he/she will always do so").

Again, good decisions require good information. The more you misperceive, the more likely you are to make poor decisions. Remember that the first perception is not necessarily the best. Rational decision making demands that you take the time and trouble to verify the accuracy of your perceptions of yourself and others. They are important building blocks for your decision-making process.

Are My Attributions of Cause Accurate?

Below are three examples of people who are making decisions on the basis of their attributions.

> Shirley, 26, has decided to get a divorce. She attributes the reason for this decision to her own growth as an assertive and independent woman while her husband remains the same spoiled little boy he has always been.

> Ron, 38, was fired a year ago. He has decided to leave the state in which he has lived all his life. He attributes the reason for this decision to a lack of opportunities in his home state for electronics engineers like himself.

> Norm, 21, has decided not to go on to graduate school. His grades in college this year have not been as good as he had wanted. He attributes this to lack of ability.

In these examples Shirley, Ron, and Norm are all making important decisions on the basis of their explanations for the situations in which they find themselves. These explanations may or may not be accurate. When making decisions—especially important ones—you need to consider carefully the explanations you give yourself for what is happening to you. Useful skills for doing this include separating facts from inferences and logically analyzing the factual underpinning of any causal inferences you make.

Are My Predictions Realistic?

When you make decisions, do you collect sufficient information to increase the probability of your predictions being realistic? You may have a general decision-making style that is overly optimistic or pessimistic. Though you make many decisions well, you may rush into others on the basis of rosy expectations and then live to regret it. Alternatively, you may fail to create or take advantage of good opportunities by being too pessimistic.

Poor decisions are often founded on faulty predictive reasoning. You jump to erroneous and simplistic conclusions. Here are some examples of faulty predictive reasoning by people contemplating their careers:

"I could never work for a woman."

"I can't stand the sight of blood; therefore I could never become a doctor."

"They didn't employ my friend, so they won't employ me."

"Some people in the company are getting fired, so I am likely to be next."

"A woman like me will never be able to compete in a man's world."

"I have received a letter of rejection; this means that I'm unemployable."

"They won't pay any attention to the fact that I've had ten jobs in eight years when I next apply for a job."

As with other thinking skills, you need to discipline your thinking to sort out facts from inferences in making predictions. You may have some basis for some of your perceptions; however, the conclusions you draw from them may be inaccurate. For example, you may have realistic evidence that as a woman it is harder to succeed in your chosen career. But it is probably a leap of logic to say that you will never be able to compete: increasingly, women succeed in areas such as medicine and law that have traditionally been dominated by males. Also, you may have strengths that you do not fully acknowledge.

Am I Articulating
My Goals Clearly, and Do They Reflect My Values?

When you begin the decision-making process, your goals may not be altogether clear. Part of the process can entail making decisions about what goals you choose as well as about how to obtain them. This is well illustrated by the earlier examples of Frank and Grace.

> Frank, the computer operator for a telephone company, had the overall goal of getting a better job. He had thought up some criteria for the job he wanted, including a 15

percent increase in salary, the chance to do more programming and less administration, staying in the city center rather than going to the suburbs, and being part of a team rather than working on his own. Frank articulated these goals at the start of his job search. He intended to use the job search process not only to find out what was available, but also to refine and add to his goals for the position he sought.

Grace, the bedding company salesperson, had goals at the start of her job search that were as much negative as positive. She wished to be less bored and to get away from Ed. Though she realized that she wanted to make more money, she never thought through specific criteria for choosing a new position. Only when she started the job selling display plants did she articulate what should have been some of her original goals: for example, having a good company car and a total income increase of 20 percent. These were her two main goals. However, as Grace now contemplated another job move, together with a counselor she articulated eight more goals. In descending order of importance to her, these goals were having a high-quality product to sell; working for a reputable company; having a boss with professional management and relationship skills; getting good secretarial and delivery-of-goods support; having her own desk and phone in a modern office; the availability of in-service training; opportunities for advancement; and being offered a clear contract, the terms of which she could negotiate. Grace admitted that she had made a poor decision in rushing into the display plants job. She very much wanted to learn how to go about making better decisions.

Ideally, your goals reflect your values. However, on occasion your values may come into conflict, making it hard for you to articulate your goals. For example, you may have materialistic values but also want to help others in your work. You then need to spend time clarifying your values and goals prior to making a more specific decision about what jobs to apply for. The trade-offs and compromises involved in articulating your goals are more likely to help than harm you if you approach your values decisions in a rational way that also takes into account your deeper feelings and ethical commitments.

Am I Using Visualizing to Best Effect?

Ways that you can use visualizing to improve your decision making include clarifying your goals, reviewing your options, using positive imagery, and considering the worst-case scenario.

• *Clarifying your goals:* It helps to have a vision of how you want your life to be. Tapping into your daydreams is one source of ideas for your goals. When you've articulated your goals, it may help to visualize what it would be like attaining them. As you do so, you may choose to modify them.

• *Reviewing your options:* As you review and weigh options for a decision, it may help you to picture implementing the main ones and experiencing their consequences. For instance, you might visualize a day in the life of different careers, what it might be like being married to someone, what it might be like being divorced, or what it might be like living with your first child. You probably do this already, but may not be sufficiently systematic about it.

• *Using positive imagery:* If you use positive imagery to visualize your strengths and coping capacities, you may feel more confident about making certain decisions. For example, if you are afraid of the consequences of accepting a promotion, visualizing yourself coping in the more demanding job might help you decide to accept rather than reject the offer.

• *Considering the worst-case scenario:* If you're avoiding making a decision, one approach is to visualize the worst-case scenario of one or more options. You should try to picture how you would cope with those difficulties and what support you would be able to call upon. Visualizing yourself coping in adversity may help you overcome blocks to making and to implementing the decision.

THINKSHEET 47

Reviewing How You Make Important Decisions

'Write out your answers to the following questions. When you have finished, list the main points that you should remember, to improve future decision making.

1. Do I make important decisions in a systematic and rational way?
2. Do I own responsibility for the authorship of my life?
3. Do I get in touch with my underlying feelings?
4. Do I use self-talk constructively?
5. Do my personal rules and directives help rather than harm me?
6. Do I perceive myself and others accurately?
7. Do I attribute cause accurately?
8. Do I make realistic predictions?
9. Do I articulate my goals clearly, and do they reflect my values?
10. Do I use visualizing to best effect?

CHAPTER HIGHLIGHTS

Poor decisions can cost you dearly in time, effort, emotional upset, and money.
Decision-making styles are characteristic patterns of making decisions.
Styles of individual decision making include the following: rational, feelings-based, hypervigilant, avoidant, impulsive, compliant, and ethical.
Styles of joint decision making include competitive, compliant, and collaborative.
Rational decision making involves (1) confronting the decision, (2) generating options and gathering information about them, (3) assessing the predicted consequences of options, (4) committing yourself to a decision, (5) planning its implementation, (6) implementing it, and (7) assessing the actual consequences of implementation.
You may improve the quality of your decision making if you (1) engage in the steps of rational decision making, (2) own responsibility for the authorship of your life, (3) use self-talk constructively, (4) have helpful personal rules and directives, (5) perceive yourself and others accurately, (6) attribute cause accurately, (7) make realistic predictions, (8) articulate your goals clearly, and (9) use visualizing to best effect.

CHAPTER 11

Preventing
and Managing Problems

No problem is so big or so complicated that it can't be run away from.

Charles Schultz, Peanuts *caption*

Definition of having a problem: Loving yourself
more than your analyst
Definition of overcoming a problem: Loving your
analyst more than yourself

Like death and taxes, problems are great equalizers: everybody has them. However, some people have more problems than others. And some are better at making the choices that prevent avoidable problems and help them to manage unavoidable ones. A chess problem is an arrangement of pieces on the board, to which a player is challenged to find an answer. Similarly, in your life there are likely to be many times when you are challenged to find answers to personal problems.

In Chapter 1 I mentioned two ways of approaching personal problems. One way is to see them as a challenge: that is, how do we prevent problems? The second way is to look for methods of managing problems: then the challenge is how best to cope with problems once they occur. Your problems have often been around for a long time. You may have tried unsuccessfully to solve them, and your attempted solutions may now have become part of your problems. Many of you may feel stuck in your problems. You want to cope and have tried to cope better, but your problems still persist. I do not wish to imply that all personal problems are capable of solution. However, if you choose to use the thinking skills described in this book, they may help you to prevent some problems, overcome others, and live more comfortably with those that are unavoidable and relatively permanent features of your life.

Decision making and problem management overlap. However, the focus in Chapter 10 was on making decisions at major and minor turning points, where you needed to decide among different options. Here the focus is on using thinking skills to prevent and manage feelings and behaviors that are problematic for you. This does not mean that you have caused all your problems. External events are often heavy contributors: other people's behavior, accidents, socioeconomic conditions, and so on. You have also been heavily influenced by your learning environment. Nevertheless, you have a choice about how you cope with your problems, whatever their origins.

Styles of Managing Problems

Though you may manage different problems in different ways, you may have a characteristic pattern or style of managing problems. As we'll see later, the skills needed to manage problems differ somewhat from those needed to make decisions. Nevertheless, the decision-making styles mentioned in the last chapter are relevant to how you manage problems. You may be rational in your approach. You may get in touch with your deeper feelings. Or you may avoid problems, impulsively find solutions, be hypervigilant and get bogged down in the details of problems, or try to manage your problems by complying with others' wishes. Some of you may also approach your problems within ethical frameworks that may either harm or help you.

As you work through this chapter, you'll learn to apply your thinking skills to preventing problems and gain a new tool: CASIE, a five-step framework for managing problems. You'll also discover how thinking skills can provide some useful "handles" for working on certain common problems.

PREVENTING PROBLEMS

Proverbs such as "An ounce of prevention is worth a pound of cure" and "A stitch in time saves nine" tell the homey truths that you are often better off preventing problems than having to deal with them later. In Chapter 1 I used the analogy of the golfer who tries to stay on the fairway to prevent the problems of having to play out of the rough. You too should try and stay on the fairway of life.

An overall approach to preventive problem management is to acknowledge that you are less predisposed to problems when you use good thinking skills in your everyday life. Good thinking skills make you a more confident person, less prone to be threatened by imaginary, as opposed to real, difficulties. Your commitment to effective thinking will help you to direct your life—for instance, your relationships—in ways that minimize the occurrence of unnecessary problems.

A more specific approach is to be able to anticipate when a certain problem may occur. A personal "early warning system" can also detect when you are in danger of making a self-oppressing move that will either create or worsen a problem on the horizon. Table 11.1 is a checklist that you may use to review how you might prevent a problem. The negative consequences of many problems are profound—from broken families to heart attacks—so time spent in trying to prevent those consequences is time well spent. You can also use the checklist for managing problems that already exist, once you have familiarized yourself with the CASIE steps presented later in this chapter.

Table 11.1. A Checklist for Preventing and Managing Problems
1. Am I engaging in the steps of effective problem management?
2. Am I owning responsibility for the authorship of my life?
3. Am I in touch with my underlying feelings?
4. Am I using self-talk constructively?
5. Are my personal rules and directives helping rather than harming me?
6. Are my perceptions of myself and others accurate?
7. Are my attributions of cause accurate?
8. Are my predictions realistic?
9. Am I articulating my goals clearly, and do they reflect my values?
10. Am I using visualizing to best effect?

Preventing Excessive Stress

Let me illustrate what I mean by using thinking skills in a preventive way by addressing a specific problem, excessive stress. Let us assume that your goal is to have an optimal level of stress: you feel sufficiently challenged yet not overwhelmed by adjustive demands made by yourself, others, and your environment. No one can banish stress entirely; consequently, your goals should be simply to choose the level of stress and activity that works best for you and to cope effectively with stresses originating outside of you. You may not feel excessively stressed now; nevertheless, you may see excessive stress as a potential problem that you wish to either avoid or contain. For instance, you may have a relative who has suffered from stress-related ailments like hypertension and heart attacks. You may decide, therefore, that for you prevention is better than a cure.

How can you use your thinking skills to prevent excessive stress? Below are some suggestions with reference to items two to ten of the checklist.

• *Am I owning responsibility for the authorship of my life?* You may need to review whether you are in danger of making faulty choices that will lead you to neglect your health and lack a balanced level of activity. You may need to become more aware of your mortality and physical limitations. The more you can assume responsibility for making your life, the less likely you are to allow yourself to be stressed beyond reasonable limits.

• *Am I in touch with my underlying feelings?* If you operate as a healthy animal, you use your feelings as a guide for your behavior. For example, if you feel you are a worthwhile person in your own right, you are less likely to overstrive to meet others' unrealistic expectations. We all have the capacity of listening to our bodies. When you start feeling tired and stressed, acknowledge this and then act, if possible, to protect your overall effectiveness.

• *Am I using self-talk constructively?* Part of preventing excessive stress is to deal with the stresses you face daily in self-supporting rather than in self-oppressing ways. One of the main uses of coping self-talk is to manage stressful events more effectively.

By talking yourself through stressful events in calming and coaching ways, you can diminish your frustration and increase your effectiveness.

• *Are my personal rules and directives helping rather than harming me?* If you make perfectionist mustabatory demands on yourself, others, and the environment, it may contribute to feelings of excessive stress and burnout. The more you can work toward having functional, realistic, and flexible personal rules that are based on preferences rather than demands, the less likely a candidate you are for stress-related misery and illness. For instance, you may have mustabatory personal rules about study and work achievement or about needing others' approval. If so, you need to challenge and reformulate those rules. Also, if you have a potentially dangerous pressurizer directive like "Hurry up," challenge it and give yourself permission to live at a pace that better suits your animal nature.

• *Are my perceptions of myself and others accurate?* What you perceive as stressful implies a pact between you and the stressor. If you can avoid negative self-labeling and acknowledge your realistic positive attributes, you should feel more able to cope with stress. Additionally, if you avoid distortions of others, you can prevent stress to yourself. For example, Lorenzo experiences his boss as much more threatening than his behavior to date has justified. In reality, Lorenzo has transferred his perception of a previous boss, who *was* difficult, to his current boss, who has not been difficult so far. If Lorenzo behaves negatively toward his new boss, he may further increase his stress.

• *Are my attributions of cause accurate?* If you realistically acknowledge your own contribution to your problems, you are in a position to work on them successfully. This relieves your stress in the long run. Additionally, if you are realistic about the causes of your successes and failures, you are in a better position to improve your performance than if your attributions of cause are inaccurate. For example, Sophie is uptight because she insists on believing that the bias of the interviewing panel, not the strength of another candidate, was the cause of her being turned down for a job. Additionally, Sophie may lose the opportunity of sharpening her interviewing skills by misattributing cause.

• *Are my predictions realistic?* You may prevent excessive stress if you adopt an "It can happen to me" instead of an "It can't happen to me" attitude toward the negative consequences of overstressing your body. Also, accurately predicting the consequences of your actions can help you avoid costly mistakes and the stresses that accompany them.

• *Am I articulating my goals clearly, and do they reflect my values?* Clear goals help prevent the stresses of confusion. Realistic goals are a protection against overstriving. Goals that reflect your values as much as possible can help prevent stress-inducing inner conflicts due to discrepancies between your goals and values. If you are able to create your future on the basis of well-thought-through goals and values, you should enjoy the beneficial, as contrasted with the harmful, effects of stress.

• *Am I using visualizing to best effect?* You can prevent stress by visualizing realistic goals for yourself, visualizing the consequences of decisions before you make them, and using visualizing to improve your relationships. You can also prevent excessive stress through visualized relaxation, in which you take time out to visualize a calm and peaceful scene.

These are only some of the ways in which you can use your thinking skills to prevent the psychological and physical miseries of self-inflicted excessive stress. Also, the more effectively you can think when actually faced with problems and decisions, the more you support yourself in avoiding and containing excessive stress.

Preventing Problems and Developing Superior Functioning

Much of the field of psychology focuses on the remediation of psychological pain rather than on how to live effectively. Living effectively means not just managing painful problems but preventing them. Humans have the capacity to transcend the unhappiness that blights so many lives and so often gets handed on from parents to children. If you can develop and use the thinking skills described in this book, you should be able to prevent many of the problems that create and sustain psychological distress. Superior human functioning entails making "smart" rather than "dumb" thinking choices. Effective people are good information processors. They realize that, if they discipline themselves to think effectively, not only will they create happiness but also avoid misery—for both themselves and others.

--- **THINKSHEET 48** ---

Using Thinking Skills to Prevent Problems

1. Think of a possible future problem—for instance, excessive stress or a deterioration of your relationship with your partner—that you wish to prevent.
2. Review the following broad areas of thinking skills to identify ways of preventing your potential problem.
   a. owning responsibility for authorship of my life
   b. being in touch with my underlying feelings
   c. using self-talk constructively
   d. having helpful personal rules and directives
   e. having accurate perceptions of myself and others
   f. attributing cause accurately
   g. making realistic predictions
   h. clearly articulating goals that reflect my values
   i. using visualizing to best effect
3. Summarize what you have learned from this analysis about how to prevent your problem. Start putting your insights into practice now.

CASIE: A FIVE-STEP FRAMEWORK FOR MANAGING PROBLEMS

Managing your problems effectively requires that you use many of the same skills for making decisions. Nevertheless, there are some important differences, especially in the areas of assessing and defining problems. Following is a five-step framework for managing problems, which I have given the acronym CASIE to make it easier to remember.

C   *Confront* your problem.
A   *Assess* and *define* your problem.
S   *Set goals* and *plan*.
I   *Implement* your plan.
E   *Evaluate* the consequences of implementation.

This framework is not intended to be a straightjacket, but a tool to be used flexibly. It can be used with varying degrees of formality and rigor, depending on how difficult and important your problem is. For many minor problems, you may rightly judge it not worth the bother of systematically going through the five steps.

Step One: Confront Your Problem

Confronting your problem requires that you keep the following considerations in mind.

• *Orientation:* Orientation refers to your attitude toward problems. These attitudes include the degree to which you think that (1) problems are a normal part of life, (2) the best approach to problems is to try to cope with them, (3) it is important to identify problems either before or as they arise rather than when they are full-blown, and (4) a "Stop...think...what are my choices?" approach is better than impulsiveness.

• *Ownership:* You own a problem when you fully acknowledge that you have one. For numerous reasons, it may be convenient to deny your problems or to dilute their significance. Acknowledging problems may mean, among other things, admitting to yourself that you were wrong, confronting the need for change, and having to develop new and better skills. It may also mean assuming responsibility for how you think, feel, and act rather than choosing to perceive others as responsible.

• *Clearing a space:* Confronting a problem goes beyond an awareness of its existence to acknowledging that you need to work on it. This necessitates clearing a space in which to do so. You may need to find a physical environment free from distractions. You also need psychological space, to give the problem the time and emotional energy it deserves.

Step Two: Assess and Define Your Problem

You may make the following statements of problems.

"I'm bored."

"I'm unhappy."

"I'm lonely."

"I'm shy."

"I can't control my anger."

"My marriage is headed for the rocks."

"I get tense and nervous about tests."

"I'm disorganized and good at procrastinating."

"I suffer from hypertension."

"I'm afraid of having another heart attack."

"I feel dominated by my parents."

All of these statements are descriptive, but none of them offer any "handles" on how you might work for change. In Chapter 2 I stressed the distinction between how you acquired your thinking skills weaknesses and how you sustain them. The former is often phrased as "what others have done to me," the latter "what I do to myself." Assessing your problems entails the detective work of searching for what you do, or fail to do, that sustains your problems. The purpose of assessment is to move from a descriptive statement to a working definition of your problem. A working definition specifies the thinking and action skills weaknesses whereby you sustain your problem or your share of it. We'll take a look at some working definitions after describing how to generate them.

Describing Problems

Once you decide to clear a space and focus on a problem, you need to develop a fuller understanding of it. One way to get such an understanding is to ask yourself questions that elicit specific information about your problem. At this stage you are *describing* your problem. Though the two stages overlap, in the next stage you'll be *explaining* how you sustain your problem.

You can elaborate your initial description of your problem by asking yourself a series of *how* questions. These include the following:

- How would I like to be?
- How long has the problem been going on?
- How severe is it?
- How important is it?
- How frequent is it?
- How do I feel in relation to it?
- How do I think in relation to it?
- How do I act in relation to it?
- How have I attempted to cope with it so far?
- How is my behavior helping or harming me?

To answer some of these "how" questions, you may need to focus systematically on your thoughts and actions. Below are three methods that may help you become more aware of your thoughts about a problem.

• *Thought listing:* Make a list of all the thoughts you have about your problem. If necessary, add to this list daily until you think you have identified most of your more important thoughts.

• *ABC analysis:* Think of a recent problem situation. Use the ABC framework to identify your thoughts, feelings, and actions in relation to this situation.

A. the problem situation (or activating event)
B. your thoughts and visual images about A
C. how you felt and acted in relation to A

You should try to be as specific as possible when describing your thoughts.

• *Double-column technique:* The double-column technique is a method of monitoring, for a specific period, your thoughts about your problem. For example, if your problem is "I can't control my anger," keep a log of times when you were angry. At the top of the left-hand column write "What happened?" and at the top of the right-hand column write "My thoughts." In the left-hand column fill in the dates, approximate times, descriptions of what happened to trigger your anger, and how you behaved. In the right-hand column fill in your thoughts before, during, and after each incident.

THINKSHEET 49

Describing Your Problems More Fully

1. Think of a problem on which you wish to work.
2. Write out your answers to the following questions:
   a. How would I like to be?
   b. How long has the problem been going on?
   c. How severe is it?
   d. How important is it?
   e. How frequent is it?
   f. How do I feel in relation to it?
   g. How do I act in relation to it?
   h. How have I attempted to cope with it so far?
   i. How is my behavior helping or harming me?
3. Review your thinking about the problem using at least one of the following methods:
   a. thought listing
   b. ABC analysis
   c. double-column technique

Explaining How You Sustain Your Problems

Defining problems entails generating and weighing different explanations of how you sustain your problems. The final product is a list of specific skills weaknesses that you can work to change. Skills for *explaining* your contribution to your problems include the following.

- *Gathering information:* In Thinksheet 49 you gathered internal information to describe your problem more fully. You may also seek information from others, such as what they think about the problem and how supportive they are likely to be.
- *Knowing what to look for:* When trying to explain how you sustain your problems, how do you know what to look for? This is a problem for professional helpers as well as for those wishing to help themselves. Professional helpers tend to rely on a mixture of theory, research findings, and professional experience. They then pragmatically adapt this to the needs of individual clients. This book has described many of the thinking skills weaknesses that a professional cognitive psychotherapist might cite to explain your problems, and the checklist in Table 11.1 can remind you of the various thinking skills weaknesses to take into account. Additionally, you can look for action skills weaknesses that sustain your problems. These vary from problem to problem: focus on specific relationship skills weaknesses to improve how you relate and on specific study skills weaknesses to improve how you study.
- *Generating explanations:* You may need to be creative to generate alternative explanations for how you sustain your problems. As with decision making, the first option is frequently not the best. You may need to brainstorm for different options. If so, remember the brainstorming rules: criticism of ideas is ruled out, free-wheeling is welcomed, and quantity is desirable.
- *Weighing explanations:* You need to decide which explanations best suit your particular problem. Which do you think are the most accurate and important? Various considerations are useful in weighing explanations. For instance, your past history in relation to other similar problems may have sensitized you to look for characteristic skills weaknesses. Some explanations may appear to fit the facts better than others. You anticipate that the predicted consequences of certain explanations are more likely to get you what you want than those of other explanations. Or you think that certain explanations will lead to changing your thoughts and actions in ways that suit your abilities better than others.

Stating Working Definitions

A working definition reflects your decisions about how you sustain all or part of your problem. It identifies specific thinking and action skills weaknesses that you can work on. You have now moved beyond description to providing yourself with specific "handles" to guide your attempts to change. Working definitions are based on the best information you have available at the time, and should be open to modification and updating in the light of any new information.

Below are two examples of working definitions.

Angry Al, a middle-aged man with two teenage daughters, had great difficulty controlling his temper. He had recently struck one of his daughters, and was afraid that his inability to control his anger would lead to the breakup of his family. A working definition of Al's anger problem included the following *thinking* skills weaknesses: (1) inadequately acknowledging his responsibility for his thoughts, feelings, and actions;

(2) not using coping self-talk when faced with provocations; (3) having rigid and unrealistic personal rules concerning standards of behavior in the family; and (4) misperceiving and insufficiently acknowledging the connection between how he behaved toward his family and how they behaved toward him. *Action* skills weaknesses that Al needed to work on included poor listening, assertion, and conflict communication skills.

Neil was a shy 22-year-old college student. A working definition of his shyness included the following *thinking* skills weaknesses: (1) using self-talk in social situations in ways that heightened his anxieties; (2) having a self-oppressing personal rule about the need for universal approval and the catastrophe of any sign of rejection; (3) being quick to perceive situations as "put-downs" without asking himself if there were other explanations; and (4) tending to think passively rather than actively about how he might assume responsibility for making things happen in his life. Neil's *action* skills weaknesses included (1) revealing very little of his thoughts and feelings to others; (2) speaking in a very quiet voice; and (3) not using "I" statements.

THINKSHEET 50

Formulating a Working Definition of Your Problem

1. Select a problem on which you wish to work, preferably the one you used for Thinksheet 49.
2. Generate and weigh different explanations of how you sustain your problem. In particular, focus on which thinking skills weaknesses may sustain your problem.
3. State a working definition of your problem that includes at least two thinking skills weaknesses and one action skills weakness.

Step Three: Set Goals and Plan

In step two you attempted to answer the question "How do I sustain the problem?" Given your working definition arrived at in step two, step three focuses on the question "How can I best manage the problem?" Step three consists of two phases: setting working goals and developing a plan.

Setting Working Goals

Goals can be stated broadly: "I want to become less angry" or "I want to become less shy." Though these descriptive statements of goals may provide an overall vision, if you are to work for change you need to state your goals more specifically. Statements of working goals are the reverse or "flip side" of your working definitions of your problems. The following examples transform Al's and Neil's working definitions of their problems into statements of working goals.

Working goals for angry Al include the following *thinking* skills strengths: (1) adequately acknowledging his responsibility for his thoughts, feelings, and actions; (2)

using coping self-talk when faced with provocations; (3) having realistic personal rules concerning standards of behavior in the family; and (4) realistically perceiving how his behavior affects his family's behavior toward him. Al also needed to acquire the *action* skills strengths of good listening, assertion, and conflict communication skills.

Working goals for shy Neil included the following *thinking* skills strengths: (1) using coping self-talk in social situations; (2) having a realistic personal rule concerning approval and acknowledging that, when others seem to reject him, he does not have to reject himself; (3) realistically perceiving others' behavior in social situations; and (4) assuming more responsibility for making things happen in his life. Neil also needed to acquire the *action* skills strengths of (1) greater self-disclosure; (2) speaking in a louder voice; and (3) using "I" statements.

In Chapter 8 I mentioned four characteristics of well-stated goals: they should reflect your values, be realistic, be specific, and give a time frame. Both Al and Neil still lacked a time frame for working on their problems. Both wished to start immediately. Because Al feared the negative consequences of a divorce and family breakup, his goal was to make significant progress in managing his anger by the end of a month. Neil gave himself 3 months to make significant progress in managing his shyness. As they grappled with their problems, Al and Neil found they still needed to spell out their working goals further: for instance, what kind of coping self-talk to use in which anger-evoking or shyness-evoking situations. However, they had sufficient information in their initial statements of working goals to give them a sense of direction. The details could be filled in later.

Developing a Plan

In the previous Chapter I listed six skills useful in planning how to implement a decision; they are also helpful in developing a plan to manage a problem.

- *Clearly state your goals and subgoals.* For instance, Al's overall goal was to become less angry. Each of his working goals might be viewed as subgoals.
- *Break down tasks.* You may need to break down the skills you need to acquire. A simple example is that of breaking down coping self-talk into coaching self-instructions and calming self-instructions.
- *Generate and assess alternative courses of action.* Generating and assessing alternatives tells you how best to attain your thinking and action working goals. You can generate alternative ways of thinking as well as of acting.
- *Anticipate difficulties and setbacks.* You need to acknowledge that difficulties may occur when you implement your plan and also decide how best to cope with them.
- *Identify sources of support.* Sometimes a problem shared is a problem doubled, if not tripled or quadrupled. For instance, someone diagnosed as having AIDS might face all sorts of unwanted reactions if this information were disclosed indiscriminately. Nevertheless, a discriminating identification of sources of support may greatly help you to manage a difficult problem better.
- *Write out your plan.* If a problem is important to you, it very likely merits the time and attention to write out your plan. Written plans can give you clarity of focus and strengthen your commitment.

Keep in mind when developing your plan that you may not be ready to act on certain parts of it right away. Consequently, a seventh skill to master is needed:

- *Build in homework, rehearsal, and practice.* You may acquire a better understanding of the thinking skills weaknesses contributing to your problem if you work through the relevant thinksheets. You can also use visualized rehearsal, in which you rehearse the thinking and action components required for successfully performing a task. Furthermore, you may be able to practice your thinking and action skills on easier problems before moving on to more difficult ones.

When you develop plans, you outline ways of approaching specific problems. Your plans need to take into account the particular circumstances of the problem under attack. Plans need to be both firm and flexible: firm so that you discipline yourself to take appropriate steps to implement them, and flexible so that you are open to realistic feedback. Thinksheet 51 is designed to give you practice in stating working goals and developing a plan to manage a problem.

THINKSHEET 51

Stating Working Goals and Developing a Plan

1. Select a problem on which you wish to work, preferably the problem you used for Thinksheet 50.
2. Translate the working definition of your problem into a statement of working goals.
3. List the negative consequences to yourself and others of not managing your problem effectively.
4. Develop and write out a plan to manage your problem. Focus especially on how to improve specific thinking skills, but also on improving at least one action skill. In developing your plan remember to do the following:
   a. State your goals and subgoals clearly.
   b. Break down tasks.
   c. Generate and assess alternative ways of thinking and courses of action.
   d. Anticipate difficulties and setbacks.
   e. Identify sources of support.
   f. Build in homework, rehearsal, and practice.

As you write out your plan, remember to avoid the twin pitfalls of giving insufficient or too much detail. Ensure that your plan is easy for you to understand and follow.

Step Four: Implement Your Plan

Again, much of what was relevant to implementing decisions is also relevant to implementing plans: paying attention to timing; working through reservations about aspects of your plan; accepting no excuses; being open to feedback; using positive self-reward; and working through the guilt you may feel if you do not adhere to your plan. Altering long-established habits of thinking and behaving can be difficult. Setbacks are to be expected. Your learning may take place in fits and starts. However, if you persist, you may like Al and Neil start reaping the rewards of your changed thinking and behavior. Success can do wonders for commitment.

Step Five: Evaluate the Consequences of Implementation

By stating your working goals clearly, you have given yourself guidelines for monitoring and evaluating the changes in how you think and act. Three important questions to ask yourself are "How well am I using my thinking and action skills?"; "What are the consequences for myself and others of changes in my thinking and action skills?"; and "Do I need to modify my plan in the light of feedback and new information?" Let's return to the example of angry Al: when he thought through the consequences of his changed thinking and actions, he was encouraged to persist in them.

> When Al started being more rational and less aggressive in approaching family problems he thought that he had lost some of his power. He did not like this. However, he evaluated the gains and losses from his changed thinking and acting. He then realized that (1) Sara, the daughter he had struck, was now more understanding and supportive of him; (2) both of his daughters were behaving more considerately at home; (3) his daughters' boyfriends were more friendly to him; (4) the family bonds had definitely been strengthened; and (5) the breakup of his family had been averted. This confirmed Al in continuing to make different and better choices in his family life.

MANAGING SPECIFIC PROBLEMS

So far in this chapter I have provided illustrations of how to use thinking skills to prevent excessive stress and manage anger and shyness. In the remainder of this chapter, I'll try to give you some "handles" for using thinking skills to manage three other common problems: test anxiety, depression, and a relationship conflict. I'll mainly focus on the thinking skills weaknesses by which people sustain these problems. If both the problem and the thinking skills weaknesses seem relevant to you, you may have a "handle" with which to open the door of change.

Managing Test Anxiety

> Angie, 18, was coming to the end of her first year at the university. Throughout the year she had been depressed and anxious each time she was required to take a test. Her marks were near the top of her class, but she still did not think that was good enough. Angie had very little social life. She worked and worked to prove that she was worthy of her parents' sacrifices in supporting her at the university. She found that as the year went on her concentration seemed poorer when she studied. Also, she was increasingly tense during tests. At the start of each test she had to struggle to hold on to her pen

because her hand shook so much. Her mouth went dry, her stomach felt knotted, her mind felt empty, and she feared she might faint.

Most people experience some anxiety when they take a test that is of any importance to them. A certain amount of anxiety tones you up and facilitates your performance. However, as in the case of Angie, too much anxiety can be debilitating, in terms of both discomfort and performance. Let's look for some "handles" for people like Angie to use in working on their test anxiety problems.

- *Am I owning responsibility for the authorship of my life?* Angie may not be fully aware of herself as a chooser. In particular, she may fail to realize that she is always making thinking choices, and that those choices influence how she feels. Angie may have the illusion that she assumes responsibility for the authorship of her life, yet not possess the knowledge and skill to be able to do so effectively.

- *Am I in touch with my underlying feelings?* There is a good chance that Angie is out of touch with her own valuing process, without realizing it. She does not appear to be listening to her needs for recreation and social companionship. Instead she treats herself like a machine. If she continues to do so, she will risk converting burnout into a full-blown breakdown.

- *Am I using self-talk constructively?* Angie could use the calming and coaching elements of coping self-talk to help her take tests. Additionally, coping self-talk might help her study more efficiently. If, when studying for or taking tests, she uses "you" messages like "you fool," she needs to replace them with coping "I" messages.

- *Are my personal rules and directives helping me?* Angie may be making mustabatory demands on herself. She may have these personal rules: "I *must* do extremely well every time I take a test" and "I *must* always obtain my parents' approval." Additionally, she may engage in unnecessary self-rating ("If I do not do well, then I am a worthless person") and catastrophizing ("If I do not do well, there will be an awful catastrophe that I will be unable to handle"). Angie may also have pressurizer directives like "Achieve at all costs," "Be in control," and "Hurry up." She may have some inhibitor directives like "Don't feel," "Don't be sensual," "Don't enjoy yourself," and "Don't take risks."

- *Are my perceptions of myself and others accurate?* Angie needs to explore whether she has a realistic perception of her academic ability. On the one hand she may be trying to reach standards that, without huge sacrifices, are too high for her. On the other hand, she may be an extremely able student whose anxieties and negative self-labeling interfere with her achievement. A logical analysis of the available evidence on her academic strengths and weaknesses should help her perceive herself more accurately. Additionally, Angie needs to test out her perceptions of her parents. They may be proud of her in her own right and not want her to feel under constant pressure to achieve for their sake.

- *Are my attributions of cause accurate?* Angie may be overworking because she makes inaccurate attributions about why she does not do well. For instance, she may think any "failure" on her part is due to lack of effort. If so, she needs to review whether there are better-fit explanations for not performing as well as she would like to in some tests. Such explanations might include insufficient ability, lack of interest in the subject, high anxiety, task difficulty, bad luck, poor teaching, emotional staleness, poor study skills, and poor test-taking skills. Angie may undermine her confidence by viewing the causes of her poor performance as internal and stable and the causes of her good performance as external and transient. In sum, she needs to carefully review her own explanations of the causes of her test anxiety problem.

• *Are my predictions realistic?* Angie may be making unrealistic predictions about the tests she takes. For example, she may be so afraid of doing poorly that it contributes to her predicting that she will not do well, thus getting even more anxious. If she were to acknowledge and assess the evidence, she might alter this prediction. Additionally, she may predict that she cannot cope with not doing well. Again, a realistic assessment of the evidence might indicate otherwise.

• *Am I articulating my goals clearly, and do they reflect my values?* Clearly, one of Angie's goals would be to manage her test anxiety better. If she has not articulated this as a goal, she needs to. Angie may have unrealistic goals about how well she expects to do. She needs to articulate specific and realistic goals for herself. Also, Angie seems to be leading an unbalanced life: she should articulate some social and recreational goals. Possibly, as Angie explores herself and her situation more deeply, she will find that much of her current behavior reflects others' values rather than what she wants for herself.

• *Am I using visualizing to best effect?* The answer is probably "No." Angie appears to imagine herself as behaving incompetently when she takes tests and as unable to cope with poor results. She might use visualizing to clarify her goals and to get in touch with her strengths. Furthermore, she could use visualized rehearsal and practice, including coping self-talk, to prepare for upcoming tests. As part of this, she might engage in goal-directed visualizing, in which she pictures herself taking tests calmly and competently.

This has been an illustrative rather than an exhaustive analysis of how Angie's thinking skills weaknesses might contribute to sustaining her test anxiety problem. Angie may also have to look at specific action skills, such as planning her study time or allocation of time in tests better, to arrive at a full working definition of her problem. Once she has confronted her problem and adequately assessed and defined it, she has laid a sound foundation to work for change.

Managing Feelings of Depression

Pete, 42, was fired from the foreman's job he had held for 6 years when the small electronics company he worked for was taken over. He was devastated. Secretly he blamed himself for his ill fortune. He felt anxious, worthless, and depressed. He kept going over in his mind how, if he had acted differently, he might have held on to his job. Pete was eating and sleeping badly. He moped around the house a lot, watched too much television, and started drinking more than he used to. His interest in sex declined. He hated being dependent on his wife, Ellie, to be the main breadwinner in the family. He thought his teenage children, Hugh and Jenny, did not understand how hurt he was and blamed them for their insensitivity. Pete wallowed in self-pity. He applied for a few jobs unsuccessfully. After a couple of months, he came to the conclusion that he was too old to ever get a good job again. The future seemed hopeless.

Pete's vulnerability to depression was exposed when he received a hard knock. His vulnerability comprised many thinking skills weaknesses that were activated by adverse circumstances. Pete was not mentally ill; he was merely confronting what numerous others have faced, too: the challenge of coming to terms with an unpredictable economic world. Let us look for some possible "handles" for Pete to use in working on his depression.

- *Am I owning responsibility for the authorship of my life?* Pete does not appear to have a clear sense of his responsibility for making the choices that support rather than oppress him. He does not seem aware that if he works on his thinking choices he can alter how he feels. Some of Pete's behavior indicates that, under high stress, he is becoming less rather than more responsible for his life, evidenced for instance by his passive TV watching.
- *Am I in touch with my underlying feelings?* Unemployment can be a frightening experience that cuts to the core of people's anxieties about existential isolation and being unable to survive. Pete appears to be in touch with some of those feelings. However, he does not appear to be fully in touch with his underlying drive to actualize his potential. There are opportunities for him in being fired, as well as drawbacks. If he listens to himself carefully he may find that he wants to change the nature of his work. Other areas of feeling of which Pete does not seem fully aware include his competence as a worker and his affection for his family.
- *Am I using self-talk constructively?* Possibly Pete puts himself down with "you" messages like "you idiot" and "you useless fool." Additionally, Pete may be talking himself into rather than out of depression. He may oppress himself with statements like "I'm not going to be able to set my life straight." He needs to use coping self-talk like "Calm down. Relax. Break down the tasks of getting a job and of handling unemployment. I can manage it if I hang in there."
- *Are my personal rules and directives helping me?* Pete appears to make a number of mustabatory demands on himself, others, and the environment, including the following.

"I *must* always be employed."

"I *must* never make mistakes at work."

"As a male I *must* always be the breadwinner."

"My children *must* always understand my difficulties."

"The environment *must* never do things to me that might cause me to feel uncomfortable."

Pete's feelings of depression are partly caused by negatively rating himself as a *person* when he, others, and/or the environment do not live up to his personal rules.

- *Are my perceptions of myself and others accurate?* Possibly Pete engages in negative self-labeling in which he dwells on his imagined weaknesses. He does not seem to be listing and affirming his resources. Pete may also be jumping to conclusions unfavorable to himself in his relationships with others. For instance, he may misperceive his children's behavior as unsupportive when, in reality, they sympathize with his position but lack the skills to show it. Pete also may exhibit perceptual errors like overgeneralizing ("The fact that I was turned down for some jobs means that I will always be turned down"), black-and-white thinking ("Either people are all for me or they are against me"), and tunnel vision ("I can only look for jobs that are just like my previous one").

• *Are my attributions of cause accurate?* Pete may unrealistically blame himself for being fired. He may be taking more responsibility for his failures than for his successes. Additionally, he may misunderstand the causes of his not getting work immediately. For instance, Pete attributes his inability to find work to his age when there may be numerous other explanations: poor information-gathering skills, living in an economically depressed area, lack of effort, out-of-date skills, and so on. Additionally, Pete appears to be waiting for his employment situation to change so that he can feel better at home. If he attributed the cause of some of his depression to his failure to use his spare time creatively, he might be in a better position to do something about it.

• *Are my predictions realistic?* Pete seems to predict that whatever he does will not improve matters. He needs to carefully review the evidence for this counsel of despair. His belief that the future is hopeless ignores his own potential, despite adverse circumstances, to create much of his future.

• *Am I articulating my goals clearly, and do they reflect my values?* Probably Pete has not thought out a clear statement of his work, family, and leisure goals. His seeming uncertainty about his underlying values and self-worth makes it harder for him to both articulate and adhere to goals. For the moment, he's allowing himself to be the victim of fate.

• *Am I using visualizing to best effect?* Pete could use visualizing to support himself in many areas. He could get a clearer picture of his goals and strengths. He could visually rehearse and practice upcoming job interviews. He could use visualizing to deepen his understanding of how his family sees his behavior. Visualizing restful scenes might be a useful self-help skill to cope with his anxieties. Additionally, visualizing himself coping with "worst-case scenarios" and imagining himself living successfully at a date in the future, say in 12 months, might enhance his confidence and motivation.

The search for Pete's possible thinking skills weaknesses has not been exhaustive; nevertheless, it turned up some thinking skills "handles" that would allow Pete to open the door of working for change. Pete would also need to review the adequacy of his action skills; how to search for jobs, use leisure time effectively, and better relate to his family.

Managing a Relationship Conflict

After 21 years, Liz and Harry's marriage was headed for the rocks. They had two children, Nick, 19, and Karen, 16. Harry thought that Liz was very critical of him as a husband, lover, father, and businessman. Liz had previously suspected and recently found out that Harry was having an affair with Martha. Whereas Harry saw Liz as uptight and angry, he experienced Martha as much less inhibited. Harry thought that he loved two people, and felt great inner conflict about what he was doing. Liz intensely disliked Harry's affair. Though she contemplated divorce, she held off for three main reasons: her love for Harry, her insecurity about making it on her own, and her hope that he might honor his commitment to her by giving up Martha. Though at each other's throats much of the time, Liz and Harry still had good times together. They enjoyed going camping, spending time with their children, and having sex. Liz had worked for the last 10 years as secretary and bookkeeper in their jointly owned company that Harry managed. However, by mutual agreement, she recently left this job. She now worked as a receptionist in a law firm. Liz and Harry went to a counselor to discuss how to save their marriage.

Harry had been referred for counseling by a minister who was concerned about the potential breakup of his family. The counselor started by having a few individual sessions with Harry and then some joint sessions with both. Harry was pleasant, but not heavily invested in the process. When Liz first came for counseling she was extremely nervous. However, she was prepared to work and thought she would gain from counseling whether or not she stayed married. Consequently, with Harry's agreement, Liz decided to come for individual sessions with the option of joint sessions when it seemed desirable to both. Liz was the more psychologically accessible of the two. In this instance, the most likely solution to the relationship conflict seemed to lie in Liz altering her thinking and behavior. This might make it easier for Harry to change and to recommit himself to their relationship. Let us now search for some thinking skills "handles" to help Liz work for change.

• *Am I owning responsibility for authorship of my life?* Liz and Harry both thought they related to each other in programmed ways that were frequently unhelpful. They had not fully acknowledged their capacity to be choosers of how they thought, felt, and acted. Liz's behavior indicated some flexibility in being prepared to make the choices that would work for her. First, when she found out about Harry's affair, she realized she had a *choice* about whether to end the relationship. Second, despite her hating his affair, she was prepared to try the personal experiment of changing her thinking and behavior in the hope that it would achieve her goal of changing Harry.

• *Am I in touch with my underlying feelings?* Liz had received a strict upbringing, especially from her martinet of a father; for instance, she was allowed to touch only the handle when she closed a door. As a result, she now insufficiently acknowledged her feelings of strength and competence and allowed herself to be overcome by feelings of powerlessness and inadequacy. Feeling bad about herself made her much more prone to feeling bad about Harry. Along with this went an insufficient sense of her own identity. She found it difficult to acknowledge her needs and to want to do things for herself. Liz felt she was primarily an appendage of others.

• *Am I using self-talk constructively?* Liz used self-talk in ways that heightened her feelings of anxiety and powerlessness. Instead of trying to calm down and make her points, she talked herself into feeling small and then overreacted by screaming and scratching. She later regretted this behavior. One of the ways in which she talked herself into feeling vulnerable was to tell herself that she couldn't cope on her own without Harry.

• *Are my personal rules and directives helping me?* Liz had a number of mustabatory personal rules that exposed her to self-denigration. They included "I *must* be approved of all the time"; "I *must* be superwoman in the home and meet everybody else's needs"; "My husband *must* always know what my needs are without my telling him"; and, though not all the time, "When Harry and I have a problem in our relationship we *must* compete with each other to find out who is right." Liz also oppressed herself with a number of inhibitor directives such as "Don't think," "Don't be different," and "Don't take risks."

• *Are my perceptions of myself and others accurate?* Both Liz and Harry admitted how quick they were to take offense at each other's behavior. Rather than giving the benefit of the doubt, they watched for slights and malevolent intentions. Liz was a mistress of negative self-labeling and putting herself down. Though sometimes she acknowledged her strengths and resources, she attached insufficient importance to them. Liz also tended to perceive Harry more negatively than was warranted. When they were working on improving their relationship, Harry asked Liz to list the things she found positive about him. He did not expect much. Both Liz and Harry were amazed by how long the list was. Liz realized that she had previously not fully acknowledged much of her appreciation, let alone communicated it. Harry was also blocked in his ability to give positive feedback.

• *Are my attributions of cause accurate?* On one level Liz blamed Harry for both causing and sustaining their marital conflict through his relationship with Martha. On another, she had deep doubts about her adequacy as a wife and, without knowing what to do, blamed herself for his affair. As she worked on the problem she realized that, what ever the *past* causes of Harry's affair, she had some power to influence *future* events in her favor. Increasingly she changed her attribution of cause from "Poor me, I am the victim of my husband, of this scheming woman Martha, and of my own inadequacies" to "I can play to win and achieve my goals by altering some of the ways I think and behave. Even if Harry and I do not manage to repair our relationship, I can still make a success of my life."

• *Are my predictions realistic?* Trusting a person requires confidence that they will behave in a trustworthy fashion. Harry's affair seriously undermined Liz's trust in his commitment to their relationship. He said he wanted their relationship to work, but was reluctant to give up seeing Martha. Liz now needed to assess not so much what Harry said as how he acted, to predict if she could trust him again. Harry was starting to become much more attentive to her, including penning a first-ever poem on her birthday. Also, Liz had some inconclusive evidence, such as Harry's coming home earlier, that he might be withdrawing from the affair with Martha. As Liz began to succeed in and enjoy her new employment away from Harry's business, she realized that her predictions of catastrophe if she were to be divorced were inaccurate. Her exaggerated fears of the consequences of abandonment had contributed to her high anxiety and tendencies to overreact.

• *Am I articulating my goals clearly, and do they reflect my values?* Liz had a much clearer idea of where she wanted to be in 5 years than Harry did. She had a strong commitment to and liking for family life. To maintain this was her first priority, but not to do so at any cost. Liz was moving toward a decision that if, despite her own best efforts, Harry did not give up Martha, she would reevaluate her goals and perhaps seek a divorce.

• *Am I using visualizing to best effect?* Liz was tense much of the time. Independent of counseling, she had started to use visualizing to relax herself. Liz had a reasonably clear vision of her goals. However, she could profit from using visualizing to rehearse and practice coping with difficult situations in a more goal-oriented fashion: for instance, when feeling criticized by Harry.

This is an abbreviated and simplified account of how Liz was able to identify some thinking choice "handles" that enabled her to work for change. As did Angie and Pete, Liz needed to review certain action skills: for instance, how she communicated with Harry in their fights and how to give positive and not mainly negative feedback. Liz had the courage, even though she thought Harry was at fault, to try changing her thinking and behavior in order to give him the opportunity to change his. Love has many faces.

Thinksheet 52 is designed to give you further practice at thinking through a problem.

THINKSHEET 52
Thinking Through a Problem

1. Select a problem that you have not used for previous thinksheets.
2. Describe the facts of your problem more fully.
3. Using the checklist in Table 11.1, conduct a thorough search for thinking skill "handles" to help explain how you may sustain your problem.
4. Formulate a working definition of your problem, focused mainly on thinking skills weaknesses but containing at least one action skills weakness.
5. Translate your working definition into working goals.
6. Write out a realistic plan for managing your problem better.

CHAPTER HIGHLIGHTS

Prevention is better than cure: effective thinking skills may make you less predisposed to problems as well as help you prevent those that are avoidable.

Whatever their origins, you have choices about how you manage your problems.

CASIE is a five-step framework for managing your problems: Confront, Assess and define, Set goals and plan, Implement, and Evaluate.

In assessing and defining your problem, your objective is to move from description to a working definition that identifies specific "handles" that enable you to work for change.

As well as identifying thinking skills weaknesses, your working definitions should
identify action skills weaknesses that sustain your problem.

When searching for "handles" to help you either prevent or manage problems better,
review the following thinking skills areas: taking responsibility for the authorship
of your life; being in touch with your feelings; using self-talk constructively;
having helpful personal rules and directives; perceiving self and others accurately;
making accurate attributions of cause; making realistic predictions; setting clear
goals; and using visualizing effectively.

Translate your working definitions of problems into statements of working goals.

When problems are important to you, time spent thinking them through and planning
how to manage them is likely to be time well spent.

CHAPTER 12

The Courage to Think for Yourself

The buck stops here.

Harry S Truman

I have nothing to offer but blood, toil, tears and sweat.

Sir Winston Churchill

Having now read about the many thinking skills for preventing and managing problems, you may feel like the centipede who came to grief because of too much thinking about which leg came after which. However, I encourage you to persist in working on your thinking skills. Hopefully, like the skills you use when driving a car, in time you will be able to use them without great self-consciousness. The *price* of having effective thinking skills with which to prevent and manage problems is eternal vigilance. Once acquired, skills need to be maintained and developed. You are constantly challenged to renew and recreate them. The *prize* of using effective thinking skills is that you are likely to realize much more of your human potential. You should spend less time and energy on the hassles of life and more on activities and relationships that you find fulfilling.

MONITORING YOUR THINKING SKILLS

Effective thinking about your problems and decisions requires that you keep monitoring your thinking choices. Some of this will be done as you think on your feet. On other occasions, you either may pause for reflection or clear a longer space to think through a problem. Also, there is a case to be made for periodically reviewing your thinking skills. As with servicing your car, there may not be anything obviously wrong, but time on upkeep and prevention is well spent.

Thinksheet 53 is a questionnaire designed to help you to systematically review your thinking skills. I suggest that you answer it now, after reading this book and completing many, if not all, of the thinksheets. Thinksheet 53 can also be used to monitor your thinking skills at points in the future.

-------------------- **THINKSHEET 53** --------------------

Monitoring Your Thinking Skills

Using the scale below, rate how satisfied you are with your skills in each of the following areas of thinking.

3   great need for improvement
2   moderate need for improvement
1   slight need for improvement
0   no need for improvement

Your Rating   **Skills**
Learning How Not to Think

_____   understanding the influence of my parents on how I prevent and manage problems

_____   having an adequate conceptual framework with which to think through problems

_____   understanding the influence of high anxiety on my thinking

_____   having insight into how I may sustain my deficient thinking skills

Owning Responsibility for Choosing

_____   being aware that I am always a chooser in my life

_____   acknowledging personal responsibility for the authorship of my life

_____   being fully aware of the finality of death and transient nature of life

_____   being aware of my significant physical sensations

_____   being able to get in touch with my feelings

Using Self-Talk

_____   using "I" self-talk that "owns" my thoughts, feelings, and actions

_____   being able to identify my negative self-talk

_____   using calming self-talk

_____   using coaching self-talk

_____   combining calming and coaching self-talk into coping self-talk

Choosing My Personal Rules

_____   being aware of my self-oppressing personal rules

_____   disputing and reformulating my self-oppressing personal rules

_____   being aware of my self-oppressing pressurizer and inhibitor directives

_____   challenging and changing my self-oppressing directives

_____   listening to and living up to my conscience

Choosing How I Perceive

_____   monitoring and recording my upsetting perceptions

_____   identifying my perceptual errors

_____   generating and evaluating different perceptions

_____   reality-testing my perceptions by conducting appropriate personal experiments

_____   being aware of my negative self-labels

_____   searching for and affirming my resources

_____   being aware of my main defensive processes

_____   letting go of my defensive processes

_____   being aware that on occasion I may not perceive others realistically

_____   being able to correct my errors to perceive others realistically

Attributing Cause

_____   being aware of my misattributions about the causes of my personal problems

_____   being able to acknowledge accurately how I contribute to my personal problems

_____   being accurate about how I attribute cause for positive and negative events

_____   being accurate in how I attribute cause for my academic or work successes and failures

Predicting and Creating My Future

_____   making accurate predictions of risk

_____   making accurate predictions of reward

_____   knowing what my values are

_____   having clear short-term, medium-term, and long-term goals

Visualizing with My Mind's Eye

_____   being aware of the power of visualizing

_____   using visualizing to relax

_____   using visualizing to manage anxiety

_____   visualizing positive images to counteract negative feelings

(continued)

THINKSHEET 53 (continued)

_____	using visualizing to perform specific tasks better
_____	using visualizing to clarify my goals
_____	using visualizing to enhance my relationships
_____	using visualizing to avoid the negative consequences of giving in to temptation

Making Decisions

_____	being aware of any self-oppressing decision-making styles I possess
_____	knowing how to make rational decisions
_____	generating options and gathering information
_____	assessing the consequences of decision options
_____	being able to commit myself to a specific decision
_____	planning the implementation of decisions
_____	evaluating the actual consequences of my decisions
_____	being aware of thinking skills weaknesses that interfere with the quality of my decision making

Preventing and Managing Problems

_____	using my thinking skills to prevent avoidable problems
_____	confronting my problems
_____	fully describing problems that I want to work on
_____	searching for thinking skills "handles" on how I contribute to sustaining my problems
_____	formulating working definitions of my problems
_____	stating working goals to manage problems
_____	developing a plan to attain my working goals
_____	evaluating my progress in managing my problems

Staying in Control of My Thinking

_____	monitoring the adequacy of my thinking skills
_____	having assertion skills
_____	developing my thinking skills
_____	having the courage to think for myself

On the basis of your responses to the above questionnaire, write out a summary statement of your thinking skills strengths and weaknesses. Then set yourself specific goals for developing your thinking skills.

MAINTAINING YOUR THINKING SKILLS

How can you maintain your thinking skills? Effective thinking about your problems and decisions of living requires courage, inner strength, and resilience. Human beings live in webs of fears and anxieties; you need courage to confront those fears. You need to face up to and work on self-oppressing aspects of your thinking, however insidious they may be. Also, you require the courage to think for and define yourself, despite the fears and relationship skills weaknesses of those who prefer to define you on their own terms. In brief, you need to assert yourself both inwardly and outwardly.

Inner Assertion

Inner assertion means acknowledging and working on those aspects of your inner self that weaken your effectiveness. It entails delving behind your public mask to struggle with the fears, insecurities, and anxieties that diminish you. It involves grappling with "the enemy within" so as to avoid being your own worst enemy.

There is no simple answer to how you can find the inner strength to stay in control of your thinking. However, here is some self-talk that may encourage you to persist in asserting the constructive rather than the destructive tendencies within you.

- *"Good thinking skills require a daily struggle."* You are born with the potential for both effective and ineffective thinking. Even people you consider to be outstandingly successful in managing their lives constantly have to strive to control their thinking. There is no easy way out. Human happiness and fulfillment comes from finding meaning in striving, not from the absence of challenge.
- *"Nobody's perfect."* Vulnerability and fallibility are universal human characteristics. You may weaken yourself by possessing a mustabatory personal rule about your own need for perfection. Awareness of your vulnerability, though often painful, may be a sign of strength rather than of weakness. Weak people lack the courage to admit their fallibility. When possible, be a friend to yourself and confront your thinking skills weaknesses—not in a spirit of self-blame, but as a chance to change them for the better.
- *"Changing my thinking skills may be difficult."* Though it's not always the case, choosing to change how you think may be a long, hard process. You risk weakening your resolve if you always expect it to be easy. By the time you decide to change, you probably have a long learning history of acquiring and sustaining your weaknesses. Ellis (1987) observes that many people sabotage themselves by thinking that changes *should* be quicker, more profound, easier, and more continuous and "so they settle for moderate rather than elegant emotional health" [p. 368].
- *"Maintaining my thinking skills involves practice."* Like many skills such as playing a musical instrument or sport, maintaining your thinking skills takes practice. Life is so full of problems and decisions that opportunities for practice are not hard to find; consciously use those opportunities to practice your skills. When faced with problems and decisions, remember the self-instruction: "Stop...Think...what are my thinking choices?"

- *"Using my thinking skills helps me."* You are more likely to persist in using your thinking skills if you perceive them as bringing rewards. If you doubt whether it is worth the struggle of maintaining your thinking skills, ask yourself the following questions: "What are the costs and consequences of maintaining my thinking skills?" "What are the costs and consequences of thinking like I used to?" Assuming that you genuinely do think more effectively, you are likely to find that many more positive than negative consequences follow from maintaining your thinking skills. Self-support rewards; self-oppression hurts.

Many people find they are better able to discipline their thinking if they make commitments that transcend what William James has called their "convulsive little ego" (Gardner, 1965, p. 96). These commitments may be to loved ones, to sources of meaning in work and leisure, to helping others, to political or social change, or to a religious faith. The existential position emphasizes that humans are meaning-seeking animals. Good thinking skills are likely to help you to both find and renew meaning in your life. This, in turn, contributes to your willingness and confidence to apply your thinking skills.

Outer Assertion

Tell the truth and you will get your head bashed in.

Hungarian proverb

Though having thoughts is a private activity, expressing your thoughts is a public or social activity. The distinction is not this simple, of course, because you may develop some of your best private thoughts in conjunction with others. Also, others may threaten you to the point at which you inhibit some of your private thoughts. In this context, outer assertion means having the courage to assert what you think to others without counterproductive inhibition or aggression. You need to counteract negative messages not only to yourself but also from others that interfere with your thinking. Numerous books have been written about assertion skills (for example, Alberti & Emmons, 1986; Bower & Bower, 1976; Butler, 1981b; Steiner, 1981). Here my goal is simply to alert you to the importance of using good assertion skills when expressing your thoughts. Also, I indicate some of the ways in which others, intentionally or otherwise, may try to "dethink" you. You will want to look elsewhere for more detailed discussions of assertion skills.

Stating What You Think

Good skills for stating what you think include inner assertion—overcoming your mental barriers—as well as outer assertion—sending clear verbal, vocal, and bodily messages to others. You seek to avoid the dangers of inhibition, or "bottling it up," and of either direct aggression—"going over the top"—or indirect aggression—"letting it come out sideways." Though you can choose to control your own behavior, at most you can only influence how others behave. Consequently, though stating what you think assertively may increase the probability of your relating well to others, this cannot be guaranteed.

Some of the main skills of assertively stating what you think are as follows.

• *Inner assertion skills:* You may need to work on thoughts that restrict your freedom of choice for defining and asserting yourself. These self-oppressing thoughts include demands on yourself ("I must be nice." "I must be liked." "I must avoid conflict."), fears about others' reactions ("Others might reject me." "Others might criticize me." "Others might think me unfeminine."), and fears about your reactions to others' reactions ("I can't handle conflict." "I can't handle rejection." "I can't handle causing pain.").

• *Verbal skills:* The words that you use to express your thoughts need to be simple and clear. Also, they need to be stated as "I" messages, indicating your ownership of your thoughts.

• *Vocal skills:* These are the messages that you send with your voice qualities: loudness, pace, stress, and enunciation. When stating your thoughts assertively you want to avoid being perceived as either weak or unnecessarily threatening. Therefore, speak so you can be heard easily, at a pace that is comfortable to follow, with a firmness appropriate to your message, and with clear enunciation.

• *Body skills:* Your body language needs to match your verbal and vocal messages. Avoid signs of weakness, such as an absence of eye contact, and of unnecessary threat, such as repeatedly jabbing your finger at another. Aim for eye contact, facial expression, gestures, and posture that appropriately support you in communicating what you think.

Counteracting Dethinking Messages

In many ways people may try to influence you not to think for yourself. These negative messages are also verbal, vocal, and bodily ones. Frequently they reflect the insecurities of those with whom you talk. What you say may challenge their picture of themselves and of you. They then "export" their fears and insecurities by threatening you. However, as anyone who has unwittingly allowed himself or herself to be seduced knows, positive messages may also dethink you.

Here is a list of some of the ways in which others may interfere with your thinking. These *dethinking messages* include the following.

• *Advising:* conveying "I know what is best for you."
• *Blaming:* put simply, "It's all your fault."
• *Distracting:* changing the subject; fidgeting
• *Flattering:* trying to hook you by conveying "Gee, you're the greatest thing since sliced bread."
• *Intellectualizing:* using the intellect to talk around rather than to the point
• *Intimidating:* psychologically or physically threatening you
• *Labeling:* telling you how you are whether you want to be that way or not: for instance, "Jane doesn't mind when I tease her, do you Jane?"
• *Playing stupid:* deliberately seeming not to understand you

- *Playing the victim:* inducing you to feel guilty through passive aggression: for instance, "I'm so disappointed with you."
- *Setting rules:* defining the rules for handling a situation in ways unfavorable to you: for instance, "Children don't talk back to their parents."
- *Talking down:* being treated by another as inferior for reasons that may include your age, size, position in the family, gender, color, status, financial position, and so on

This is only a partial list of manipulations and power plays. Furthermore, it does not illustrate the many vocal and bodily messages that others can use to interfere with your thinking. All these dethinking messages are "put-downs" of you, of varying degrees of subtlety. They show a lack of respect for your right to express your opinions in an open and honest way. Also, they may insidiously block your inner thinking in ways that alienate you from yourself.

How can you counteract attempts to interfere with your thinking? It can be very difficult, especially when there are big discrepancies of power in the relationship; for instance, between parents and dependent children or between bosses and employees. If possible, you can avoid threatening people unnecessarily, so that they will be less likely to adopt dethinking tactics. Preventive assertion skills include using honest positives and making initial statements assertively.

- *Using honest positives:* Kassorla (1984) uses the term *honest positives* for positive feedback that you can honestly give to others. You may build up an emotional climate in which you are more likely to be listened to if you use this skill. Honest positives can be used before, during, and after a problem involving another person.

- *Making initial statements assertively:* Aggressively stating your opinion sets you up for someone to use dethinking tactics on you. The world is full of easily threatened people who are only too ready to punish themselves and you. This may happen anyway if you assertively state your opinions. However, why trigger others' defenses unnecessarily by being aggressive? Recognize the distinction between aggression and assertion.

A number of other skills can be used once you are actually confronted with dethinking tactics.

- *Being aware:* Awareness of others' manipulative tendencies implies a realistic appraisal of their behavior. Two extremes to avoid are paranoia, imagining dethinking tactics when they are not being used, and Pollyannaism, being blind to dethinking tactics when they are used. If you are aware that others are manipulating you, you can then choose how to respond.

- *Calmly persisting in asserting what you think:* You may choose to keep asserting what you think at the same time that you show you have understood another's position. Others may try to power-play you because they expect you to give in. However, by having the courage of your convictions you may be able to get them to accept your thinking. Even if they do not, you are likely to feel better about yourself. This is true because you have both stated your thoughts and done so assertively rather than aggressively.

• *Confronting others with how you perceive their behavior:* One option, if you think someone is trying to prevent you from doing your own thinking, is to point it out to them. Again, success cannot be guaranteed, but doing this assertively may help the way you feel about yourself.

• *Using handling feedback skills:* You have a range of other skills to use if you sense someone is using dethinking tactics on you. At the simplest level you can assess whether the issue is worth bothering about, count to ten, relax yourself by regulating your breathing and using calming self-talk, or back off. You may also choose to gather more information about why he or she reacts negatively to your thoughts, clear up misperceptions and misunderstandings, agree to disagree, or try to work on the conflict between you. If all else fails, you may choose to seek more congenial company.

───────────────── **THINKSHEET 54** ─────────────────

Maintaining Your Thinking Skills

1. *Inner assertion*
   a. Write down the main ways in which you think you are in danger of not maintaining your thinking skills through deficient inner assertion.
   b. Set yourself goals and develop a plan to combat these inner self-sabotaging tendencies.
2. *Outer assertion*
   a. To what extent do you think you have the courage to express your thoughts to others?
   b. Assess the extent to which you possess and use assertion skills.
   c. To what extent and in what ways do you think you allow others, by using dethinking tactics, to interfere with your thinking?
   d. Set yourself goals and develop a plan to counter any weaknesses you may have in assertively expressing your thoughts.

DEVELOPING YOUR THINKING SKILLS

The previous sections on monitoring and maintaining your thinking skills also apply to developing them. Below are some additional suggestions.

• *Working with another person:* You may choose to work with another person on a regular basis to improve the thinking skills of both. If you are in a relationship, this other person may be your partner. One approach is for each of you to be available to support and help the other as and when you wish to think through a problem or decision. Another approach is to meet on a regular basis for, say, an hour a week. There are many ways in which you can divide the time; the point is for each of you to have "air time" in which you can explore and work on your problems and decisions with the help of the other.

• *Developing a support network:* You can develop a support network of trusted people to whom you can turn when thinking through your problems and decisions: relatives, friends, work colleagues, ministers, helping service professionals, and others. When possible, they should have some insight into how people oppress rather than support themselves through ineffective thinking. Additionally, they should be able to help you to do your own thinking rather than do it for you. As well as receiving help, you may develop your own thinking skills by offering help to other members of your support network.

• *Peer support groups:* You may choose to meet on a regular basis with a group of congenial people to work on your thinking skills. Here you have many people to give you support and feedback, and, if there are effective thinkers in your group, you can learn from observing how they think through their problems. Alternatively, within the context of a particular focus, you can work on the thinking skills pertinent to the group's main task. Such peer support groups might focus on bereavement, living with spouses with Alzheimer's disease, being homosexual, overcoming alcohol or drug addiction, or many other concerns.

• *Workshops and training courses:* Interest in and acknowledgment of the importance of thinking skills is rapidly increasing among helping service professionals and academics. Consequently, there is a growth in the availability of thinking skills training courses and workshops. Ways to find out about such courses and workshops include looking in papers and journals; contacting educational institutions, personnel offices, counseling services, and helping service agencies; and getting in touch with professional associations in psychology, counseling, and social work. However, let the buyer beware! Before joining any training course or workshop, make inquiries about its goals and training methods, the training and experience of the people running it, how large the group will be, the frequency and duration of the sessions, and what fees are required. Since acquiring, maintaining, and developing your thinking skills demands a lot of work and practice, courses offering miracle cures should be avoided.

• *Counseling and psychotherapy:* Counseling and psychotherapy are terms that tend to be used interchangeably. Some of you may think you need the service of a professional therapist to help you think through your problems and decisions more effectively. Therapists operate in different ways, and many therapeutic approaches do not focus primarily on how people think. The term *cognitive approach* is the professional jargon for therapy that focuses on a client's thinking. There is no single preeminent cognitive approach, but rather a range of cognitive therapies. If you wish to find a therapist whose work is roughly in accord with the philosophy of this book, look for someone who emphasizes helping you take more effective responsibility for your life by making better thinking, feeling, and action choices. Be prepared to shop around for a therapist with whom you will be comfortable—but not too comfortable! Good therapy includes being challenged within the context of a caring and supportive relationship.

Group therapy may be appropriate for some of you instead of, concurrently with, or after individual work. Therapy groups tend to have a leader and six to ten members. Their length and the duration of their sessions vary: for instance, 2-hour sessions may be held weekly for 6 months. Therapy groups, with their smaller memberships, provide a more intense opportunity for working on your thinking skills than that found in many training courses and workshops.

You may not be immediately aware of a therapist you can try. As with training courses and workshops, inquiries to helping service agencies, professionals, and professional associations may bear fruit. Additionally, many therapists list their services in the phone book. Again, the message is buyer beware.

• *Thinking skills reading:* Though it is no substitute for practice, you can learn much about thinking skills from reading relevant books and articles. In the bibliography at the end of this book I have starred books likely to be of interest to nonprofessional readers.

─────────────────── **THINKSHEET 55** ───────────────────

Developing Your Thinking Skills

At the end of Thinksheet 53 you were asked to write out a summary statement of your thinking skills strengths and weaknesses for preventing and managing problems and making decisions. You were then asked to set yourself specific goals for developing your thinking skills. There are many different ways to develop your skills, including the following:

• inner assertion
• outer assertion
• working with another person
• developing a support network
• peer support groups
• training courses and workshops
• individual and/or group therapy
• thinking skills reading

Make a plan for developing at least one of your thinking skills. Write out as specifically as you can the following:

• your goals
• the methods you intend to use to achieve each goal
• a realistic time schedule
• how you intend to monitor and evaluate your progress

───

HAVING THE COURAGE TO THINK FOR YOURSELF

Life only demands from you
the strength you possess. Only one feat is possible—not to have run away.

Dag Hammarskjöld

The thinking skills described in this book do not require intelligence so much as courage and integrity. Based on his experience in Nazi concentration camps, Frankl (1959) concluded, "From all this we may learn that there are two races of men in this world, but only these two—the 'race' of the decent man and the 'race' of the indecent man" [p. 137]. Another way of phrasing this is that humans fall into two broad categories: those who are aware of the fallibility of their thinking and strive to think rationally, and those who are psychologically toxic because they do not.

Those who strive to think rationally have some insight into their vulnerability as human beings. They seek to affirm themselves without damaging others. They attach as much, if not more, importance to giving as they do to receiving. They are committed to meaningful activities. Those afraid to think rationally are preoccupied with themselves. They are, psychologically, children who lack the courage to admit their vulnerability when faced with problems and decisions. Much of their thinking seeks to avoid rather than assume personal responsibility for their lives. Lacking insight and self-respect, they may seek to damage others by attacking them if they do not support their fantasies about themselves.

Most people fall at some point between these two extremes. However, lying beyond the problem of preventing and managing problems is the problem of personal excellence. This is a problem that faces people whatever their gender, socioeconomic status, or race. It is not a matter of an outer achievement, but of the inner achievement of continuously striving to think constructively. You have the courage to choose to assert your inner freedom to think for yourself. You do not demand perfection and you do not run away.

Where do you stand? Having the courage to think for yourself means a lifelong commitment. It is one thing to read about thinking skills and another to apply them conscientiously in your daily life, even when nobody's looking. The world is a beautiful place filled with a lot of ugliness. If the human race is going to fulfill its potential, more and more people will have to commit themselves to the inner struggle to think for themselves. As the Berkeley, California, street poster of the 1960s said, "To make a better world, make yourself a better person."

CHAPTER HIGHLIGHTS

Monitoring your thinking skills can help you to identify and work on skills weaknesses.
Maintaining your thinking skills requires inner assertion—confronting your own fears
    and anxieties—and outer assertion—being able assertively to express your
    thoughts despite others' fears and anxieties.
In many ways, others may try to interfere with your thinking, or "dethink" you.
Skills for counteracting dethinking tactics include (1) using honest positives, (2) mak-
    ing initial statements assertively, (3) being aware of when you are being manipu-
    lated, (4) calmly persisting in asserting what you think, (5) confronting others
    with how you perceive their behavior, and (6) using handling feedback skills.
Ways of developing your thinking skills include working with another person, devel-

oping a support network, peer support groups, training courses and workshops, counseling and psychotherapy, and reading about thinking skills.

Thinking skills for facing problems and decisions require courage and integrity more than intelligence.

Having the courage to think for yourself is a lifelong commitment.

Bibliography

References likely to be of special interest to the self-help reader are indicated with an asterisk.

Abramson, L. Y., Seligman, M. E. P., & Teasdale, J. D. (1978). Learned helplessness in humans; Critique and reformulation. *Journal of Abnormal Psychology,
87,* 49–74.

*Alberti, R. E., & Emmons, M. L. (1986). *Your perfect right: A guide to assertive
living* (5th ed.). San Luis Obispo, Calif.: Impact Press.

Argyle, N. (1988). The nature of cognitions in panic disorder. *Behaviour Research
& Therapy, 26*(3), 261–264.

Arroba, T. (1977). Styles of decision making and their use: An empirical study.
British Journal of Guidance & Counselling, 5(2), 149–158.

Bandura, A. (1977). *Social learning theory.* Englewood Cliffs, N.J.: Prentice-Hall.

*Barnard, M. E. (1986). *Staying rational in an irrational world.* Melbourne:
McCulloch Publishing.

*Beck, A. T. (1976). *Cognitive therapy and the emotional disorders.* New York:
New American Library.

Beck, A. T. (1987). Cognitive models of depression. *Journal of Cognitive Psychotherapy, 1*(1), 5–37.

Beck, A. T., & Emery, G. (1985). *Anxiety disorders and phobias: A cognitive perspective.* New York: Basic Books.

*Beck, A. T., & Greenberg, R. L. (1974). *Coping with depression.* New York: Institute for Rational Living.

Beck, A. T., Laude, R., & Bohnert, M. (1974). Ideational components of anxiety neurosis. *Archives of General Psychiatry, 31,* 319–325.

Beck, A. T., Rush, A. J., Shaw, B. F., & Emery, G. (1979). *Cognitive therapy of depression.* New York: Wiley.

*Berne, E. (1964). *Games people play.* New York: Grove Press.

*Berne, E. (1972). *What do you say after you say hello?* London: Corgi Books.

*Bower, S. A., & Bower, G. H. (1976). *Asserting yourself: A practical guide for positive change.* Reading, Mass.: Addison-Wesley.

Brewin, C. R. (1986). Internal attribution and self-esteem in depression: A theoretical note. *Cognitive Therapy and Research, 10*(4), 469–475.

Brewin, C. R., & Furnham, A. (1987). Dependency, self-criticism and depressive attributional style. *British Journal of Clinical Psychology, 26,* 225–226.

*Bry, A. (1978). *Visualization: Directing the movies of your mind.* New York: Harper & Row.

Burns, D., Shaw, B. F., & Croker, W. (1987). Thinking styles and coping strategies of depressed women: An empirical investigation. *Behaviour Research & Therapy, 25*(3), 223–225.

*Butler, P. E. (1981a). *Talking to yourself: Learning the language of self-support.* New York: Harper & Row.

*Butler, P. E. (1981b). *Self-assertion for women* (rev. ed.). San Francisco: Harper & Row.

Camper, P. M., Jacobson, N. S., Holtzworth-Munroe, A., & Schmaling, K. B. (1988). Causal attributions for interactional behaviours in married couples. *Cognitive Therapy and Research, 12*(2), 195–209.

Carkhuff, R. R. (1973). *The art of problem solving.* Amherst, Mass.: Human Resource Development Press.

Cautela, J. (1967). Covert sensitization. *Psychological Reports, 20,* 459–468.

Clark, D. M. (1986). A cognitive approach to panic. *Behaviour Research & Therapy, 24*(4), 461–470.

Deffenbacher, J. L., & Suinn, R. M. (1988). Systematic desensitization and the reduction of anxiety. *The Counseling Psychologist, 16,* 9–30.

Dryden, W., & Ellis, A. (1986). Rational-emotive therapy (RET). In W. Dryden & W. Golden (Eds.), *Cognitive-behavioural approaches to psychotherapy* (pp. 129–168). London: Harper & Row.

*Dyer, W. W. (1976). *Your erroneous zones.* London: Sphere.

D'Zurilla, T. J., & Goldfried, M. R. (1971). Problem solving and behavior modification. *Journal of Abnormal Psychology, 78*(1), 107–126.

D'Zurilla, T. J., & Nezu, A. (1980). A study of the generation-of-alternatives process in social problem solving. *Cognitive Therapy and Research, 4*(1), 67–72.

Egan, G. (1986). *The skilled helper* (3rd ed.). Pacific Grove, Calif.: Brooks/Cole.

Eidelson, R. J., & Epstein, N. (1982). Cognition and relationship maladjustment: Development of a measure of dysfunctional relationship beliefs. *Journal of Consulting and Clinical Psychology, 50,* 721–726.

Ellis, A. (1962). *Reason and emotion in psychotherapy.* New York: Lyle Stuart.

Ellis, A. (1980). Overview of the clinical theory of rational-emotive therapy. In

R. Grieger & J. Boyd. (Eds.) *Rational-emotive therapy: A skills-based approach* (pp. 1–31). New York: Van Nostrand Reinhold.

Ellis, A. (1985). *Rational humorous songs.* New York: Institute for Rational-Emotive Therapy.

Ellis, A. (1987). The impossibility of achieving consistently good mental health. *American Psychologist, 42*(4), 364–375.

*Ellis, A., & Harper, R. A. (1975). *A new guide to rational living.* Hollywood: Wilshire.

*Emery, G. (1982). *Own your own life.* New York: New American Library.

Fincham, F. D. (1985). Attribution processes in distressed and nondistressed couples: 2. Responsibility for marital problems. *Journal of Abnormal Psychology, 94*(2), 183–190.

Fincham, F. D., Beach, S., & Nelson, G. (1987). Attribution processes in distressed and nondistressed couples: 3. Causal and responsibility attributions for spouse behavior. *Cognitive Therapy and Research, 11*(1), 71–86.

Flavell, J. H. (1985). *Cognitive development* (2nd ed.). Englewood Cliffs, N.J.: Prentice-Hall.

*Frankl, V. E. (1959). *Man's search for meaning.* New York: Washington Square Press.

Frankl, V. E. (1969). *The doctor and the soul.* Harmondsworth, England; Penguin Books.

Fricker, P. (1987, July). Quoted in an anonymous article: The will to win. *The Australian Weekend Magazine,* pp. 1–2.

*Friedman, M., & Rosenman, R. H. (1974). *Type A behavior and your heart.* New York: Knopf.

Fuqua, D., Seaworth, T. B., & Newman, J. L. (1987). The relationship of career indecision and anxiety: A multivariate examination. *Journal of Vocational Behavior, 30,* 175–186.

Gardner, J. (1965). *Self-renewal: The individual and the innovative society.* New York: Harper & Row.

Gendlin, E. T. (1981). *Focusing* (2nd ed.). New York: Bantam Books.

Glasser, W. (1984). *Control theory.* New York: Harper & Row.

Goldfried, M. R., Decenteceo, E. T., & Weinberg, L. (1974). Systematic rational restructuring as a self-control technique. *Behavior Therapy, 5,* 247–254.

*Gordon, T. (1970). *Parent effectiveness training.* New York: Wyden.

*Howe, M. A. (1986). *Imaging.* Melbourne: Spiral.

Ivey, A. E., Ivey, M. B., & Simek-Downing, L. (1987). *Counseling and psychotherapy: Integrating skills, theory, and practice* (2nd ed.). Englewood Cliffs, N. J.: Prentice-Hall.

Jacobson, E. (1938). *Progressive relaxation* (2nd ed.). Chicago: University of Chicago Press.

Jacobson, N. S., McDonald, D. W., Follette, W. C., & Berley, R. A. (1985). Attributional processes in distressed and nondistressed married couples. *Cognitive Therapy and Research, 9*(1), 35–50.

Janis, I. L. (1982). *Counseling on personal decisions.* New Haven, Conn.: Yale University Press.

Janis, I. L., & Mann, L. (1977). *Decision making: A psychological analysis of conflict, choice, and commitment*. New York: The Free Press.

Jarrett, R. B., & Nelson, R. O. (1987). Mechanisms of change in cognitive therapy of depression. *Behavior Therapy, 18*, 227–241.

Kassorla, I. C. (1984). *Go for it!* New York: Dell.

Kelly, G. A. (1955a). *The psychology of personal constructs*. New York: Norton.

Kelly, G. A. (1955b). *A theory of personality*. New York: Norton.

Kinnier, R. T. (1987). Development of a values conflict resolution assessment. *Journal of Counseling Psychology, 34*(1), 31–37.

Kohlberg, L., & Gilligan, C. (1971). The adolescent as philosopher: The discovery of the self in a postconventional world. *Daedalus, 100*, 1051–1086.

Kulik, J. A., & Mahler, H. I. M. (1987). Health status, perceptions of risk, and prevention interest for health and nonhealth problems. *Health Psychology, 6*(1), 15–27.

Laing, R. D. (1969). *The politics of the family*. London: Tavistock.

Lang, P. J. (1977). Imagery in therapy: An information processing analysis of fear. *Behavior Therapy, 8*, 862–886.

*Lazarus, A. (1977). *In the mind's eye*. New York: The Guilford Press.

Leong, S. L., Leong, F. T., & Hoffman, M. A. (1987). Counseling expectations of rational, intuitive and dependent decision makers. *Journal of Counseling Psychology, 34*(3), 261–265.

*Lewisohn, P. M., Munoz, R. F., Youngren, M. A., & Zeiss, A. M. (1986). *Control your depression*. New York: Prentice-Hall.

Lopez, F. G., & Thurman, C. W. (1986). A cognitive behavioral investigation of anger among college students. *Cognitive Therapy and Research, 10*(2), 245–256.

Lucock, M. P., & Salkovskis, P. M. (1988). Cognitive factors in social anxiety and its treatment. *Behaviour Research & Therapy, 26*(4), 297–302.

Mahoney, M. J., & Lyddon, W. J. (1988). Recent developments in cognitive approaches to counseling and psychotherapy. *The Counseling Psychologist, 16*, 190–234.

Marsh, H. W. (1986). Self-serving effect (bias?) in academic attributions: Its relation to academic achievement and self-concept. *Journal of Educational Psychology, 78*(3), 190–200.

Maslow, A. H. (1962). *Toward a psychology of being*. Princeton, N. J.:Van Nostrand.

Maslow, A. H. (1970). *Motivation and personality* (2nd ed.). New York: Harper & Row.

Maslow, A. H. (1971). *The farther reaches of human nature*. Harmondsworth, England: Penguin Books.

May, R. (1953). *Man's search for himself*. New York: Norton.

Meichenbaum, D. (1977). *Cognitive-behavior modification: An integrative approach*. New York: Plenum.

*Meichenbaum, D. (1983). *Coping with stress*. London: Century.

Meichenbaum, D. (1985). *Stress inoculation training*. New York: Pergamon Press.

Meichenbaum, D. (1986). Cognitive-behavior modification. In F. H. Kanfer & A. P.

Goldstein (Eds.), *Helping people change* (3rd ed., pp. 346–380). New York: Pergamon Press.

Meichenbaum, D., & Deffenbacher, J. L. (1988). Stress inoculation training. *The Counseling Psychologist, 16*, 69–90.

Mitchell, L. K., & Krumboltz, J. D. (1987). The effects of cognitive restructuring and decision-making training on career indecision. *Journal of Counseling and Development, 66*, 171–174.

Moon, J. R., & Eisler, R. M. (1983). Anger control: An experimental comparison of three behavioral treatments. *Behavior Therapy, 14*, 493-505.

Mowrer, O. H. (1964). *The new group therapy*. Princeton, N. J.: Van Nostrand.

Nelson-Jones, R. (1984). *Personal responsibility counselling and therapy*. London & Sydney: Harper & Row; New York: Hemisphere.

Nelson-Jones, R. (1988). Choice therapy. *Counselling Psychology Quarterly, 1*(1), 41–53.

Nezu, A. M., & Ronan, G. F. (1988). Social problem solving as a moderator of stress-related depressive symptoms: A prospective analysis. *Journal of Counseling Psychology, 35*(2), 134–138.

Novaco, R. W. (1977). Stress inoculation: A cognitive therapy for anger and its application to a case of depression. *Journal of Consulting and Clinical Psychology, 45*(4), 600-688.

*Peale, N. V. (1953). *The power of positive thinking*. Kingswood, England: The World's Work.

Perry, W. G. (1970). *Forms of intellectual and ethical development in the college years*. New York: Holt, Rinehart & Winston.

Peterson, C., Semmel, A. Baeyer, C. von, Abramson, L., Metalsky, G. I., & Seligman, M. E. P. (1982). The attributional style questionnaire. *Cognitive Therapy and Research, 6*(3), 287–300.

Peterson, C., Villanova, P., & Raps, C. S. (1985). Depression and attributions: Factors responsible for inconsistent results in the published literature. *Journal of Abnormal Psychology, 94*(2), 165–168.

Piaget, J. (1970). Piaget's theory. In P. H. Mussen (Ed.), *Carmichael's manual of child psychology* (3rd ed., Vol. 1, pp. 703–732). New York: Wiley.

Pietromonaco, P. R., & Rook, K. S. (1987). Decision style in depression: The contribution of perceived risks versus benefits. *Journal of Personality and Social Psychology, 52*(2), 399–408.

Platt, J. J., Pout, M. F., & Metzger, D. S. (1986). Interpersonal cognitive problem solving therapy (ICPS). In W. Dryden & W. Golden (Eds.), *Cognitive-behavioural approaches to psychotherapy* (pp. 261–289). London: Harper & Row.

*Rogers, C. R. (1961). *On becoming a person*. Boston: Houghton Mifflin.

*Rogers, C. R. (1980). *A way of being*. Boston: Houghton Mifflin.

Ross, S. M., Gottfredson, D. K., Christensen, P., & Weaver, R. (1986). Cognitive self-statements in depression: Findings across clinical populations. *Cognitive Therapy and Research, 10*(2), 159–166.

Sanford, N. (1962). Developmental status of the entering freshman. In N. Sanford (Ed.), *The American college* (pp. 253–282). New York: Wiley.

Sartre, J. P. (1956). *Being and nothingness*. New York: Philosophical Library.

Schulman, P., Seligman, M. E. P., & Amsterdam, D. (1987). The attributional style questionnaire is not transparent. *Behaviour Research & Therapy, 25*(5), 391–395.

Seligman, M. E. P., Abramson, L. Y., Semmel, A., & Baeyer, C. von (1979). Depressive attributional style. *Journal of Abnormal Psychology, 88,* 242–247.

*Simonton, O. C., Matthews-Simonton, S., & Creighton, J. L. (1978). *Getting well again.* New York: Bantam Books.

Skovolt, T. M., & Hoenninger, R. W. (1974). Guided fantasy in career development. *Personnel and Guidance Journal, 52,* 693–696.

Skovolt, T. M., & Thoen, G. A. (1987). Mental imagery and parenthood decision-making. *Journal of Counseling & Development, 65,* 315–316.

*Steiner, C. M. (1974). *Scripts people live.* New York: Bantam Books.

*Steiner, C. M. (1981). *The other side of power.* New York: Grove Press.

Szasz, T. S. (1973). *The second sin.* London: Routledge & Kegan Paul.

Teasdale, J. D., & Dent, J. (1987). Cognitive vulnerability to depression: An investigation of two hypotheses. *British Journal of Clinical Psychology, 26,* 113–126.

*Tillich, P. (1952). *The courage to be.* New Haven, Conn.: Yale University Press.

Tresemer, D. W. (1977). *Fear of success.* New York: Plenum.

Ward, C. H., & Eisler, R. M. (1987). Type A achievement striving and failure to achieve personal goals. *Cognitive Therapy and Research, 11*(4), 463–471.

Warren, R., McLellarn, R., & Ponzoha, C. (1988). Rational-emotive therapy vs. general cognitive-behavior therapy in the treatment of low self-esteem and related emotional disturbances. *Cognitive Therapy and Research, 12*(1), 21–38.

Watson, J. (1986). Parental attributions of emotional disturbance and their relation to the outcome of therapy: Preliminary findings. *Australian Psychologist, 21,* 271–282.

Weiner, B., & Kukla, A. (1970). An attributional analysis of achievement motivation. *Journal of Personality and Social Psychology, 15,* 1–20.

Weinstein, N. D. (1980). Unrealistic optimism about future life events. *Journal of Personality and Social Psychology, 39*(5), 806–820.

Weinstein, N. D. (1984). Why it won't happen to me: Perceptions of risk factors and susceptibility. *Health Psychology, 3*(5), 431–457.

Wessler, R.L., & Hankin-Wessler, S. W. R. (1986). Cognitive appraisal therapy (CAT). In W. Dryden & W. Golden (Eds.), *Cognitive-behavioural approaches to psychotherapy* (pp. 196–223). London: Harper & Row.

Witmer, J. M., & Young, M. E. (1985). The silent partner: Uses of imagery in counseling. *Journal of Counseling & Development, 64,* 187–190.

Wolpe, J. E. (1982). *The practice of behavior therapy* (2nd ed.). New York: Pergamon Press.

Woolfolk, R. L., Parish, M. W., & Murphy, S. M. (1985). The effects of positive and negative imagery on motor skill performance. *Cognitive Therapy and Research, 9*(3), 335–341.

Yalom, I. D. (1980). *Existential psychotherapy.* New York: Basic Books.

Young, R. A. (1986). Counseling the unemployed: Attributional issues. *Journal of Counseling and Development, 64,* 374–378.

Index